MVS/TSO
Mastering CLISTs

Books and Training Products From QED

DATABASE

Data Analysis: The Key to Data Base Design
The Data Dictionary: Concepts and Uses
DB2: The Complete Guide to Implementation
and Use
Logical Data Base Design
DB2 Design Review Guidelines
DB2: Maximizing Performance of Online
Production Systems
Entity-Relationship Approach to Logical Data
Base Design
How to Use ORACLE SQL*PLUS
ORACLE: Building High Performance
Online Systems
Embedded SQL for DB2: Application Design
and Programming
SQL for dBASE IV
Introduction to Data and Activity Analysis
ORACLE Design Review Guidelines
Using DB2 to Build Decision Support Systems
How to Use SQL for DB2

SYSTEMS ENGINEERING

Handbook of Screen Format Design
Managing Projects: Selecting and Using PC-
Based Project Management Systems
The Complete Guide to Software Testing
A User's Guide for Defining Software
Requirements
A Structured Approach to Systems Testing
Practical Applications of Expert Systems
Expert Systems Development: Building
PC-Based Applications
Storyboard Prototyping: A New Approach to
User Requirements Analysis
The Software Factory: Managing Software
Development and Maintenance
Data Architecture: The Information Paradigm
Advanced Topics in Information Engineering

MANAGEMENT

CASE: The Potential and the Pitfalls
Strategic and Operational Planning for
Information Services
The State of the Art in Decision Support Systems
The Management Handbook for Information
Center and End-User Computing
Disaster Recovery: Contingency Planning and
Program Analysis

MANAGEMENT (cont'd)

Winning the Change Game
Information Systems Planning for Competitive
Advantage
Critical Issues in Information Processing
Management and Technology
Developing the World Class Information
Systems Organization
The Technical Instructor's Handbook: From
Techie to Teacher
Collision: Theory vs. Reality in Expert System
How to Automate Your Computer Center:
Achieving Unattended Operations
Ethical Conflicts in Information and Computer
Science, Technology, and Business

DATA COMMUNICATIONS

Data Communications: Concepts and Solutions
Designing and Implementing Ethernet Networks
Network Concepts and Architectures
Open Systems: The Guide to OSI and its
Implementation
VAX/VMS: Mastering DCL Commands and
Utilities

PROGRAMMING

VSAM Techniques: Systems Concepts and
Programming Procedures
How to Use CICS to Create On-Line
Applications: Methods and Solutions
DOS/VSE/SP Guide for Systems Programming:
Concepts, Programs, Macros, Subroutines
Systems Programmer's Problem Solver
VSAM: Guide to Optimization and Design
MVS/TSO: Mastering CLISTS
MVS/TSO: Mastering Native Mode and ISPF
VAX/VMS: Mastering DCL Commands
and Utilities

SELF-PACED TRAINING

SQL as a Second Language
Building Online Production Systems with DB2
(Video)
Introduction to UNIX (CBT)
Building Production Applications with ORACLE
(Video)

For Additional Information or a Free Catalog contact

QED INFORMATION SCIENCES, INC. • P. O. Box 82-181 • Wellesley, MA 02181
Telephone: 800-343-4848 or 617-237-5656

MVS/TSO
Mastering CLISTs

Barry K. Nirmal

QED Information Sciences, Inc.
Wellesley, Massachusetts

© 1990 by QED Information Sciences, Inc.
P.O. Box 82-181
Wellesley, MA 02181

Library of Congress Catalog Number: 89-24367
International Standard Book Number: 0-89435-319-5

Printed in the United States of America
90 91 92 10 9 8 7 6 5 4 3 2

Library of Congress Cataloging-in-Publication Data

Nirmal, Barry K., 1949-
  MVS/TSO : Mastering CLISTs/ Barry K. Nirmal.
      p.   cm.
  Includes bibliographical references.
  ISBN 0-89435-319-5
  1. Time-sharing computer systems. 2. MVS (Computer system)
I. Title.
QA76.53.N57   1990
004'.32--dc 20

The following are reprinted by permission from IBM Corporation — page 237, Figure A.5; page 238, Figure A.6; page 256, Figure B.1; page 258, Figure B.2; pages 260-261, Figure C.1. Figures 6, 7, 15, 16 and 18 have been reprinted from *MVS Extended Architecture — TSO Extensions — TSO Command Language Reference (SC28-1134)* © 1983.

Limits of Liability and Disclaimer of Warranty: The author and publisher of this book have used their best efforts in preparing this book. These efforts include the development, research, and testing of the theories and programs to determine their effectiveness. The author and publisher make no warranty of any kind, expressed or implied, with regard to these programs or the documentation contained in this book. The author and publisher shall not be liable in any event for incidental or consequential damages in connection with, or arising out of, the furnishing, performance, or use of these programs.

Dedicated to
my mother, Sheo Tiwary, and my late
father, Kailash Tiwary, for their
unselfish love which provided
support and encouragement,
whenever I needed it.

Table of Contents

Chapter 5:   FILE INPUT/OUTPUT AND OTHER
ADVANCED CLIST TOPICS 111

Chapter 6:   SOME USEFUL CLISTs ESPECIALLY
FOR SYSTEMS PROGRAMMERS 137

Preface

After seeing my first book on programming standards and guidelines published by Prentice Hall Inc. of New Jersey, U.S.A., people have often asked me, 'What motivated you to write this book?' I wish to answer this question regarding this book on CLISTs. This book arose out of my frustration in working with CLISTs, both as an MVS Systems Programmer and as a Senior Programmer/Analyst in applications. While working in Calgary, Canada as an MVS Systems Programmer, during 1984, I frequently had to make modifications to the existing CLISTs either in the course of installing program products or while solving problems related to applications running under TSO. Then again, during 1982-1983, while working as a Senior Programmer/Analyst in Calgary, I had to understand the CLISTs written by a programmer/analyst who had left the company. We used these CLISTs to do such things as define the base of a generation data group and assemble online CICS programs.

On both these jobs, I was severely handicapped due to the inavailability of good textbooks on the subject. The IBM Corporation manuals that were available to me were more reference manuals than tutorials. Trying to understand a technique without first having firmly grasped the basic concepts and terminology of the CLIST language was a painful task. It was not easy to find all the basic concepts and definitions of the terms and concepts in one book or even in one or two chapters of a book. Information in the IBM Corporation manuals that were available to me on the job were scattered. So I decided that after I had mastered the techniques related to CLISTs, I would write a book that could be of use to the programmers and analysts, both in systems and applications programming, all over the world.

This is how this book was conceived and started. It is a result of years of painstaking work, research, experimentation and testing. After I came to Saudi Arabia in 1987, I had plenty of spare time after returning home from work. This is because my family had not yet arrived due to the slow preparation and processing of papers required to obtain entry visas for them. In the hot summer evenings of 1987, I decided to make use of the great amount of spare time by writing this book. This is how this book was completed.

All concepts, techniques, and tools given in this book have been tested on an MVS/TSO system. This was done to ensure that no mistakes of any kind remain in the final text.

ACKNOWLEDGMENTS

I am thankful to Mr. Yahya S. Al-Dhukair, EDP Department Manager, SCECO East, Mr. Max Seirawan, Administrator, Computer Science Division, SCECO East and Mr. Saud Al-Shammari, Administrator, Applications Division, SCECO East, for giving me opportunities to advance myself professionally, and for making IBM Corporation manuals and other books freely available to me so that I could educate myself.

I am grateful to Mohammed Z. Ghory for providing me with material related to CLISTs. The material he provided was of great help in my own understanding of the subject and in developing the techniques and tools that this book contains. I am also grateful to IBM Corporation for promptly granting me permission to include in this text some figures from one of their manuals on MVS/TSO.

The review of this book by Mr. Michael Haupt of Haupt M.I.S. Consultants of Mt. Prospect, Illinois was well-received. It was his suggestion to transform this book from a tutorial for the beginners to an advanced tools and techniques book. The following comments by him inspired me to add more practical examples as well as useful tools and techniques in the text:

"There is a large audience of self-taught CLIST users. They know the basics and have a small set of CLISTs they use frequently. This audience would be receptive to the large number of useful examples in this text. Not only does the text demonstrate advanced CLIST options, but it gives them many CLISTs which they can tailor and use quickly. . . . The superb examples accompanied by detailed explanations are the primary strength of this book."

I would be failing in my duty if I did not thank Edwin F. Kerr, Executive Vice President and Publisher of QED Information Sciences, Inc., for accepting my proposal and acting fast to ensure that this book saw the light of day at an early date. The staff at QED deserve special thanks for their professionalism and efficiency. My special thanks also go to Beth A. Roberts of QED for her professional work.

Finally, to Gargi, who on many occasions was more enthusiastic about this book than I, my love and thanks.

Barry K. Nirmal

Note to the Reader

If you have any comments to make regarding the usefulness of this book, or have any ideas for improving it, e.g., by giving some specific CLIST example that you have in mind, please write to me at the following address:

P.O. Box 649
Marlborough Postal Centre
Calgary, Alberta, T2A 7L5
Canada

Conventions

1. Since all CLISTs, COBOL programs and MVS JCL are coded using only uppercase characters, whenever lowercase words are used in program, CLIST or JCL statements, the user should replace the lowercase words with appropriate, meaningful words.

2. The system of notation used to describe the syntax and formats of TSO commands and CLIST statements is as follows:

Notation	Example	Meaning
Uppercase words	ALLOC	Required reserved word. Should be coded exactly as shown.
Lowercase words	ddname	Word or entry must be supplied by the user.
Brackets	[SYSOUT(class)]	Optional parameter. If more than one is enclosed and stacked vertically, one or none can be chosen.

Braces	$\begin{Bmatrix} \text{ALLOC} \\ \text{ALLOCATE} \end{Bmatrix}$	Alternatives. Unless a default is indicated, one of the entries must be supplied by the user.
Ellipses	. . .	Multiple entries of the type immediately preceding the ellipses are allowed.
Punctuation: Period, parentheses, commas, spaces, colon, semi-colon		Must be entered as shown.

Note:

- Required parameters (without alternatives) will not be enclosed in brackets.

- If a word is underlined, it is the default. If the parameter is omitted by the user, the system assumes the under⁻ lined value.

Chapter 1
INTRODUCTION

IS THIS BOOK FOR YOU?

As you read this introduction, you may be trying to decide if this book is for you and whether or not you should spend your own or your company's money to buy it. If you are a supervisor, administrator, or a manager of programmers and system analysts, you may be wondering whether you should purchase copies of this book for all members of your group, division or department.

As the title of this book suggests, it is a "tools and techniques" book. It contains many tools for the active professional. These tools are the many CLISTs and the accompanying COBOL programs that solve the problems encountered by programmers and analysts on the job. These CLISTs and programs can be easily copied to your own datasets and executed with little or no change. These CLISTs are accompanied by detailed explanation. This will help in acquiring a good understanding of these CLISTs, which will enable you to easily modify these CLISTs so that they meet your unique needs on the job. This book also contains many examples. These examples, along with short as well as long CLISTs and the accompanying COBOL programs, and MVS JCL illustrate the techniques of writing CLISTs for solving problems on the job.

If you are a programmer, a programmer/analyst, a systems analyst, or a supervisor of programmers, programmer/analysts or systems analysts, and you work with MVS/TSO, this book is definitely for you. If you are a student or an instructor and you use MVS/TSO at your school, college, or university, this book is also for you. If you are an engineer or a scientist and you use MVS/TSO in your day-to-day work, this book can be helpful to you in understanding the CLIST language and in learning to write CLISTs for your unique needs.

MVS/TSO is a very important subject for anyone who uses TSO or ISPF on a computer terminal for programming or programming-related work. TSO has been said to bring MVS on your terminal. TSO and its companion product, ISPF/PDF, make many facilities of MVS available right on your terminal. The CLIST language is a high level language which allows you to build very simple or highly sophisticated commands for execution under TSO or ISPF. Hence, sound knowledge of the CLIST language will pay handsome dividends to anyone who uses MVS/TSO in his or her day-to-day work.

That is all there is to deciding whether this book is for you. If this book is for you, then it is worth its weight in gold. It will serve as a useful reference on MVS/TSO CLISTs. The sample CLISTs and programs presented throughout this book are of a highly practical nature. They cannot only be put to immediate use, but they will also give you valuable insights into the kind of needs for which CLISTs can be written. This will hopefully inspire you to write similar CLISTs that will meet your own unique needs and that will be suitable and relevant to your own unique environment and application.

HOW TO PROFIT THE MOST FROM THIS BOOK

This book is more of a reference than a tutorial. Being a "tools and techniques" book, it can be beneficial to both the inexperienced and the experienced CLIST user. However, if you are not familiar with the basic concepts and terminology of the CLIST language, you will have to refer to some other book or an IBM manual for definitions of terms and concepts and detailed descriptions of TSO commands and CLIST statements mentioned in this book. In order to write a computer program in any language, one must understand the basic rules of the language. Similarly, in order to write CLIST programs, you must understand the basic concepts of the language such as symbolic variables, labels and expressions. Some introductory material is given in this chapter. A summary of built-in functions, and control variables, is given in Appendix B, and TSO commands commonly used in CLISTs are discussed in Appendix A. However, you may refer to the following manuals (or equivalent manuals suitable to your installation's software release) while reading this book:

IBM Manual	Topic
MVS/Extended Architecture TSO Extensions, TSO Command Language Reference	Syntax and detailed explanations of TSO commands, such as ALLOCATE, EDIT, as well as CLIST statements, e.g., ATTN, ERROR, GOTO, and CLIST built-in functions and control variables
MVS/Extended Architecture Access Method Services Reference	Syntax and detailed descriptions of Access Method Services commands such as DEFINE, DELETE, and LISTCAT.

Recommended Reading Plans for the Experienced CLIST User

If you are already familiar with the CLIST concepts, you may read only those sections of the book that are of interest to you. For example, suppose you are an applications programmer who has just moved to systems programming, and you are unfamiliar with how TSO log-on processing works. In this case, you may read CLISTs in TSO Log-On Processing in Chapter 4, but you may skip CLISTs and ISPF Panels in the same chapter if you are knowledgeable about setting up on-line applications using CLISTs and ISPF panels. If you are an applications programmer, Chapter 6 will be of little interest to you because the CLISTs given there are intended mainly for the systems programmers.

If you are an inexperienced CLIST user, you should begin with Chapter 1 and continue reading sequentially. You may skip a section if it is of little interest to you. You should refer to Appendix A whenever the CLISTs presented in this book use a TSO command that is described in Appendix A. You should also refer to Appendices B and C for brief descriptions of built-in functions, and control variables. An inexperienced CLIST user will find the CLISTs given in Chapter 2 to be interesting because each CLIST is discussed in detail, and the short CLISTs are easy to understand.

If you are an inexperienced CLIST user, it is also recommended that as you progress through the book, you use your TSO terminal to try out the examples so that your knowledge of the topics becomes sound. This will help you better understand the topics presented in subsequent sections and chapters. It has been said that practice makes a person perfect, and the practice of writing and running CLISTs on your terminal will make you a perfect professional possessing sound knowledge of the CLIST language.

It is not correct to think: 'let me first read the whole book and then I will try out some CLISTs on my terminal.' Learning to write CLISTs using this 'tools and techniques' book will become easy when you read some topics, then write and execute some CLISTs using the material just learned and then read further.

WHAT IS A CLIST?

The term CLIST (pronounced "sea list") stands for command list, which is also called command procedure. A command procedure is a set of TSO commands, subcommands, and CLIST statements that have been arranged in an executable sequence. We use the CLIST language or the command procedure language for writing CLISTs. This high-level language is different from the other high-level languages such as COBOL or PL/I in that the program written in the command procedure language is not compiled or assembled and a load module created by using the linkage-editor prior to executing a CLIST. A program written in the command procedure language, i.e., a CLIST, gets executed 'on the fly.' It gets interpreted and executed at the same time. Any error detected during execution gets displayed on the terminal, unlike a COBOL program where errors detected during compilation are displayed at compilation time and these errors are corrected and the program link-edited before executing the load module.

So, it is important to understand that with a high-level interpretive language like the CLIST language, there are no intermediate steps of compilation or assembly followed by the creation of a load module using the linkage-editor program.

To understand the concept of CLIST, let us consider a simple example. Suppose that a TSO user with prefix RF has to delete five datasets with prefix RF every time one of his batch jobs fails before submitting that job again. Rather than issuing five DELETE commands from TSO, he can save himself considerable time and typing by doing the following:

a. Allocating a dataset 'RF.DELFILES.CLIST' with the following attributes:
   Dataset Organization = Physical Sequential (PS)
   Record Format = Fixed Blocked

Logical Record Length = 80
Block Size = 3200 or some multiple of 80
(This allocation can be done using option 3.2 of ISPF or by executing program IEFBR14 in a batch job.)

b. Editing this dataset using the ISPF Editor and entering the following five lines, where each line starts at column 1:

```
DELETE TEST.FILE01
DELETE TEST.FILE02
DELETE TEST.FILE03
DELETE TEST.FILE04
DELETE TEST.FILE05
```

(Note that the dataset names are not enclosed within quotes, which means that the DELETE commands are issued against datasets with names 'RF.TEST.FILE01', 'RF.TEST.FILE02', and so on, because RF happens to be the dataset name prefix of the TSO user executing this CLIST.)

c. Saving the dataset

Now, every time the job fails and the user has to delete the five datasets, the user can issue the following command from native mode TSO or from TSO within ISPF:

```
EXEC DELFILES
```

Note: from ISPF screen, the user must issue the command: TSO EXEC DELFILES.

The command above expands into EXECUTE 'RF.DELFILES.CLIST', which results in the execution of the CLIST contained in 'RF.DELFILES.CLIST'. This CLIST causes the deletion of the five datasets listed in the CLIST. The real advantages of CLISTs will become more apparent when we examine more complex examples of CLISTs in subsequent chapters.

WHY DO WE NEED CLISTs?

CLISTs are used for a variety of tasks by application programmers, system programmers, and computer operations and data control personnel. Most importantly, they are used to save the operator time and effort. For example, in many situations a TSO user has to repeatedly enter the same sequence of commands. A CLIST can save the user considerable time and effort in typing the commands and each to finish before he enters the next command. He can build a CLIST and enter all the commands in it. Then all he has to do is to execute the CLIST which will result in the execution of the command sequence contained in the CLIST. The commands we are talking about here are usually TSO commands, but they can also be access method commands such as VTAM commands to display the status of a logical unit or to VARY a logical unit active or inactive.

CLISTs are also used in connection with running production systems. For example, consider a regular month-end cycle of an application system that consists of several sets of JCL (Job Control Language), each of which requires minor changes each month (for example, the dates on control cards). An operations clerk can invoke a CLIST which will automatically make these changes without the risk of accidental changes to production JCL caused by human error. CLISTs are also used to invoke software systems such as FOCUS and Report Management and Distribution System (RMDS). They are also indispensible when building on-line systems using ISPF dialogs.

WHERE ARE CLISTS STORED?

A CLIST can be stored in either a sequential dataset or a member of a partitioned dataset (PDS). If a partitioned dataset is used, it is advisable that all members of the PDS contain CLISTS only, even though this is not a system requirement.

If a dataset containing CLISTs has fixed-length records, for example, Record Format (RECFM) of Fixed Blocked (FB), Logical Record Length (LRECL) of 80 and Block Size (BLKSIZE) of 3120, the lines in the CLIST should start in column 1. Also, each line in the CLIST should have a proper sequence number in columns 73 thru 80. This happens automatically under ISPF if the profile of the TSO user is properly set up. The TSO user should not attempt to write onto the sequence numbers in columns 73 thru 80 as this will make the CLIST unexecutable.

However, if the dataset has variable length records, such as Record Format (RECFM) of Variable Blocked (VB), Logical Record Length (LRECL) of 255 and Block Size (BLK-SIZE) of say 3120, then the lines in the CLIST should start in column 9. Also columns 1 thru 8 of each line should contain a proper sequence number. This happens automatically under ISPF if the dataset containing the CLIST is edited with proper profile. The TSO user should not attempt to write into columns 1 thru 8 as this will make the CLIST unexecutable.

For this reason, when you copy a CLIST using ISPF option 3.3 from a dataset with one record format to another dataset with another record format, you may encounter problems when trying to execute the CLIST in the 'copied to' dataset. You may get one of the following messages depending on whether a dataset with Fixed Blocked records was copied into another with Variable Blocked records or vice versa:

```
A COMMAND ENTERED OR CONTAINED IN A CLIST HAS INVALID SYNTAX
***


INVALID KEYWORD, ---------
LASTCC=12
***
```

If this happens, a slight editing of the CLIST in the 'copied to' dataset may be necessary to make the CLIST executable.

HOW TO CREATE AND MODIFY CLISTs?

Suppose you want to write a small CLIST called MYCLIST. The first step is to allocate a PDS (also called a library) to contain this CLIST. Now suppose that SYS2.CLIST is a production CLIST library containing CLISTs that you are authorized to execute. Then it is a good idea for you to create your own CLIST dataset with the same characteristics (fixed-block or variable-block records) as SYS2.CLIST. This will allow you to concatenate your own CLIST dataset with the production CLIST library under DDname SYSPROC. To allocate your own dataset, go to option 3.2 (Utilities - Dataset) of ISPF/PDF:

- View the characteristics of your production CLIST library (e.g., SYS2.CLIST) and then allocate your own CLIST library with the same record format, logical record length and block size. Suppose your TSO prefix is H4ABC then you may name this dataset 'H4ABC.CLIST'. Here the dataset type is CLIST which simplifies execution as you will see later.
- Go to option 2 (Edit) of ISPF/EDIT and create member MYCLIST in your CLIST library that you have just allocated. While creating the CLIST, you need not enter the line number. The system automatically assigns line numbers to each line you enter, provided your profile is properly set up.
- Save the dataset by pressing the key assigned to the END command (commonly PF3 or PF15)
- Now to execute this CLIST, type one of the following from the command line of any ISPF panel:

```
TSO EX (MYCLIST)
       or
TSO EX 'H4ABC.CLIST(MYCLIST)'
```

- If you want to modify this CLIST, select option 2 (Edit) of ISPF/PDF and edit this member. Make any changes you want and then save the changes by pressing the key assigned to the END command.

TWO TYPES AND THREE CATEGORIES OF CLISTs

There are two types of CLISTs. A CLIST can be either a simple CLIST consisting of only TSO commands and subcommands or a complex one consisting of all the facilities available with command procedures. The CLIST described above which contained only five DELETE commands of TSO is an example of a simple CLIST. A complex CLIST uses facilities such as built-in functions, control variables and CLIST statements. The built-in functions perform immediate evaluations of character strings. They are listed in Appendix B. The control variables which provide information about the environment, such as the TSO log-on ID of the user executing the CLIST are also listed in Appendix B. The CLIST statements give the writer of CLISTs the capabilities of a high-level language.

CLISTs fall into three general categories:

CLISTs That Perform Routine Tasks

These are used to save the TSO user time, effort and keystrokes involved in entering commands for performing routine tasks such as checking on the status of his jobs or datasets, allocating files required to execute a program or printing files.

CLISTs that are Structured Applications

The CLIST language of today is a highly evolved language. It has all the facilities available in a high-level language. A CLIST can invoke another CLIST, which in turn can invoke another CLIST. A CLIST can also contain separate routines called subprocedures. CLISTs can also issue commands of the Interactive System Productivity Facility (ISPF) to display full-screen panels. And ISPF panels can also invoke CLISTs based on input entered by the user on panels.

CLISTs that are Front-end for Applications Written in Other Languages

You may have applications written in other languages. But you may not have user-friendly interfaces to those applications. In such instances, you may write CLISTs that let you interface easily with those applications, thus making it easier for you and your users to access those applications.

HOW IS A CLIST EXECUTED?

A CLIST can be executed in one of the three ways described below.

Explicit Form of the EXEC Command

There are several different ways to invoke a CLIST; however, any CLIST residing in a member of a PDS or in a sequential dataset can be executed using the EXEC command of TSO or the EXEC subcommand of EDIT. For example, suppose there exists a partitioned dataset called SYS2.PROD.CLIST which is a collection of CLISTs. We can invoke a CLIST member of this partitioned dataset by issuing the following TSO command:

```
EXEC 'SYS2.PROD.CLIST(member-name)'
```

(Note: EXEC can be abbreviated as EX)

It should be noted here that the name of the CLIST dataset need not have the word CLIST as the last qualifier, even though this is advisable. The reason for this will become clear shortly. Now to illustrate the point that the name of the dataset containing CLIST program can be anything, suppose that dataset 'SYS2.TEST.FILE' is a sequential dataset containing a CLIST. Then this CLIST can be executed by issuing the following EXEC command:

```
EX 'SYS2.TEST.FILE'
```

Suppose that the TSO user NIRMABK whose prefix is RF has created a sequential dataset called 'RF.ALLOC.CLIST'. The TSO user NIRMABK can execute this CLIST by issuing the following TSO command:

```
EXEC ALLOC
```

The command above expands into EXEC 'RF.ALLOC.CLIST' because the name of the dataset was not enclosed within quotation marks. This feature which allows you not to enter the first qualifier or the third qualifier of the dataset name helps to reduce typing and hence chances of error caused by mistyping.

To take another example, suppose a TSO user with prefix RF has a PDS 'RF.CLIST'. Then he can execute any member of this CLIST library by issuing the following command:

```
EX (member-name)
```

And, if that user has a PDS 'RF.LIB.CLIST', then he can execute a member of this CLIST library by executing:

```
EX LIB(member-name)
```

The explicit method of executing a CLIST is the most general, though not the most practical method. It is most general in the sense that whether or not a CLIST dataset is allocated under DDname SYSPROC during your TSO session, you can use the explicit form of the EXEC command described above to execute it. This method is not used frequently because it involves a lot of typing. The two other methods of executing CLISTs described below require much less typing and are therefore more frequently used.

Implicit Form of the EXEC Command

In this method, the user simply enters the name of the CLIST he or she wants to execute as if it was a TSO command. For example, suppose that partitioned dataset SYS2.PROD.CLIST is allocated under DDname SYSPROC during a TSO user's session and that this dataset contains member FOCUS, and, suppose further, that none of the libraries assigned to DDname STEPLIB nor any of the other MVS areas including the LINKLIST libraries contains member FOCUS. To execute member FOCUS of SYS2.PROD.CLIST, the user enters the following on native mode TSO screen or on TSO within ISPF panel and presses the Enter key:

```
FOCUS
```

(On any ISPF panel, one has to key in 'TSO FOCUS' and press the Enter key. This is true for any TSO command, as well.)

In this case the system first tries to determine if FOCUS is a TSO command. To do this it searches all the libraries allocated to DDname STEPLIB; then it searches other MVS areas such as LINKLIST. Failing to find member FOCUS in any of them, the system then searches the libraries allocated to DDname SYSPROC. In this example, the system will find FOCUS as a member in SYS2.PROD.CLIST and will execute it. The results of the execution will depend on what CLIST FOCUS does.

If the user knows that FOCUS is a CLIST, he can direct the system to search the libraries allocated under DDname SYSPROC directly without having to search system libraries such as STEPLIB datasets by using the extended implicit form of the EXECUTE command as described below.

Extended Implicit Form of the EXEC Command

This method is the fastest and most practical method of executing a CLIST. In this method the user simply enters a percent sign followed by the name of the CLIST he wants to execute as a TSO command and presses the Enter key. For example suppose that during a TSO user's session, partitioned dataset SYS2.PROD.CLIST is allocated under DDname SYSPROC and that this dataset consists of CLIST members. To invoke member FOCUS of SYS2.PROD.CLIST, it is sufficient to enter the following as a TSO command:

```
%FOCUS
```

The system will search only the libraries assigned to DDname SYSPROC, and, finding member FOCUS in SYS2.PROD.CLIST in this example, will execute this CLIST. This results in much faster response on the user's terminal compared to the implicit method described above.

But you may ask, how can I make sure that my CLIST library is one of the datasets assigned to DDname SYSPROC? The answer is this. Suppose your CLIST is in the partitioned dataset 'RF.LIB.CLIST'. Then to check whether this dataset is allocated under DDname SYSPROC, issue this command:

```
LISTA STAT H
```

This command will list the names of all the datasets that are currently allocated and the DDnames under which they are allocated. Suppose that DDname SYSPROC appears in this list but your dataset 'RF.LIB.CLIST' does not appear under DDname SYSPROC. You can issue the following command to first free the SYSPROC DDname:

```
FREE F(SYSPROC)
```

Next, you can allocate your CLIST dataset by issuing this command:

```
ALLOC DA('RF.LIB.CLIST') F(SYSPROC) SHR
```

However, if RF happens to be your TSO prefix, then the following command is sufficient:

```
ALLOC DA(LIB.CLIST) F(SYSPROC) SHR
```

Here we have allocated the dataset with shared disposition because this allows other TSO or batch users to use this dataset concurrently.

CONCATENATING CLIST LIBRARIES UNDER SYSPROC

Suppose that a TSO user has written several CLISTs and stored them in dataset 'RF.LIB.CLIST'. He would like to be able to execute CLISTs stored in this dataset as well as those stored in SYS1.CLIST and SYS2.CLIST which contain CLISTs for use by all TSO users at the installation. By concatenating these three datasets under SYSPROC, the user will be able to invoke any CLIST using the extended implicit form of the EXEC command. This concatenation can be done either in the log-on procedure or in a CLIST or directly on the terminal. To do this allocation, the TSO user first issues the FREE F(SYSPROC) command to free up SYSPROC if it is already allocated. Next, he issues the following command from within a CLIST which concatenates the datasets in the same order as they appear in the list:

```
ALLOC F(SYSPROC) DA('RF.LIB.CLIST' +
                    'SYS2.CLIST'   +
                    'SYS1.CLIST') SHR
```

The plus sign at the end of the first and the second line indicates that the command is continued on the next line. The single quotation marks are needed to make the dataset names fully-qualified names. Without the quotation marks, TSO would append the TSO user's dataset name prefix to the beginning of the dataset name supplied before doing the allocation. The disposition of SHR permits these datasets to be concurrently used by other users. Note that if the user wants to issue this ALLOC command directly from option 6 of ISPF, he should type the entire command continuously without using the plus character, but separating the dataset names by at least one space.

Note that after this allocation, the user can invoke member DISPTI of RF.LIB.CLIST by issuing:

```
%DISPTI
```

If member DISPTI was also present in the partitioned dataset SYS2.CLIST, that member will not be executed since TSO searches the datasets in the same order in which they appear in the allocation.

Rules for Concatenating Datasets Under SYSPROC

1. Only partitioned datasets should be concatenated.
2. The order of datasets appearing in the ALLOCATE command or in the JCL under DDname SYSPROC is important, since the concatenation order determines the order in which TSO searches the datasets for the specified CLIST. Hence, the most frequently used dataset should appear first in the concatenation order.
3. The block sizes of datasets also determine the concatenation order. It is best to make block sizes of all datasets the same. However, where block sizes vary, the MVS/370 (but not MVS/XA) system requires that the dataset with the largest block size appear first in the concatenation order. This is true for the ALLOCATE command used in a CLIST or on a terminal as well as for DDname SYSPROC appearing in the log-on procedure.

For example, if you want to concatenate your own CLIST dataset to the common CLIST library available at your installation so that your CLIST library appears first, make sure that the block size of your library is at least as large as the block size of the installation CLIST library. To find the block size of the installation CLIST library, use the following command to display all the attributes of the dataset:

```
LISTDS 'system-CLIST-data-set-name'
```

THINGS TO REMEMBER WHEN COPYING CLISTs FROM ONE DATASET TO ANOTHER

If you copy a CLIST from a dataset with fixed-blocked records into another with variable-blocked records thru ISPF/PDF, the line numbers in columns 73-80 also get copied. This data must be removed in order to make the

CLIST in the target dataset executable. You can do this removal thru ISPF/PDF Option 2 (Edit).

Similarly when you copy a CLIST from a dataset with variable-blocked records into another with fixed-blocked records thru ISPF/PDF, the line numbers in columns 1-8 of the input dataset also get copied. (When you edit a variable-blocked dataset, you do not normally see the line numbers). This data also must then be removed in order to make the CLIST in the target dataset executable. You can do this removal thru ISPF/PDF Option 2 (Edit).

Chapter 2
SOME SIMPLE BUT USEFUL CLIST EXAMPLES

In this chapter we will examine a number of CLISTs that have the following characteristics:

- they are useful in day-to-day work, and can be copied to your own CLIST library and executed with no or little change.
- they illustrate the techniques of writing CLIST programs.
- they can be easily modified to meet your unique needs at work.

Each CLIST will be explained in detail.

A CLIST TO DISPLAY THE TIME OF DAY IN A USER-FRIENDLY FORMAT

Let us examine a simple CLIST that can be used to display the time of the day in a user-friendly format. This CLIST is shown in Figure 2.1. This CLIST when executed at 4.45.20 p.m. will display the messages as shown in Figure 2.2, and when executed at 9.21.32 a.m. will display the lines as shown in Figure 2.3.

19

How Does this CLIST Work?

We will examine this question by referring to the line numbers shown on the left side in Figure 2.1. It should be noted that these line numbers are not coded in the CLIST. In the dataset you would only code the CLIST lines starting at column one or column 9 depending on whether the dataset has fixed blocked (FB) records or variable blocked (VB) records.

Now let us proceed to examine the question of how this CLIST works. Let us understand that &SYSTIME which is a

```
Line   Statement
Number

1      PROC 0
2      CONTROL NOMSG NOLIST
3      /*===============================================================*
4      /* THIS CLIST WILL DISPLAY THE TIME OF THE DAY IN A USER-FRIENDLY   *
5      /* FORMAT. IT WILL ALSO REMIND YOU TO GO HOME IF TIME OF DAY IS AFTER*
6      /* FOUR IN THE AFTERNOON.                                          *
7      /*===============================================================*
8      SET &HOUR = &SUBSTR(1:2,&SYSTIME)
9      SET &MIN  = &SUBSTR(4:5,&SYSTIME)
10     SET &SEC  = &SUBSTR(7:8,&SYSTIME)
11     SET &TOT  = &HOUR&MIN&SEC
12     IF &HOUR = 0 THEN SET &HRPRT = MIDNIGHT
13     IF &HOUR > 12 THEN SET &HOUR1 = &HOUR - 12
14     IF &HOUR > 12 THEN SET &HRPRT = &HOUR1. PM
15     IF &HOUR = 12 THEN SET &HRPRT = &HOUR. NOON
16     IF &HOUR < 12 THEN SET &HRPRT= &HOUR. AM
17     IF &MIN > 1 THEN +
18        WRITE IT IS NOW &MIN MINUTES
19     IF &MIN NG 1 THEN +
20        WRITE IT IS NOW &MIN MINUTE
21     WRITE             AND
22     IF &SEC > 1 THEN +
23        WRITE            &SEC   SECONDS
24     IF &SEC NG 1 THEN +
25        WRITE            &SEC   SECOND
26     WRITE
27     WRITE AFTER &HRPRT
28     WRITE
29     IF &TOT > 160000 THEN +
30        WRITE IT'S AFTER FOUR ALREADY, DON'T YOU WANT TO GO HOME??
31     END
```

Figure 2.1.   A CLIST to display the time of the day in an user-friendly format.

```
IT IS NOW 45 MINUTES
            AND
            20 SECONDS

AFTER 4 PM

IT'S AFTER FOUR ALREADY, DON'T YOU WANT TO GO HOME??
***
```

Figure 2.2. Shows messages displayed by executing the CLIST in Figure 2.1 at 4.45 p.m.

control variable used to obtain the present time of the day in format hh:mm:ss, where hh is hours, mm is minutes and ss is seconds, is 16:10:08. The statement on line 8 moves into variable &HOUR that portion of &SYSTIME which starts at position 1 and ends at position 2. So variable &HOUR assumes a value of 16. Similarly line 9 causes 10 to be moved into variable &MIN and line 10 causes 08 to be moved into variable &SEC. Line 11 causes variable &TOT to assume a value of 161008 as a result of concatenation of the three variables, &HOUR, &MIN and &SEC.

```
IT IS NOW 21 MINUTES
            AND
            32 SECONDS

AFTER 09 AM

***
```

Figure 2.3. Shows messages displayed by executing the CLIST in Figure 2.1 at 9.21 a.m.

The THEN clause of line 12 does not get executed because &HOUR is not zero. And since &HOUR is greater than 12, the THEN clauses of lines 13 and 14 are executed causing &HRPRT to assume a value of '4 PM'. The THEN clauses of lines 15 and 16 are not executed since &HOUR is neither equal to nor less than 12. Since &MIN is greater than one, line 18 gets executed causing the following line to appear on the terminal:

```
IT IS NOW 10 MINUTES
```

Line 21 gets executed unconditionally causing the following line to appear on the terminal:

```
AND
```

And since &SEC is greater than one, line 23 gets executed causing the following line to appear on the terminal:

```
08  SECONDS
```

Line 26 results in a blank line to appear on the screen. Line 27 causes the following line to appear on the screen:

```
AFTER 4 PM
```

Line 28 causes a blank line to appear on the screen unconditionally. Next, since &TOT happens to be greater than 160000, line 30 gets executed causing the following line to appear on the screen:

```
IT'S AFTER FOUR ALREADY, DON'T YOU WANT TO GO HOME??
```

The statement on line 31 signals the end of the CLIST and the CLIST execution terminates which causes TSO to display a line with three asterisks on the terminal. At this point, the TSO user is free to use the terminal for any other work.

You can enter this CLIST in your own dataset and execute it using the methods of executing CLISTs described in Chapter 1. This will convince you that this CLIST works at all times of the day. If you are an inexperienced CLIST user, this will also give you a chance to become familiar with the process of writing and testing CLISTs.

A CLIST TO DISPLAY INFORMATION SUCH AS JULIAN DATE, USER ID AND LOG-ON PROCEDURE, ETC.

Figure 2.4 shows a CLIST that can be used to obtain important information such as User ID, Julian Date, etc. If this CLIST is stored as member INFO in a PDS allocated to DDname SYSPROC under your TSO session, you can invoke it from any ISPF panel by typing the following on the command line:

```
TSO %INFO
```

This CLIST will display a number of message lines. One such display is shown in Figure 2.5. This CLIST uses the ISPEXEC command of ISPF to obtain current values of

```
CONTROL NOMSG NOLIST
ISPEXEC VGET (ZUSER,ZPREFIX,ZTIME,ZDATE,ZJDATE,ZTERM)
WRITE YOUR TSO USER ID IS ==================> &ZUSER
WRITE YOUR TSO USER PREFIX IS ==============> &ZPREFIX
WRITE YOUR TSO LOG-ON PROCEDURE NAME IS ===> &SYSPROC
WRITE CURRENT DATE (YY/MM/DD) IS ==========> &ZDATE
WRITE CUREENT DATE IN JULIAN FORMAT IS ====> &ZJDATE
WRITE CURRENT TIME (HH:MM) IS =============> &ZTIME
WRITE YOUR TERMINAL TYPE IS ===============> &ZTERM
EXIT
```

Figure 2.4.   A CLIST to display important information on the terminal.

```
YOUR TSO USER ID IS ================> Z7BJN
YOUR TSO USER PREFIX IS ============> Z7BJN
YOUR TSO LOG-ON PROCEDURE NAME IS ===> @LGN2
CURRENT DATE (YY/MM/DD) IS =========> 89/08/30
CURRENT DATE IN JULIAN FORMAT IS ====> 89.242
CURRENT TIME (HH:MM) IS ============> 14:00
YOUR TERMINAL TYPE IS ==============> 3278
***
```

Figure 2.5.   One example of the messages displayed by executing the CLIST of Figure 2.4.

ISPF system variables, which are described fully in the following IBM publication:

> *Interactive System Productivity Facility (ISPF)*
> *Dialog Management Services (MVS, VM/SP, and VSE/AF)*
> (Publication Number: SC34-2088-2)

Note that variables whose name starts with character Z are ISPF variables that are obtained by executing the ISPEXEC command, while &SYSPROC is a CLIST control variable that is listed in Appendix B. The ISPF variables are described in the IBM publication listed above.

This CLIST can be very helpful especially in displaying the current Julian date. Of course, the current date (in YY/MM/DD format) and time can be easily obtained by issuing the TSO command TIME. But the TIME command does not display the current date in the Julian format. And very often programmers and systems analysts do not have a calendar on their desks that shows the current date in the Julian format. You will agree that the Julian format is used in many system displays. For example, when you issue the LISTCAT command against a dataset, its creation date is shown in the Julian format. So, you can use the CLIST in Figure 2.4 to get a rough idea of the date of creation of that dataset. Of course, what would be really desirable is to have a CLIST that could accept a Julian date as input, convert it into the YY/MM/DD format and display the result. This CLIST should also be able to accept a date in the YY/MM/DD format and convert it into the Julian format. If you have a date conversion routine (commonly written in the Assembly language) available at your installation, you can easily write a CLIST that does the conversion from the Julian format into the YY/MM/DD format, and vice versa by calling the date routine.

A CLIST TO DELETE A NUMBER OF DATASETS WITH VARYING FIRST QUALIFIER

Suppose that every user at an installation has a dataset named prefix.LIB.CLIST where prefix stands for the TSO dataset name prefix of the user. A CLIST is to be written which will ask the user for the dataset name prefix. It will read in the value entered by the user on the terminal. If no value was entered (the user just pressed the ENTER key) the CLIST will ask the user for the dataset name prefix again, otherwise it will issue the TSO DELETE command to delete prefix.LIB.CLIST, where prefix is replaced by the value supplied by the user. It will then ask the user for another value for prefix. When the word QUIT is entered for the prefix, the CLIST will end. A CLIST which performs the function described is shown in Figure 2.6.

In this CLIST, note the use of two periods on line 15. Here we are concatenating a literal to a symbolic variable, the literal being a period followed by LIB.CLIST. According to the rule for concatenating a literal to a symbolic variable, the symbolic variable must be followed by a period and then the literal. Thus, the first period on line 15 serves as a delimiter, while the second period is part of the literal being concatenated.

```
1    PROC 0
2    CONTROL MSG NOLIST
3    WRITE ===================================================================
4    WRITE THIS CLIST WILL ASK YOU FOR A DATA SET NAME PREFIX. IT WILL THEN
5    WRITE ISSUE A DELETE AGAINST PREFIX.LIB.CLIST WHERE PREFIX IS THE
6    WRITE VALUE YOU SUPPLIED. IT WILL THEN ASK YOU FOR ANOTHER VALUE FOR
7    WRITE PREFIX. YOU CAN ENTER QUIT AS THE PREFIX VALUE, WHICH WILL
8    WRITE TERMINATE THIS CLIST. NO DELETE WILL BE ISSUED AGAINST
9    WRITE QUIT.LIB.CLIST.
10   WRITE ===================================================================
11   LOOP: WRITE PLEASE ENTER THE DATA SET NAME PREFIX (ENTER QUIT TO END).
12   READ PREFIX
13   IF &PREFIX = THEN GOTO LOOP
14   IF &PREFIX = QUIT THEN GOTO ENDCLIST
15   DELETE '&PREFIX..LIB.CLIST'
16   GOTO LOOP
17   ENDCLIST: EXIT
```

Figure 2.6.   A CLIST to delete a dataset with any specified first level qualifier.

Also, note that if the user simply pressed the Enter key without entering anything on the terminal in response to query by the CLIST, or if he entered one or more blanks and then pressed the Enter key, the value of symbolic variable &PREFIX after the execution of the READ statement on line 12 will be blank. The statement on line 13 is checking whether the value of &PREFIX is blank, and, if so, it branches to the line with label LOOP. This is a useful technique to detect if the user entered a blank value for a symbolic variable by simply pressing the Enter key without entering even a single character on the terminal or by entering only spaces before pressing the Enter key. In this connection note that there is one space before the word THEN on line 13 in Figure 2.3. But more than one space before THEN on this line will not change the way the comparison works.

Another point to note is that when the DELETE command issued by this CLIST is unsuccessful because the dataset does not exist, the following message will be dis-

```
PROC 0
CONTROL MSG,NOLIST
WRITE ===================================================================
WRITE THIS CLIST WILL RENAME  CT161.FILE1, CT161.FILE2..... CT161.FILEN
WRITE TO CP161.FILE1....CP161.FILEN WHERE N IS THE VALUE YOU WILL
WRITE SUPPLY. (NOTE: N SHOULD BE BETWEEN 1 AND 100, OTHERWISE THIS
WRITE CLIST WILL TERMINATE WITHOUT DOING ANY RENAMING.)
WRITE ===================================================================
WRITE HOW MANY FILES DO YOU WANT TO RENAME?
READ &LIMIT
IF &LIMIT LT 1 OR &LIMIT GT 100 THEN GOTO ERROR1
SET &NUM = 0
LOOP: SET &NUM = &NUM + 1
RENAME 'CT161.FILE&NUM.'  'CP161.FILE&NUM.'
IF &NUM = &LIMIT THEN GOTO ENDCLIST
GOTO LOOP
ERROR1: WRITE THE VALUE OF N SUPPLIED IS NOT WITHIN RANGE
WRITE THIS CLIST TERMINATES WITHOUT DOING ANY RENAME OPERATION.
ENDCLIST: EXIT
```

Figure 2.7.   A CLIST to rename multiple datasets without using multiple RENAME commands.

played on the terminal and the CLIST execution will abnormally terminate:

```
IKJ56709I INVALID DATA SET NAME 'data-set-name'
```

Later we will discuss how to prevent the CLIST from terminating in such situations, because it would be better if a message was displayed and the operator was prompted for another value for the dataset name prefix.

A CLIST TO RENAME MULTIPLE NON-VSAM DATASETS

Suppose that there exist non-VSAM datasets named CT161.FILE1, CT161.FILE2, CT161.FILE3, and so on up to CT161.FILE100. The task is to write a CLIST which will rename all these datasets to CP161.FILE1, CP161.FILE2, CP161.FILE3, and so on up to CP161.FILE100 respectively. One brute-force approach to solving this problem would be to write a CLIST with 100 RENAME commands. However, a smart programmer could use concatenation to achieve the same thing with a CLIST with fewer than twenty lines, as shown in Figure 2.7. This CLIST is flexible in allowing the operator to rename any number of datasets, from one to one-hundred. The user is asked to supply the number of datasets to be renamed. This flexibility is a desirable feature of well-written CLISTs.

Note that the TSO RENAME command used to rename non-VSAM datasets has this format:

```
RENAME old-data-set-name   new-data-set-name
```

where there should be at least one blank between the old dataset name and the new dataset name. Also note that a fully-qualified dataset name must be enclosed within quotation marks.

In CLISTs, TSO commands and subcommands are frequently used. We have therefore included a discussion of the commonly used TSO commands and subcommands in Appendix A. However, for a more detailed discussion of the commands presented in Appendix A as well as other commands, please refer to the following IBM manual:

MVS/ Extended Architecture TSO Extensions
TSO Command Language Reference
(Manual # SC28-1134)

or an equivalent manual applicable to the software environment at your installation.

You will note that the CLISTs of Figure 2.6 and Figure 2.7 are written so that they will display a number of lines explaining how the CLIST works right in the beginning. This way the user of the CLIST will become aware of what to expect from the CLIST execution. This too is a very desirable feature of well-written CLISTs and interactive programs written in any language. The idea is to maintain a good level of communication between the program and the user. Good, effective communication is not only a key factor in maintaining healthy relations between spouses, coworkers and people, it is also a key factor in ensuring that the man-machine dialog is effective and productive, eliminating confusion and surprises for the user. Effective man-machine dialog is profitable for the company and enjoyable for the users of computer programs and systems.

Another point is that if any RENAME operation carried by this CLIST ended in failure, the following message would be displayed on the terminal and the CLIST execution would abnormally terminate:

```
IKJ58201I DATA SET 'data-set-name' NOT IN CATALOG OR AMOUNT OF DATA SETS
     EXCEEDS WORKAREA FOR GENERIC RENAME
```

Later in this book, we will discuss how to prevent the CLIST from terminating altogether in such situations. This will be helpful when we want to use this CLIST to rename say 20 or 50 datasets, knowing that some datasets in this range may not exist.

A CLIST TO DISPLAY N AND 2 TO THE POWER OF N FOR N=0,1,2...20

Suppose we want to write a CLIST which prints the value of two raised to the power of N for all values of N from zero to twenty. Such a CLIST will be of great interest to all programmers, who can use this CLIST rather than look up a booklet such as IBM's well-known yellow card that contains codes and other information for the IBM 370 family of computers. Figure 2.8 shows such a CLIST. The following notes describes how this CLIST works. The result of executing this CLIST is shown in Figure 2.9 (Note that the lines with dashes in this figure represent lines not shown in order to keep this figure short. In reality, all lines with values of N from zero to twenty are displayed on the terminal.) The

```
1    SET N = 0
2    WRITE   N        2**N
3    WRITE
4    LOOP: SET RESULT = 2 ** &N
5    WRITE &N        &RESULT
6    SET &N = &N + 1
7    IF &N = 21 THEN GOTO ENDCLIST
8    GOTO LOOP
9    ENDCLIST: EXIT
```

Figure 2.8.   A CLIST to display N and 2 to the power of N, for N = 0,1,2...20.

```
N       2**N

0       1
1       2
2       4
3       8
4       16
5       32
-  -  -  -  -
-  -  -  -  -
-  -  -  -  -
18      262144
19      524288
20      1048576
```

Figure 2.9.   The display on the terminal shown by executing the CLIST in Figure 2.8.

number on the left below refers to the line number in the CLIST of Figure 2.8. Note that when you enter this or any other CLIST in a dataset, you do not enter the line numbers shown on the left in Figure 2.8.

1. The symbolic variable &N is initialized to zero.
2. The heading line is written on the terminal.
3. A blank line is written on the terminal.
4. The SET statement computes 2 raised to the power of &N and assigns the result of computation to symbolic variable &RESULT.
5. The values of &N and &RESULT are written on the terminal.
6. &N is incremented by 1 through this SET statement.
7. A test is made if &N has become 21. If so, control is transferred to label ENDCLIST otherwise control flows to line 8 which is the next sequential line.
8. Control is unconditionally transferred to the line with label LOOP.
9. The EXIT statement causes the termination of this CLIST.

TWO CLISTs TO ILLUSTRATE THE DO-END AND DO-WHILE-END SEQUENCES

Let us suppose that we are writing a CLIST and we want to test if the employee's nationality is Canadian, and, if so, we want to do the following things:

- Increment counter &TOTCANADIANS which keeps count of Canadian employees.
- Turn on &FLAGCANADA to indicate that a Canadian employee has been encountered.
- Write a message on the terminal.

If the employee's nationality is not Canadian, we just want to do one thing, that is increment the counter &TOTOTHERS. The code in Figure 2.10 will achieve this objective. In this figure you will notice that the statements to be executed if the condition tested is true, have been placed in a DO-Group.

The rules governing the DO-WHILE sequence can be best described through a sample CLIST given in Figure 2.11. The number on the left in the following description refers to the line number given in this figure.

Descriptions of the CLIST in Figure 2.11

1 thru 6	These are comment lines.
7	Initializes symbolic variable &NOTHING to nulls (i.e., blanks).
8,9	Send prompt to the terminal.
10	Reads the text entered by the user and stores it in &STATEMENT.
11	Tests if &STATEMENT is not equal to null(i.e., blanks). If so, statements on line 12 thru 24 are executed. When the END on line 25 is encountered, control goes back to the DO-WHILE on line 11 where this condition is tested again.

```
IF &NATIONALITY = 10       /* 10 = CANADIAN  */   +
   THEN DO
      SET &TOTCANADIANS = &TOTCANADIANS + 1
      SET &FLAGCANADA = 1
      WRITE PROCESSING CANADIAN EMPLOYEE, EMPLOYEE NUMBER = &NUMBER
      END
   ELSE +
      SET &TOTOTHERS = &TOTOTHERS + 1
```

Figure 2.10. A CLIST segment showing the use of DO group in an IF-THEN-ELSE sequence.

```
Line
Num
1      /*======================================================================
2     /* THIS CLIST WILL ASK THE USER FOR A STATEMENT. IT WILL THEN
3     /* DISPLAY THAT STATEMENT TEN TIMES ON THE TERMINAL. IT WILL THEN
4     /* REPEAT THE ABOVE PROCESS. WHEN A STATEMENT OF NULL IS ENTERED, THIS
5     /* CLIST TERMINATES.
6      /*======================================================================
7     SET &NOTHING =
8     WRITE ENTER THE STATEMENT YOU WANT DISPLAYED 10 TIMES. IF YOU WANT TO
9     WRITE QUIT, SIMPLY PRESS THE ENTER KEY WITHOUT ENTERING ANYTHING.
10    READ &STATEMENT
11    DO WHILE &STATEMENT NE &NOTHING
12       WRITE &STATEMENT
13       WRITE &STATEMENT
14       WRITE &STATEMENT
15       WRITE &STATEMENT
16       WRITE &STATEMENT
17       WRITE &STATEMENT
18       WRITE &STATEMENT
19       WRITE &STATEMENT
20       WRITE &STATEEMNT
21       WRITE &STATEMENT
22       WRITE DO YOU WANT TO PLAY THIS GAME AGAIN? IF SO, ENTER YOUR STATEMENT
23       WRITE PLEASE. (SIMPLY PRESS ENTER KEY IF YOU WANT TO QUIT.)
24       READ &STATEMENT
25    END
26    EXIT
```

Figure 2.11. A CLIST showing the use of DO-WHILE sequence to control a loop.

If the condition tested is false, that is if &STATEMENT is nulls (i.e., blanks), the statements demarcated by the DO on line 11 and the END on line 25 are bypassed and control goes to line 26, that is to the line following the END.

12 thru 21   Writes the value of &STATEMENT on the terminal.

22,23   Writes prompt to the user.

24   Reads the text entered by the user and stores it in &STATEMENT.

25   This indicates the end of the DO-Group initiated by the DO on line 11.

26   This statement causes the CLIST execution to terminate.

A CLIST ILLUSTRATING THE USE OF AN EXPRESSION ON THE GOTO STATEMENT

Let us consider a CLIST which reads in an employee's nationality code and displays the nationality in words. This CLIST is given in Figure 2.12. In this program you will notice that if the nationality code entered by the user is blank, the statement on line 6 will cause a branch to label ENDCLIST, since the value of &FINISHED at that point is ENDCLIST. The GOTO statement on line 12 causes an unconditional branch, but the destination depends on what the value of &NATCODE happens to be at that point. If &NATCODE has a value of 04, the branch will be to label LAB04; and if &NATCODE happens to be 50, then GOTO LAB&NATCODE will cause a branch to label LAB50, since the value of LAB&NATCODE after symbolic substitution will be LAB50.

```
1              SET &FINISHED = ENDCLIST
2     LOOP:    WRITE ENTER TWO DIGIT NATIONALITY CODE PLEASE. (E.G. ENTER 02 AND
3              WRITE NOT 2 FOR NATIONALITY CODE=02)
4              WRITE (SIMPLY PRESS ENTER KEY WITHOUT ENTERING ANYTHING TO QUIT.)
5              READ &NATCODE
6              IF &NATCODE =   THEN GOTO &FINISHED
7              IF &NATCODE = 00 THEN +
8                DO
9                   WRITE NATIONALITY CODE = 00 IS INVALID
10                  GOTO LOOP
11               END
12             GOTO LAB&NATCODE
13    LAB01: WRITE THIS NATIONALITY CODE = CANADIAN
14             GOTO LOOP
15    LAB02: WRITE THIS NATIONALITY CODE= U.S.
16             GOTO LOOP
17    LAB03: WRITE THIS NATIONALITY CODE = THAI
18             GOTO LOOP
- - - - - - - - - - -
- - - - - - - - -
      LAB99: WRITE THIS NATIONALITY CODE = LIBYAN
               GOTO LOOP
      ENDCLIST: EXIT
```

Figure 2.12.   A CLIST showing the use of an expression as destination on a GOTO statement.

AVOIDING CONFUSION ABOUT THE ROLE OF AN END

The END command of TSO when used in a called CLIST, terminates the CLIST execution and control goes back to the calling CLIST. In a CLIST which is at the top of the hierarchy, that is a CLIST which is not called by another CLIST, the END command terminates the CLIST execution. This function is better done thru the EXIT statement. It is advised that the EXIT statement be used to transfer control to the calling CLIST, or to TSO, along with a return code if desired. The calling CLIST can check the return code and take appropriate action.

Often confusion can arise regarding whether an END is meant to end a DO-Group or to be interpreted as an END command to terminate the CLIST. For example, consider the code in Figure 2.13. Here it is possible that the programmer had intended to use the first END to end the CLIST, the second END to end the second DO-Group, and the third END to end the first DO-Group. This is what appears to be the intention from the way the code is indented. But this is not how the computer 'thinks.' The system interprets the first END to end the second DO

```
IF &STATUS = MARRIED THEN +
  DO
    SET &FLAG1 = Y
    IF &NATIONALITY = SAUDI THEN +
      DO
        SET &FLAG2 = Y
        WRITE A SERIOUS ERROR HAS BEEN ENCOUNTERED.
        WRITE THIS CLIST TERMINATES ABNORMALLY.
        END
      END
  END
WRITE GOOD MORNING, DEAR USER.
```

Figure 2.13. A CLIST segment showing possible confusion about role of END statement.

group, the second END to end the first DO group and the third END as a TSO END command ending the CLIST execution altogether. Hence the 'GOOD MORNING' message never gets written to the terminal. The system does not use indentation of code in interpreting the role of various END or any other statements. The indentation of code is for us humans to be able to make sense of the programs quickly and easily. It is not meant for the computer to use in its interpretation of our code.

One way to avoid this kind of confusion about the role of the END statement is to use the END option on the CONTROL statement. When a literal of up to four characters is used on the END operand of the CONTROL statement, that literal becomes the termination indicator for all DO-Groups (DO-END and DO-WHILE-END sequences) within the CLIST. For example, consider the code in Figure 2.14 which is exactly identical to the code in Figure 2.13 except that the literal ENDX has been used a termination indicator to end the DO-Groups and a CONTROL statement has been added right on top of this code. Now there is only

```
CONTROL END(ENDX)
IF &STATUS = MARRIED THEN +
  DO
    SET &FLAG1 = Y
    IF &NATIONALITY = SAUDI THEN +
      DO
        SET &FLAG2 = Y
        WRITE A SERIOUS ERROR HAS BEEN ENCOUNTERED.
        WRITE THIS CLIST TERMINATES ABNORMALLY.
        END
      ENDX
  ENDX
WRITE GOOD MORNING, DEAR USER.
```

Figure 2.14.   A CLIST segment showing use of CONTROL statement to avoid possible confusion about role of END statement.

one END statement in this code and that is interpreted as the END command of TSO to end CLIST execution. There is no more confusion. Now the CLIST will terminate due to the END command only if &STATUS is MARRIED and &NATIONALITY is SAUDI. In all other cases, the 'GOOD MORNING' message will be written to the terminal. Two points should be noted in this regard:

1. Even though we have used ENDX in Figure 2.14, you can use any literal of up to four characters, as long as the first character is alphabetic and the rest alphameric. But you would be advised to choose a meaningful name, and not use a literal like MOON or STAR as termination indicator. Choosing meaningful names for variables, labels etc. is a universal principle applicable to all computer languages including the TSO CLIST language.
2. In order for the system to interpret the literal ENDX properly, the CONTROL statement must be executed first. Hence the CONTROL statement should be placed near the top of the CLIST. The convention is to have PROC statement as the first statement and the CONTROL statement as the second statement in every CLIST program.

THREE CLIST EXAMPLES ILLUSTRATING THE USE OF PROC STATEMENT

Example 1. Take a look at the CLIST in Figure 2.1 that we discussed earlier in this chapter. As you will recall, this CLIST can be used to display the time of day. Assuming that this CLIST was stored as member DISPTI in a partitioned dataset which is allocated under DDname SYSPROC during your TSO session, you can execute this CLIST by entering the following as a TSO command:

```
%DISPTI
```

Note that the PROC statement in this CLIST (PROC 0) specifies that there are no positional parameters to be passed
to this CLIST. Since there are neither positional nor keyword parameters to be passed, we could have omitted the
PROC statement altogether. But keeping the PROC statement helps. It allows us to add positional or keyword
parameters on the PROC statement later, in case it is
deemed necessary.

Example 2.   Consider the CLIST in Figure 2.8. This CLIST
displays N and 2 raised to the power of N for all values of N
from 0 to 20. Suppose we want to modify this CLIST so that
it would accept two values X and Y and will display N and 2
raised to the power of N for values of N from X to Y, inclusive. The modified CLIST is given in Figure 2.15. Assuming
that CLIST is stored as member POWER2 in partitioned
dataset 'SYS2.CLIST', it can be invoked as follows:

```
EXEC 'SYS2.CLIST(POWER2)' '10 15'
```

```
PROC 2 LOWLIM HIGHLIM
SET N = &LOWLIM
WRITE    N        2**N
WRITE
LOOP: SET RESULT = 2 ** &N
WRITE &N     &RESULT
SET &N = &N + 1
IF &N = (&HIGHLIM + 1) THEN GOTO ENDCLIST
GOTO LOOP
ENDCLIST: EXIT
```

Figure 2.15.   A CLIST to display N and 2 to the power of N, for N from
LOWLIM to HIGHLIM inclusive, where LOWLIM and
HIGHLIM are variable.

Here we have entered all the parameters in quotation marks, because the explicit form of EXEC command has been used. When CLIST starts executing, LOWLIM has the value 10 and HIGHLIM has the value 15. Hence the CLIST displays N and 2 raised to the power of N for all values of N from 10 to 15 inclusive. But what if we omitted the parameters from the EXEC command? This is what would happen.

```
OPERATOR:  EXEC 'SYS2.CLIST(POWER2)'
SYSTEM:    ENTER POSITIONAL PARAMETER LOWLIM -
OPERATOR:  10
SYSTEM:    ENTER POSITIONAL PARAMETER HIGHLIM -
OPERATOR:  21
```

At this point the system will execute the CLIST and the result of execution will be displayed on the terminal. If we want to use the implicit or the extended implicit form of the EXEC command, we must not enter the parameters in quotation marks, as is done with the explicit form of the EXEC command. Supposing that SYS2.CLIST, a PDS containing this CLIST is allocated under DDname SYSPROC in your TSO session, you could execute this CLIST as follows:

```
%POWER2 10 20
```

Example 3. Now let us change the CLIST of Figure 2.15 so that it computes not 2 raised to the power of N but 16 raised to the power of N, for all values of N from LOWLIM to HIGHLIM, inclusive. We want to make this modification in such a way that this CLIST can be easily changed to compute say 8 raised to the power of N or 4 raised to the power of N. The modified CLIST is shown in Figure 2.16. You will note that we have used a keyword parameter BASE on the PROC statement. This keyword parameter has been assigned a default value of 16 on the PROC statement. In the rest of the CLIST, we use the symbolic variable &BASE

```
PROC 2 LOWLIM HIGHLIM BASE(16)
SET N = &LOWLIM
WRITE   N        &BASE**N
WRITE
LOOP: SET RESULT = &BASE ** &N
WRITE &N      &RESULT
SET &N = &N + 1
IF &N = (&HIGHLIM + 1) THEN GOTO ENDCLIST
GOTO LOOP
ENDCLIST: EXIT
```

Figure 2.16.   A CLIST to display N and 16 to the power of N, for N from
LOWLIM to HIGHLIM inclusive, where   LOWLIM and
HIGHLIM are variable.

rather than the literal 16. Supposing that this CLIST is
stored in member &POWERB of a partitioned dataset which
is allocated under DDname SYSPROC, we can invoke this
CLIST by typing the following:

```
%POWERB 2 6
```

This will display N and 16 raised to the power of N for all
values of N from 2 to 6, inclusive. Now suppose that we
want to cause this CLIST to use 8 as the base rather than
16, this can be easily achieved by specifying the value of
keyword parameter BASE on the EXEC command:

```
%POWERB 2 6 BASE(8)
```

It can also be done by changing the default value of BASE
from 16 to 8 on the PROC statement. It should be noted
that the CLIST of Figure 2.16 can not be used to compute
16 raised to the power of N where N is 8 or greater. If this is
attempted, the CLIST will produce an error message and
terminate. This is because 16 raised to the power of 8 is

```
PROC 2 A B
CONTROL SYMLIST CONLIST
TIME
SET &R1 = &A * &B
WRITE THE PRODUCT OF &A AND &B  = &R1
EXIT
```

Figure 2.17. A CLIST to display A*B where A and B are supplied by the user.

```
ENTER POSITIONAL PARAMETER A - 2
ENTER POSITIONAL PARAMETER B - 5
TIME
TIME-04:25:41 PM. CPU-00:00:01 SERVICE-12089 SESSION - - - -
SET &R1 = &A * &B
SET &R1 = 2 * 5
WRITE THE PRODUCT OF &A AND &B =  &R1
WRITE THE PRODUCT OF 2 AND 5 =  10
THE PRODUCT OF 2 AND 5 =  10
EXIT
EXIT
***
```

Figure 2.18. One display written to terminal as a result of executing the CLIST in Figure 2.17.

```
TIME
TIME-04:28:45 PM. CPU-00:00:02 SERVICE-15702 SESSION-00:04:43. . . . .
THE PRODUCT OF 10 AND 20 =  200
***
```

Figure 2.19. One display written to terminal as a result of executing the CLIST in Figure 2.17 with revised PROC and CONTROL statements.

equal to 2 raised to the power of 32, which exceeds the maximum number that can be handled in command procedures. It should be remembered that an integer to be handled within a CLIST can only have value within the range:

```
- (2 ** 31)   to   (2 ** 31) - 1
```

A CLIST ILLUSTRATING THE USE OF THE CONTROL STATEMENT

Consider the CLIST in Figure 2.17. This CLIST has the options SYMLIST and CONLIST. CONLIST specifies that all CLIST statements excluding TSO commands or subcommands will be displayed at the terminal before execution but after symbolic substitution. SYMLIST specifies that all executable statements including TSO commands and subcommands will be displayed at the terminal once prior to scanning for symbolic substitution. If this CLIST is stored as member TEST99 in a CLIST library allocated under DDname SYSPROC, it can be executed thru the command %TEST99. The output displayed at the terminal as a result of the execution is shown in Figure 2.18. You will notice that the user has been prompted for positional parameters A and B. Note that TIME is a TSO command which displays the current time of the day as well as other statistical data.

Now let us change the PROC and the CONTROL statements in Figure 2.17 to the following:

```
PROC 0 A(0) B(0)
CONTROL LIST
```

In the revised CLIST the two parameters have been made into keyword parameters. If the revised CLIST is executed and 10 and 20 are passed as the values for the keyword parameters A and B respectively (e.g. thru the command: %TEST99 A(10) B(20)), the output will appear as shown in

Figure 2.19. Note that this time the LIST option is in effect which causes only TSO commands and subcommands and not the command procedure statements to be displayed at the terminal.

A CLIST TO ILLUSTRATE THE USE OF CONTROL VARIABLE &LASTCC

Control variable &LASTCC provides the return code from the last operation performed within the CLIST, whether a TSO command, a subcommand or a CLIST statement. It also can be a return code passed by a called (nested) CLIST, or a called program. The return codes returned from executing a TSO command or a subcommand are:

0   Normal completion of the command or subcommand.

12 A severe error occurred during the execution but TSO command processor might have been able to prompt the user for information needed to recover from the error.

The return codes returned by command procedure statements are given in Appendix C in this book. Note that &LASTCC is in decimal format and can be changed within a CLIST.

Example 1. Consider the CLIST given in Figure 2.20. In this CLIST, if the ALLOC command did not complete successfully due to any reason, two lines of message would be written to the terminal and the CLIST execution would terminate. If this CLIST was executed from TSO, control will go to TSO which will display the prompt sign, which is READY under native mode of TSO and three asterisks under TSO within ISPF. It should be noted that if we did not test for the non-zero value of &LASTCC after the

```
10    CONTROL MAIN MSG LIST
20    ALLOC F(INPUT) DA('TRMRS.MASTFILE.CLUSTER') SHR
30    IF &LASTCC NE 0 THEN +
40      DO
50      WRITE ERROR ON ALLOCATING DDNAME INPUT HAS OCCURRED.
60      WRITE THIS CLIST IS UNABLE TO CONTINUE NORMALLY.
70      GOTO ENDCLIST
80      END
90    ALLOC F(OUTPUT) DA(*)
100   CALL 'Z2BKN.MLOAD(LISTFILE)'
110   ENDCLIST: EXIT
```

Figure 2.20. A CLIST showing the use of &LASTCC to control processing.

ALLOC command, the ALLOC F(OUTPUT) would be executed followed by the execution of the CALL command. And since the program LISTFILE most likely requires that DDname INPUT be allocated, this program will terminate abnormally.

Example 2. Now consider the scenario in Figure 2.21 where CLIST A calls CLIST B to test whether the time of the day is before 12 noon (A.M.) or after 12 noon (P.M.). If the time of the day happens to be exactly 12 noon or after noon, CLIST B returns a return code of 44 to the calling CLIST, otherwise it returns a return code of 33. CLIST B returns this information thru the EXIT statement. CLIST A then displays an appropriate message depending on whether the time is exactly 12 noon, before noon or after noon. Note that when control comes to CLIST A from CLIST B, the return code passed by B thru the CODE operand of EXIT statement is available in symbolic variable &LASTCC in CLIST A.

It is assumed that CLIST B is stored as member B in a partitioned dataset (PDS) allocated under DDname

```
CLIST A
-------
10    CONTROL MAIN MSG NOLIST
20    %B
30    SET &RETCODE = &LASTCC
40    IF &RETCODE = 33 THEN +
50      WRITE CURRENT TIME OF DAY IS BEFORE NOON.
60    IF &RETCODE = 44 THEN +
70      WRITE CURRENT TIME OF THE DAY IS AFTER NOON OR EXACTLY 12 NOON.
80    IF &RETCODE EQ 33 OR &RETCODE EQ 44 THEN
90    ELSE WRITE ** INVALID RETURN CODE PASSED BY CLIST B *****
100   EXIT

CLIST B
-------
10    CONTROL MSG NOLIST
20    SET &HOUR = &SUBSTR(1:2,&SYSTIME)
30    IF &HOUR GE 12 THEN +
40       SET &RETURN = 44
50    ELSE +
60       SET &RETURN = 33
70    EXIT CODE(&RETURN)
```

Figure 2.21. Two CLISTs to illustrate the technique of passing return code in control variable &LASTCC.

SYSPROC. This allows us to invoke CLIST B as shown on line 20 in CLIST A. Note that %B can be thought of as a TSO command. Also note how immediately upon return from CLIST B, the content of &LASTCC is saved in user-defined symbolic variable &RETCODE. If this saving is not done, the content of &LASTCC will soon be over-written because as you will remember &LASTCC contains the return code of the last command, subcommand or CLIST statement executed, and hence by definition its value dynamically changes as the CLIST execution proceeds.

It should be noted that if the EXIT statement on line 70 in CLIST B did not have any operand, it would pass back as return code the content of &LASTCC which in this case would be zero because the last statement executed prior to the EXIT statement would be either of the two 'SET &RETURN = ' statements.

RESTRICTING THE USE OF A CLIST TO SPECIFIC USERS OR GROUP OF USERS

Control variable &SYSUID contains the TSO User ID of the user currently executing this CLIST. It can be helpful in restricting access to the CLIST and also in allocating private datasets belonging to the user. As an example, consider a CLIST that displays sensitive information. If the TSO User ID structure at an installation is such that the first two characters of the user ID indicates the group or department of the user, then one may code the following at the beginning of the CLIST to ensure that only those users with user ID starting with characters Z2 can execute this CLIST:

```
SET &PREF = &SUBSTR(1:2,&SYSUID)
IF &PREF NE Z2 THEN +
  DO
  WRITE YOU ARE NOT AUTHORIZED TO EXECUTE THIS CLIST.
  WRITE ANY FURTHER ATTEMPTS TO EXECUTE THIS CLIST WILL RESULT IN DATA
  WRITE BEING LOGGED AND A VIOLATION REPORT FORWARDED TO YOUR SUPERVISOR.
  GOTO ENDCLIST
  END
- - - - -
- - - - -
ENDCLIST: EXIT
```

ILLUSTRATING THE USE OF CONTROL VARIABLE &SYSPREF

Control variable &SYSPREF contains the dataset name prefix of the user stored in the user profile table (UPT). To see what is stored in the UPT, issue the TSO command PROFILE. One display from this command might be as follows:

```
IKJ566881 CHAR(0) LINE(0) PROMPT INTERCOM NOPAUSE MSGID NOMODE WTPMSG
  NORECOVER PREFIX(Z2BKN)
```

This display indicates that the dataset name prefix of the user is Z2BKN. (The dataset name prefix of a user is usually the same as his user ID, but this is not a system requirement.) It also lists other entries from the UPT. If you want to nullify the dataset name prefix, you can issue the command: PROFILE NOPREFIX. But it is a good practice not to nullify the dataset name prefix and also to keep the dataset name prefix same as the TSO user ID.

Note that if your dataset name prefix in the UPT is, for instance, Z2BKN, then the TSO command DELETE CLIST will result in the system attempting to delete dataset with the fully-qualified name of 'Z2BKN.CLIST'. But if you set your prefix to nulls by issuing command PROFILE NOPREFIX, this command will cause the system to attempt to delete the dataset with the fully-qualified name of 'CLIST'.

A CLIST THAT CAN BE EXECUTED IMPLICITLY UNDER DIFFERENT NAMES

Control variable &SYSICMD is used to obtain the name by which the user implicitly invoked this CLIST. If it was invoked explicitly, that is through the explicit form of the

```
10    PROC 0
20    CONTROL MSG NOLIST END(STOP)
30    IF &SYSICMD = DISP1  THEN +
40      DO
50      WRITE CURRENT TIME OF DAY IS &SYSTIME
60      GOTO ENDCLIST
70      STOP
80    IF &SYSICMD = DISP2 THEN +
90      DO
100     WRITE CURRENT TIME OF DAY IS &SYSTIME
110     WRITE TODAY'S DATE IN MM/DD/YY = &SYSDATE
120     STOP
130   ENDCLIST: EXIT
```

Figure 2.22.   A CLIST to display either current time or both current time and date depending on the name by which it is implicitly invoked.

EXEC command, the value of &SYSICMD will be null. To illustrate the use of this control variable, let us consider a simple CLIST shown in Figure 2.22 and suppose that it is stored in partitioned dataset SYS2.CLIST as member DISP2. Issue the following command to create member DISP1 as the alias for member DISP2 in the same PDS:

```
RENAME 'SYS2.CLIST(DISP2)' (DISP1) ALIAS
```

The same CLIST can be invoked by using one of these commands, provided that SYS2.CLIST is allocated under DDname SYSPROC:

```
%DISP1
%DISP2
```

As you can see from the CLIST in Figure 2.22, when %DISP1 is used to invoke this CLIST, the value of &SYSICMD is DISP1 and only the time of day is displayed. However if %DISP2 is used, the value of &SYSICMD is DISP2 and both the current date and time are displayed. The question is: will this CLIST display anything if it is not implicitly invoked? We leave it up to the reader to experiment with this CLIST on his terminal and see what happens when this CLIST is executed by the following command:

```
EXEC 'SYS2.CLIST(DISP2)'
```

The technique discussed here is essentially a technique of assigning multiple entry points to a CLIST. By assigning multiple aliases to a member of the CLIST library, one can execute the same CLIST member by different names. And in the CLIST one can use control variable &SYSICMD to take a different path through the CLIST and do different things depending on the name by which it was invoked.

From the CLIST in Figure 2.22, one should not conclude that control variables such as &SYSICMD are only useful in writing trivial CLISTs which do trivial things like displaying current time and date. After all, why do you need a CLIST like that in Figure 2.22 if you have a good watch which can display current time and date without requiring you to issue a command to it? The reason we have taken as an example a trivial CLIST such as the one in Figure 2.22 is that we want to clarify how and when control variables such as &SYSICMD can be used. We did not want to take as an example a complex CLIST and thereby divert from the main issue here, which is to clarify the use of control variable &SYSICMD. When we present really useful and non-trivial CLISTs in later chapters, you will have the need to put into practice all the ideas and concepts discussed in the earlier chapters.

A CLIST THAT SERVES AS A SIMPLE CALCULATOR

Let us write a simple CLIST that accepts three positional parameters: an integer, an arithmetic operator and a second integer. It does the calculation requested and displays the result on the terminal. For example, suppose that this CLIST is stored as member CALC in a partitioned dataset allocated under DDname SYSPROC during your TSO session, you can use this calculator CLIST in the following manner:

```
OPR:    %CALC 15 + 90
SYS:    105
        ***
OPR:    %CALC 209 * 45
SYS:    9405
        ***
```

```
PROC 3 &NUM1 &OPER &NUM2
IF &DATATYPE(&NUM1) NE NUM OR &DATATYPE(&NUM2) NE NUM THEN +
  WRITE BOTH THE OPERANDS MUST BE NUMERIC.
ELSE +
  DO
  SET &RESULT = &EVAL(&NUM1 &OPER &NUM2)
  WRITE &RESULT
  END
EXIT
```

Figure 2.23. A CLIST that can be used as a simple calculator.

(Note that OPR and SYS in this dialog stand for operator and system, respectively. The system displays two lines in response to one line input entered by the operator.)

The CLIST is shown in Figure 2.23. As you can see, this CLIST can be used as a simple calculator, in case you do not have a calculator handy. But this CLIST will not handle numbers with fractions, and is, therefore, not a good substitute for a $10 calculator. But this is not to say that the concepts presented here are not useful. In fact, in the next chapter we will present a number of useful CLISTs which will highlight the fact that CLISTs are a great tool for boosting productivity of all computer professionals who use TSO.

In fact, the following two line CLIST is much better than a $10 calculator for integers provided it is passed numeric operands only, that is if we assume that there are no errors in the expression passed to it:

```
PROC 1 EXPRESSION
WRITE &EVAL(&EXPRESSION)
```

Here is how this CLIST can be used, assuming that it is stored as member CALC1 in a CLIST library allocated under DDname SYSPROC:

```
OPR:   %CALC1 20+30-10
SYS:   40
OPR:   %CALC1 13987//41
SYS:   6
OPR:   %CALC1 2*4/8+10
SYS:   11
```

It should be noted that when executing this CLIST, no space should be present between the characters of the expression. This is because a space will signal the end of the positional parameter EXPRESSION passed to the CLIST. For example, if you invoke this CLIST as follows:

```
%CALC1 201 * 4
```

the system will respond with this message:

```
EXTRANEOUS INFORMATION WAS IGNORED: * 4
201
```

WHEN TO USE BUILT-IN FUNCTION &STR?

The &STR is used when the character string enclosed within parentheses is to be used as a real value. Nested built-in functions are evaluated and symbolic substitution is carried out to replace any symbolic variables enclosed, but no other evaluation, arithmetic or otherwise, is carried out. To see how this built-in function is indispensible, let us suppose that we issue a READ statement to read in an answer entered by the user, and then we want to see if the answer is 1 followed by a plus sign, followed by 10. The following statement will not work:

```
IF &ANSWER = 1 + 10 THEN +
```

because if the user entered say Z as the value for &ANSWER, the CLIST processor will issue an error message when it tries to execute this statement:

```
IF Z = 1 + 10
```

but the following statement using the &STR built-in function will do the job:

```
IF &STR(&ANSWER) = &STR(1+10) THEN +
```

To understand the way &STR built-in function works, consider some more examples given below:

```
SET &A = 1 + 1          /* SETS &A TO 2, THE RESULT OF EVALUATING */
                        /* EXPRESSION ON THE RIGHT OF EQUAL SIGN  */
SET &A = &STR(1+1)      /* SETS &A TO CHARACTER STRING "1+1"       */
SET &X = 20
SET &A = &STR(&X + &X)  /* SETS &A TO CHARACTER STRING "20 + 20"   */
                        /* REMEMBER SYMBOLIC SUBSTITUTION IS DONE  */
                        /* BUT ARITHMETIC OPERATION IS NOT DONE.   */
```

Below are given some examples of statements in error and the same statements rewritten using &STR so as to eliminate error:

```
STATEMENT IN ERROR              REASON FOR ERROR
SET &VAR1 = *                   Asterisk is an arithmetic operator as
                                far as CLIST Processor is concerned.
IF &OPER = +   THEN GOTO LAB1   Plus sign gets interpreted as an
                                arithmetic operator.
IF &OPER = &STR(+) THEN +       If &OPER equals say /, the CLIST
                                processor will issue an error
                                message when it tries to execute the
                                statement IF / = + THEN +  saying
                                THIS STATEMENT HAS AN OPERATOR OUT
                                OF SEQUENCE.
```

The same three statements have been rewritten below so as
to eliminate error:

```
SET &VAR1 = &STR(*)
IF &STR(&OPER) = &STR(+) THEN GOTO LAB1
IF &STR(&OPER) = &STR(+) THEN +
```

It is important to remember that whenever an error occurs
which is hard to understand, it is safe to use &STR as
illustrated above. Usually such errors have to do with the
use of special characters such as the arithmetic operators.
Also worth noting is the fact that if you enter a plus
or a minus sign as the value for a symbolic variable
when prompted by the CLIST or at the time of executing
the CLIST, TSO will interpret it as a line continuation
character. In such cases, you are better off entering your
input as (+) or (-), i.e. by enclosing the input in quotes or
parentheses.

Chapter 3
LET US WRITE SOME MORE USEFUL CLISTs

In this chapter we will examine a number of problems which can be solved through CLISTs. We will present the CLISTs which solve these problems and discuss the thought process involved in developing solutions to these problems and the techniques employed in writing these CLISTs. We will also discuss certain guidelines which make CLISTs user-friendly and fun to use, rather than user-hostile and difficult to use. This is because a very important principle of contemporary data processing is that the interactive programs and systems must be designed and written so that they are easy to use by the human operators and take into consideration the way a human being thinks and behaves.

This is opposed to the erroneous principle which many people used to follow in the early days of data processing and which some people follow to this day, that says the programs and systems need not pay any attention to the human factors, and the human operators must learn to adapt themselves to the idiosyncrasies of the system. This quotation from a speculative article entitled "Science in 2006" by Lewis M. Branscomb (*American Scientist*, Volume 74, November-December, 1986), who was vice president and chief scientist at IBM Corporation, is worth noting. "By 2006 you could not earn a Ph.D. in computer science without studies in depth in psychology. To design machines to help people, you had to know something about people."

Let us now take up the problems to be solved through CLISTs one-by-one.

A CLIST TO CONVERT A DECIMAL INTEGER INTO ITS HEXADECIMAL EQUIVALENT

The Problem

This problem is to write a CLIST which can be used as a TSO command to convert a decimal number into its hexadecimal equivalent.

How is this CLIST to be executed? Suppose that this CLIST is stored as member DECTOHEX in a CLIST library (i.e. a partitioned dataset) allocated under DDname SYSPROC, then the following TSO command can be issued from any of the ISPF panels to convert decimal number 99 into its hexadecimal equivalent:

```
TSO %DECTOHEX 99
```

The response from the CLIST will be as follows:

```
DECIMAL NUMBER 99 IN HEX = 0 0 0 0 0 0 6 3
***
```

(Note that if you want to issue the above command from TSO mode, you should remove the word TSO from the command.)

Any number from zero to 2,147,483,647 can be passed to this CLIST. (Note that commas can not be imbedded in the number when used on the command to invoke this CLIST.) If a number greater than 2,147,483,647 is passed, an error will occur on account of the fact that a number greater than 2,147,483,647 cannot be handled by the CLIST processor.

In what way can this CLIST be useful in day-to-day work? This CLIST can be useful when one does not have a calculator that performs decimal to hexadecimal and reverse conversions. An Assembly language programmer has to do decimal to hexadecimal and reverse conversions many times while understanding and debugging the programs. Similar conversions must also be performed by both systems and applications programmers and analysts while going through dumps of files, storage areas and executable code.

What is the thought process involved in writing this CLIST? The first step in solving any problem through a computer program is to arrive at an algorithm; that is, to develop a systematic method of solving the problem. Developing an algorithm becomes easy when one organizes his thought process clearly and analyzes the problem systematically and methodically. Let us discuss now how we organize our thoughts and arrive at a solution to this problem.

A hexadecimal number consists of a number of characters written one after another from left to right. The characters in the hexadecimal representation of any number can only be 0 through 9, A, B, C, D, E or F, where A is symbolic representation for decimal number 10, B for decimal number 11, C for decimal number 12, D for decimal number 13, E for decimal number 14 and F for decimal number 15. To calculate the decimal equivalent of a hexadecimal number, we use the following formula :

```
Value in Decimal = CHAR1 * W1 + CHAR2 * W2 + CHAR3 * W3 + CHAR4 * W4 +
                  - - - - CHARn * Wn
where it is assumed that all values of CHARm for m = n+1, n+2. are zero.
```

Here CHAR1 stands for the character at the first position from the right, CHAR2 for the character at the second position from the right and so on, and W1 is the weight of the character at the first position from the right, W2 is the weight of the character at the second position from the right and so on. The weights of characters at various positions are as follows:

Character position	Character weight at this position	
1	16 raised to the power of zero	= 1
2	16 raised to the power of one	= 16
3	16 raised to the power of two	= 256
4	16 raised to the power of three	= 4,096
5	16 raised to the power of four	= 65,536
6	16 raised to the power of five	= 1,048,576
7	16 raised to the power of six	= 16,777,216
8	16 raised to the power of seven	= 268,435,456
9	16 raised to the power of eight	= 4,294,967,296

So, if we have a hexadecimal number A2B90, its decimal equivalent is calculated as:

```
0 * 1 + 9 *16 + B * 256 + 2 * 4096 + A * 65,536
```

which is equivalent to:

```
0 * 1 + 9 *16 + 11 * 256 + 2 * 4096 + 10 * 65,536 =
0 + 144 + 2816 + 8192 + 655360 = 666,512
```

Since the weight of the character at the 9th position from the right is greater than the maximum allowable under the CLIST language, we can safely assume that the character at this position in the hexadecimal number generated by our CLIST will be always zero. This means we have to worry only about determining characters in position 1,2,3 . . . 8. Let us call the decimal number to be converted DEC and suppose that its hexadecimal equivalent can be represented as follows:

CHAR8 CHAR7 CHAR6 CHAR5 CHAR4 CHAR3 CHAR2 CHAR1

We also know that if the decimal number is less than W8 (268,435,456), then CHAR8 is zero, otherwise CHAR8 is the quotient (an integer) obtained by dividing DEC by 268,435,456. Once CHAR8 has been determined, we calculate a new value for DEC which is same as the original value of DEC if it was less than 268,435,456 otherwise it is the remainder obtained by dividing DEC by 268,435,456. Now we apply this same logic to the new value of DEC for determining CHAR7. This means that if the new value of DEC is less than W7 (16,777,216), then CHAR7 is zero, otherwise CHAR7 is the quotient obtained by dividing DEC by 16,777,216. This process is applied repeatedly for determining values of CHAR6, CHAR5 . . . CHAR1.

Let us illustrate the algorithm we have just described by applying it for converting decimal number 102345 into its hexadecimal representation. The starting value of DEC is 102345.

Determining CHAR8
Since DEC is less than W8 (268,435,456), CHAR8 is zero. The value of DEC remains unchanged.

Determining CHAR7
Since DEC is still less than W7 (16,777,216), CHAR7 is zero. The value of DEC remains unchanged.

Determining CHAR6
Since DEC is still less than W6 (1,048,576), CHAR6 is zero. The value of DEC remains unchanged.

Determining CHAR5
Since DEC is greater than W5 (65,536), CHAR5 will be non-zero. Dividing 102345 by W5 (65536) yields a quotient of 1 and a remainder of 36809. So, CHAR5 equals 1 and the new value of DEC is 36809.

Determining CHAR4

Since the new value of DEC is greater than W4 (4096), CHAR4 will be non-zero. Dividing 36809 by W4 (4096) yields a quotient of 8 and a remainder of 4041. So, CHAR4 = 8 and the new value of DEC is 4041.

Determining CHAR3

Since the new value of DEC is greater than W3 (256), CHAR3 will be non-zero. Dividing 4041 by W3 (256) yields a quotient of 15 and a remainder of 201. So, CHAR3 = F and the new value of DEC is 201.

Determining CHAR2

Since the new value of DEC is greater than W2 (16), CHAR2 will be non-zero. Dividing 201 by W2 (16) yields a quotient of 12 and a remainder of 9. So, CHAR2 = C and the new value of DEC is 9.

Determining CHAR1

At this point, the value of DEC is also the value of CHAR1 because W1 = 1. So, CHAR1 = 9.

We have determined all the characters in the hexadecimal number and can state with confidence that the hexadecimal representation of 102345 = 00018FC9.

The CLIST Solutions

One CLIST that implements the algorithm illustrated above is shown in Figure 3.1. But the CLIST in Figure 3.1 is too long. It is natural to ask if we can somehow rewrite it so that it becomes more compact. And indeed we can. If you will examine the method described above for determining various values of CHARn, you will notice that this method is very systematic. Determining CHARn for n = 8,7,6, . . . upto 1 is based on the same formula and hence it can be done in a single routine. The CLIST in Figure 3.1 has been rewritten in Figure 3.2 using two DO-WHILE-END sequences so that all values of CHARn for n = 8,7,6, . . . 1 are calculated by the code inside the second DO-WHILE-END sequence. You will notice that the CLIST in Figure 3.2 is much shorter compared to the one in Figure 3.1.

```
PROC 1 DEC
/*===============================================================*
/* THIS CLIST WILL CONVERT A DECIMAL INTEGER TO ITS HEXADECIMAL*
/* REPRESENTATION. THE DECIMAL NUMBER IS SUPPLIED TO THIS CLIST*
/* AS A POSITIONAL PARAMETER. IF DECIMAL NUMBER IS NOT SUPPLIED*
/* WHEN WORKING THIS CLIST, THE USER WILL BE PROMPTED FOR IT   *
/* PROVIDED THE PROMPT OPTION IS IN EFFECT IN THE UPT.         *
/* NOTE THAT ANY DECIMAL NUMBER UPTO THE MAXIMUM ALLOWED UNDER *
/* THE CLIST LANGUAGE CAN BE CONVERTED BY THIS CLIST.          *
/*===============================================================*
SET &DECSAVE = &DEC
   IF &DEC LT 268435456 THEN SET &CHAR8 = 0
      ELSE DO
            SET &CHAR8 = &DEC / 268435456
            IF &CHAR8 = 10 THEN SET &CHAR8 = A
            IF &CHAR8 = 11 THEN SET &CHAR8 = B
            IF &CHAR8 = 12 THEN SET &CHAR8 = C
            IF &CHAR8 = 13 THEN SET &CHAR8 = D
            IF &CHAR8 = 14 THEN SET &CHAR8 = E
            IF &CHAR8 = 15 THEN SET &CHAR8 = F
            SET &DEC = &DEC // 268435456
         END
   IF &DEC LT 16777216 THEN SET &CHAR7 = 0
      ELSE DO
            SET &CHAR7 = &DEC / 16777216
            IF &CHAR7 = 10 THEN SET &CHAR7 = A
            IF &CHAR7 = 11 THEN SET &CHAR7 = B
            IF &CHAR7 = 12 THEN SET &CHAR7 = C
            IF &CHAR7 = 13 THEN SET &CHAR7 = D
            IF &CHAR7 = 14 THEN SET &CHAR7 = E
            IF &CHAR7 = 15 THEN SET &CHAR7 = F
            SET &DEC = &DEC // 16777216
         END
   IF &DEC LT 1048576 THEN SET &CHAR6 = 0
      ELSE DO
            SET &CHAR6 = &DEC / 1048576
            IF &CHAR6 = 10 THEN SET &CHAR6 = A
            IF &CHAR6 = 11 THEN SET &CHAR6 = B
            IF &CHAR6 = 12 THEN SET &CHAR6 = C
            IF &CHAR6 = 13 THEN SET &CHAR6 = D
            IF &CHAR6 = 14 THEN SET &CHAR6 = E
            IF &CHAR6 = 15 THEN SET &CHAR6 = F
            SET &DEC = &DEC // 1048576
         END
```

Figure 3.1.   A CLIST to convert a decimal integer into its hexadecimal representation.

```
         IF &DEC LT 65536    THEN SET &CHAR5 = 0
            ELSE DO
                 SET &CHAR5 = &DEC / 65536
                 IF &CHAR5 = 10 THEN SET &CHAR5 = A
                 IF &CHAR5 = 11 THEN SET &CHAR5 = B
                 IF &CHAR5 = 12 THEN SET &CHAR5 = C
                 IF &CHAR5 = 13 THEN SET &CHAR5 = D
                 IF &CHAR5 = 14 THEN SET &CHAR5 = E
                 IF &CHAR5 = 15 THEN SET &CHAR5 = F
                 SET &DEC = &DEC // 65536
            END
         IF &DEC LT 4096     THEN SET &CHAR4 = 0
            ELSE DO
                 SET &CHAR4 = &DEC / 4096
                 IF &CHAR4 = 10 THEN SET &CHAR4 = A
                 IF &CHAR4 = 11 THEN SET &CHAR4 = B
                 IF &CHAR4 = 12 THEN SET &CHAR4 = C
                 IF &CHAR4 = 13 THEN SET &CHAR4 = D
                 IF &CHAR4 = 14 THEN SET &CHAR4 = E
                 IF &CHAR4 = 15 THEN SET &CHAR4 = F
                 SET &DEC = &DEC // 4096
            END
         IF &DEC LT 256      THEN SET &CHAR3 = 0
            ELSE DO
                 SET &CHAR3 = &DEC / 256
                 IF &CHAR3 = 10 THEN SET &CHAR3 = A
                 IF &CHAR3 = 11 THEN SET &CHAR3 = B
                 IF &CHAR3 = 12 THEN SET &CHAR3 = C
                 IF &CHAR3 = 13 THEN SET &CHAR3 = D
                 IF &CHAR3 = 14 THEN SET &CHAR3 = E
                 IF &CHAR3 = 15 THEN SET &CHAR3 = F
                 SET &DEC = &DEC // 256
            END
         IF &DEC LT 16       THEN SET &CHAR2 = 0
            ELSE DO
                 SET &CHAR2 = &DEC / 16
                 IF &CHAR2 = 10 THEN SET &CHAR2 = A
                 IF &CHAR2 = 11 THEN SET &CHAR2 = B
                 IF &CHAR2 = 12 THEN SET &CHAR2 = C
                 IF &CHAR2 = 13 THEN SET &CHAR2 = D
                 IF &CHAR2 = 14 THEN SET &CHAR2 = E
                 IF &CHAR2 = 15 THEN SET &CHAR2 = F
                 SET &DEC = &DEC // 16
            END
         SET &CHAR1 = &DEC
         IF &DEC = 10 THEN SET & CHAR1 = A
         IF &DEC = 10 THEN SET & CHAR1 = B
         IF &DEC = 10 THEN SET & CHAR1 = C
         IF &DEC = 10 THEN SET & CHAR1 = D
         IF &DEC = 10 THEN SET & CHAR1 = E
         IF &DEC = 10 THEN SET & CHAR1 = F
         WRITE DECIMAL NUMBER &DECSAVE IN HEX = +
          &CHAR8. &CHAR7. &CHAR6. &CHAR5. &CHAR4. &CHAR3. &CHAR2. &CHAR1
         EXIT
```

Figure 3.1.   A CLIST to convert a decimal integer into its hexadecimal
representation (continued).

How Does the CLIST in Figure 3.2 Work?

The CLIST in Figure 3.2 illustrates the use of concatenation for creating new variable names. The statement on line 15 defines variables &W1, &W2 . . . &W8 and assigns them values of 1, 16, 256, . . .268435456 respectively. In the

```
Line    CLIST Statement


1       PROC 1 DEC
2       CONTROL END(ENDX) LIST MSG
3       /*=====================================================================*
4       /* THIS CLIST WILL CONVERT A DECIMAL NUMBER TO ITS HEXADECIMAL REPRE- *
5       /* SENTATION. THE DECIMAL NUMBER IS SUPPLIED TO THIS CLIST AS A POSI- *
6       /* TIONAL PARAMETER. IF DECIMAL NUMBER IS NOT SUPPLIED WHEN INVOKING  *
7       /* THIS CLIST, THE USER WILL BE PROMPTED FOR IT, PROVIDED THE PROMPT  *
8       /* OPTION IS IN EFFECT IN THE USER PROFILE TABLE. NOTE THAT ANY DECI- *
9       /* MAL NUMBER UPTO THE MAXIMUM ALLOWED UNDER THE CLIST LANGUAGE CAN   *
10      /* BE CONVERTED BY THIS CLIST.                                        *
11      /*=====================================================================*
12      SET &DECSAVE = &DEC
13      SET &N = 1
14      DO WHILE &N LE 8
15        SET &W&N = 16 ** (&N - 1)
16        SET &N = &N + 1
17      ENDX
18      SET &N = 8
19      DO WHILE &N GE 1
20        SET &WEIGHT = &EVAL(&&W&N)
21        IF &DEC LT &WEIGHT THEN SET &CHAR&N = 0
22          ELSE DO
23            SET &VALUE = &DEC / &WEIGHT
24            SET &DEC = &DEC // &WEIGHT
25            IF &VALUE = 10 THEN SET &VALUE = A
26            IF &VALUE = 11 THEN SET &VALUE = B
27            IF &VALUE = 12 THEN SET &VALUE = C
28            IF &VALUE = 13 THEN SET &VALUE = D
29            IF &VALUE = 14 THEN SET &VALUE = E
30            IF &VALUE = 15 THEN SET &VALUE = F
31            SET &CHAR&N = &VALUE
32          ENDX
33        SET &N = &N - 1
34      ENDX
35      WRITE DECIMAL NUMBER &DECSAVE IN HEX = +
36        &CHAR8. &CHAR7. &CHAR6. &CHAR5. &CHAR4. &CHAR3. &CHAR2. &CHAR1
37      EXIT
```

Figure 3.2. A compact version of the CLIST to convert a decimal integer into its hexadecimal representation.

second DO-WHILE-END sequence, the values of CHAR8, CHAR7, . . . CHAR1 are determined one by one. Let us see how this is done, assuming that the decimal number to be converted is 1090.

On line 18, &N is set to 8. Since &N is greater than 1, statement on line 20 gets executed. This statement sets &WEIGHT to the value of &W8. Note the use of the built-in function &EVAL and the use of two ampersands within the parentheses. While evaluating the expression within the parentheses, the CLIST processor replaces two ampersands with a single ampersand, which results in &W8, since &N has a value of 8. If we had used &EVAL(&W&N), this would be interpreted as concatenating symbolic variable &W with symbolic variable &N. And since the value of &W is blank, because it is undefined, the result of EVAL(&W&N) would be same as the value of &N, i.e., 8.

So on line 20, &WEIGHT is assigned a value of 268435456. And since &DEC is less than &WEIGHT, line 21 sets &CHAR8 to 0 and lines 22 through 32 which belong to the ELSE clause are bypassed. On line 33, &N is set to 7, and line 34 sends the computer back to line 19. Now, since &N is still greater than 1, line 20 is executed. Here &WEIGHT is set to the value of &W7, i.e., 16777216. Line 21 is executed causing &CHAR7 to be set to zero.

In this manner &CHAR6, &CHAR5 and &CHAR4 will also be set to zero. When &N becomes 3, line 20 sets &WEIGHT to 256. Now &DEC (1090) is not less than &WEIGHT (256), causing lines 23 through 32 to be executed. On line 23, &VALUE is set to the quotient obtained by dividing 1090 by 256, which is 4, and on line 24, &DEC is set to the remainder obtained by dividing 1090 by 256, which is 66. Line 31 sets &CHAR3 to 4.

Line 33 sets &N to 2 and line 34 sends the computer back to line 19. Since &N is still greater than 1, line 20 is executed which sets &WEIGHT to the value of &W2 which is 16. Since &DEC (66) is not less than &WEIGHT, lines 23 through 32 are executed. On line 23, &VALUE is set to 4 and on line 24, &DEC is set to 2. Next on line 31, &CHAR2 is set to 4.

Line 33 sets &N to 1 and line 34 sends the computer back to line 19. Since &N is equal to 1, line 20 is executed. Here &WEIGHT is set to the value of &W1 which is 1. Since &DEC (2) is not less than &WEIGHT (1), line 23 is executed next. Here &VALUE is set to 2 and on line 24, &DEC is set to 0. Line 31 causes &CHAR1 to be set to 2 and line 33 sets &N to zero. Line 34 sends the computer back to line 19. Now &N is less than 1, which means that lines 20 through 34 which belong to the DO-WHILE-END sequence are bypassed and control comes to line 35. Line 35 causes the following line to be displayed at the terminal:

```
DECIMAL NUMBER 1090 IN HEX = 0 0 0 0 0 4 4 2
```

Next line 37 is executed which causes control to be transferred to TSO.

If you think about it, you will conclude that in this CLIST we have actually used two one-dimensional arrays, W(1), W(2), . . . W(8) and CHAR(1), CHAR(2), . . . CHAR(8). Both these arrays have 8 elements. As is shown by this CLIST, the method of using concatenation to create new symbolic variables is used to handle one-dimensional arrays. In Chapter 8 we will discuss the method of handling two-dimensional arrays in CLIST programs, which is also done through concatenation of symbolic variables.

A CLIST TO DISPLAY CHARACTERISTICS OF VARIOUS DASD DEVICES

The Problem

The problem is to write a CLIST that can be used to display the characteristics of IBM 3380 and 3375 direct access storage devices (DASDs). Suppose that at an installation the majority of DASDs are IBM 3380's. Then this CLIST can be of great help to every TSO user who can find the characteristics of either a 3380 or a 3375 merely by issuing a simple TSO command, rather than having to first search for the proper book or booklet and then look up the information in it. This CLIST is given in Figure 3.3.

How can this CLIST be executed?

If this CLIST is stored in member INFODASD in a CLIST library (i.e., a partitioned dataset) allocated under DDname SYSPROC, it can be used to find 3380 characteristics by issuing the following TSO command:

```
%INFODASD 3380
```

The CLIST will display characteristics of either an IBM 3380 DASD or an IBM 3375 DASD depending on the parameter passed to it. It can be easily adapted to display characteristics of another DASD such as an IBM 3350.

A CLIST TO DISPLAY GUIDELINES FOR SELECTING BLOCK SIZES OF NON-VSAM FILES

Let us write a CLIST that can display the guidelines for choosing block sizes of non-VSAM datasets to reside on an IBM 3380 DASD. Block size of a dataset is an important factor that determines whether or not efficient utilization of track capacity is being made. This is because a block of data can not cross track boundary, i.e., it has to be fully contained within a single track. Block sizes of sequential datasets to be used in batch jobs also has significant effect on CPU time and channel time required for job processing. As I have said in my book, "The optimization of the block sizes of sequential datasets is the most important factor in

```
PROC 1 DASDTYPE
CONTROL MSG, LIST, END(ENDX)
IF &DASDTYPE = 3380 THEN DO
   SET &MBPERVOL   = 630
   SET &TOTCYL     = 885
   SET &TRACKSPC   = 15
   SET &BYTESPT    = 47,476
   SET &BYTESPC    = 712,140
   SET &TRACKSPV   = 13,275
   ENDX
ELSE -
IF &DASDTYPE = 3375 THEN DO
   SET &MBPERVOL   = 409.8
   SET &TOTCYL     = 959
   SET &TRACKSPC   = 12
   SET &BYTESPT    = 35,616
   SET &BYTESPC    = 427,392
   SET &TRACKSPV   = 11,508
   ENDX
ELSE DO
   WRITE =================================================================
   WRITE &DASDTYPE IS AN INVALID DEVICE OR NOT SUPPORTED BY THIS CLIST.
   WRITE THE ONLY DEVICES SUPPORTED BY THIS CLIST ARE IBM 3380 AND 3375.
   WRITE =================================================================
   EXIT QUIT
   ENDX
WRITE =================================================================
WRITE THE FOLLOWING ARE THE CHARACTERISTICS OF IBM &DASDTYPE DASD:
WRITE =================================================================
WRITE MEGABYTES CAPACITY PER VOLUME                  &MBPERVOL
WRITE NUMBER OF CYLINDERS PER VOLUME                 &TOTCYL
WRITE NUMBER OF TRACKS PER CYLINDER                  &TRACKSPC
WRITE NUMBER OF BYTES PER TRACK                      &BYTESPT
WRITE NUMBER OF BYTES PER CYLINDER                   &BYTESPC
WRITE NUMBER OF DATA TRACKS PER VOLUME               &TRACKSPV
WRITE
WRITE NOT ALL BYTES AVAILABLE ON A TRACK OR A CYLINDER ARE USED FOR
WRITE STORING USER DATA. THIS IS BECAUSE THERE ARE INTER-BLOCK GAPS.
WRITE A BLOCK OF DATA CAN NOT CROSS TRACK BOUNDARY. HENCE SELECTION
WRITE OF BLOCKSIZE FOR NON-VSAM DATA SETS GREATLY AFFECTS TRACK
WRITE UTILIZATION. CHOOSE BLOCKSIZES OF YOUR NON-VSAM DATA SETS VERY
WRITE CAREFULLY SO AS NOT TO WASTE DISK SPACE AND MINIMIZE CPU AND
WRITE CHANNEL TIME REQUIREMENTS FOR YOUR JOBS.
WRITE =================================================================
EXIT
```

Figure 3.3.   A CLIST to display the characteristics of IBM 3380 and 3375 direct access storage devices.

reducing CPU utilization. No other factor has anywhere near the potential for saving CPU cycles. It has been reported that one experiment increasing the block size of a sequential dataset from 200 bytes to 6K reduced CPU utilization by more than 87 percent and reduced channel time (EXCP) by 65 percent." (Barry Nirmal, *Programming Standards and Guidelines, COBOL Edition,* Englewood Cliffs, NJ: Prentice-Hall, Inc., 1987, p. 203.)

Since datasets are allocated very frequently by programmer/analysts both while developing new applications and while supporting existing applications, this CLIST can be of invaluable aid to the professionals who can, by issuing a simple TSO command, obtain guidelines for choosing block sizes of their datasets. The desired CLIST is shown in Figure 3.4. If this CLIST is stored as member BLKSIZE in a

```
        PROC 0
        WRITE  =================================================================
        WRITE   SUMMARY OF RECOMMENDED BLOCKSIZES FOR DATA SETS ON IBM 3380 DASD:
        WRITE  =================================================================
        WRITE  TYPE OF DATA SET                                     RECOMMENDED
        WRITE                                                       BLOCKSIZE
        WRITE
        WRITE  SOURCE DATA FOR ONLINE USE (E.G. WITH TSO/ISPF)         6,320
        WRITE            (LRECL=80,RECFM=FB)
        WRITE  SOURCE DATA FOR USE BY BATCH JOBS (LRECL=80,RECFM=FB)  23,440
        WRITE  COBOL COPY LIBRARIES(LRECL=80,RECFM=FB)                15,440
        WRITE  PL/I INCLUDE LIBRARIES (LRECL=80,RECFM=FB)              4,240
        WRITE  ALL LOAD MODULE DATA SETS (LRECL=0,RECFM=U)            15,476
        WRITE  ALL OBJECT DATA SETS (LRECL=80,RECFM=FB)                3,120
        WRITE  ALL CLIST DATA SETS (LRECL=255,RECFM=VB)                6,356
        WRITE  ONLINE (E.G TSO/ISPF) DATA SETS FOR STORING TEXT        6,356
        WRITE            (LRECL=255,RECFM=VB)
        WRITE  =================================================================
        WRITE  FOR VALUES OF LOGICAL RECORD LENGTH NOT MENTIONED ABOVE, BLOCK
        WRITE  SIZES BETWEEN 4000 AND 8000 BYTES ARE MOST PRACTICAL FOR THE
        WRITE  3380. CONSULT REFERENCE SUMMARY FOR IBM 3380 DASD (MANUAL #
        WRITE  GX26-1678-1) FOR CHOOSING EXACT VALUES OF BLOCKSIZE.
        WRITE  =================================================================
        WRITE  DATA SETS TO RESIDE ON TAPE SHOULD BE BLOCKED TO 8K, 12K OR
        WRITE  SOMETIMES EVEN UPTO 32,760 WHICH IS THE MAXIMUM ALLOWED.
        WRITE  =================================================================
        WRITE  NOTE: EVEN THOUGH A BLOCK OF 47,476 BYTES CAN BE PLACED ON A
        WRITE  3380 TRACK, THE LARGEST BLOCKSIZE HANDLED BY AN IBM-SUPPLIED
        WRITE  ACCESS METHOD IS 32,760 BYTES.
        WRITE  =================================================================
        EXIT
```

Figure 3.4.   A CLIST to display the guidelines for choosing blocksizes of non-VSAM datasets to reside on an IBM 3380 DASD.

CLIST library (a partitioned dataset) allocated under DDname SYSPROC during your TSO session, you can execute it by issuing this TSO command:

```
%BLKSIZE
```

It should be noted that this CLIST does not make specific recommendations for choosing block sizes of datasets where logical record length is other than 80 or 255. For such decisions, the reader should consult an appropriate publication. My book, mentioned above, offers some guidelines in this regard. The CLIST presented in Figure 3.12 in this chapter can be profitably employed to calculate a suitable block size for a non-VSAM, fixed blocked dataset, based on the value of logical record length supplied by the user.

A CLIST TO AUTOMATE THE TASK OF SUBMITTING BATCH JOBS TO MVS

Let us suppose that dataset 'PRMRS.LIB.CNTL' contains jobs to be submitted for execution for one application called Material Request System. A TSO user submits various jobs from this dataset for batch execution for various purposes. The user has two options. The first is to edit the desired member using TSO/ISPF EDIT option and, when the detail edit panel is displayed, to issue the SUBMIT command from the top line of the panel; and, when the job has been submitted, to exit from the edit panel. This process is definitely a lengthy one requiring many actions on the part of the user. The second option is to set up a CLIST to automate the task of submitting batch jobs. This CLIST is shown in Figure 3.5. Supposing that this CLIST is stored as member JOBSUB in a CLIST library (i.e., a partitioned dataset) allocated under DDname SYSPROC during the user's TSO session, the user can simply issue the following

```
PROC 1 MEMBER
SUBMIT 'PRMRS.LIB.CNTL(&MEMBER.)'
EXIT
```

Figure 3.5.   A CLIST to submit any member of a partitioned data set as a job to MVS for batch execution.

TSO command from any of the ISPF panels to submit any member of PRMRS.LIB.CNTL as a job to MVS:

```
TSO %JOBSUB member-name
```

where member-name is a variable of one to eight characters which stands for the name of the member whose contents are to be submitted as a job to MVS for batch execution. This second option is definitely much less time-consuming than the first one, requiring the user to issue only one TSO command from any of the TSO/ISPF panels to submit any member of the PDS as a job to MVS.

Now let us take this process of automation one step further. Suppose that this user submits members COPYQ and REPORT1 of PRMRS.LIB.CNTL as batch jobs frequently. This smart user can save himself considerable time and typing by assigning any two of the program function (PF) keys to the following commands:

```
TSO %JOBSUB COPYQ
TSO %JOBSUB REPORT1
```

This assignment of PF keys is usually done through option 0.3 of ISPF. One example of such an assignment is shown in Figure 3.6. Assuming the PF key assignment of Figure 3.6, the user can submit member COPYQ as a job merely by pressing the PF11 key (Program Function Key 11) from any of the ISPF panels. And he can just press the PF12 key

```
--------------- PF KEY DEFINITION - ALTERNATE KEYS ---------------
COMMAND ===>

NOTE: THE DEFINITIONS BELOW APPLY ONLY TO TERMINALS WITH 24 PF KEYS.

PF1   ===>  HELP
PF2   ===>  SPLIT
PF3   ===>  END
PF4   ===>  RETURN
PF5   ===>  RFIND
PF6   ===>  RCHANGE
PF7   ===>  UP
PF8   ===>  DOWN
PF9   ===>  SWAP
PF10  ===>  LEFT
PF11  ===>  TSO %JOBSUB COPYQ
PF12  ===>  TSO %JOBSUB REPORT1

INSTRUCTIONS:
  PRESS ENTER KEY TO PROCESS CHANGES AND DISPLAY PRIMARY KEYS.
  ENTER END COMMAND TO PROCESS CHANGES AND EXIT.
```

Figure 3.6. Shows the panel under ISPF option 0.3 used to assign PF keys 11 and 12 to TSO commands SUBJOB COPYQ and SUBJOB REPORT1, respectively.

from any of the ISPF panels to submit member REPORT1 of 'PRMRS.LIB.CNTL' as a job to MVS for batch execution.

Now you might ask, how did we arrive at the CLIST in Figure 3.5? In other words, what was the thought process in arriving at a solution to the problem of automating the submitting of jobs for the Material Request System? It was mentioned in Chapter 1 that a CLIST consists of TSO commands, subcommands and CLIST statements. Looking up the little booklet, OS/VS2 TSO Command Language Reference Summary by IBM (Manual # GX28-0647) that contains a summary of IBM-supplied TSO commands, we found that SUBMIT is a TSO command that is used to submit contents of a dataset as a batch job to MVS. So, we decided to use this command to automate the task of submitting jobs for our Material Request System. You can use the SUBMIT and the other TSO commands supplied by IBM or developed by non-IBM programmers for automating the tasks that you execute for the applications or software systems you support or manage.

Since we mentioned that a CLIST can contain TSO commands and subcommands, let us clarify this term 'TSO Command'. TSO Commands are of three kinds:

a. those supplied by IBM, either as part of MVS or as program products which an installation has to separately purchase for a license fee. Most of these commands are documented in *MVS/ Extended Architecture TSO Extensions TSO Command Language Reference* (Manual # SC28-1134-0) or an equivalent manual. These commands are also summarized in a little, very useful booklet mentioned above.
b. those developed by non-IBM sources including past or present programmers working at your installation. These commands mostly consist of programs written in IBM Assembly language. These programs can be stored in system load libraries or in private load libraries. If stored in private load libraries, these have to be allocated under DDname STEPLIB or DDname ISPLLIB during your TSO session in order for you to be able to execute them.
c. CLISTs stored in one or more CLIST libraries (i.e., partitioned datasets) allocated to DDname SYSPROC during your TSO session. A CLIST usually makes one or more dataset allocations and then calls a program stored in a load library. This program may be written in the IBM Assembly language or in a high level language such as COBOL or PL/I.

As regards the SUBMIT command that we used in Figure 3.5, the simplest form of SUBMIT command is as follows:

```
 ⎰   SUB     ⎱       data-set-name
 ⎱   SUBMIT  ⎰
```

where dataset-name specifies the name of the dataset whose contents are to be submitted as a job. It is best to specify fully-qualified dataset names by enclosing them in quotes as shown in Figure 3.5. The dataset name must refer to a sequential dataset or a member of a partitioned dataset. The dataset being submitted should be fixed blocked with record length of 80 bytes. The contents of the dataset should be a complete job with job cards, even though the job cards may not be present, in which case TSO builds job cards for you. The dataset must not contain lowercase characters.

A CLIST TO DISPLAY SELECTED FIELDS FROM A SPECIFIED RECORD ON A VSAM KSDS

The Problem

The problem is to write a CLIST and a program in a high-level language which can be used to display the following fields from the record of any desired employee on the Payroll/ Personnel Master file, which is a VSAM key-sequenced dataset (KSDS):

```
Employee Name
Employee's Permanent Address
Basic Salary
Grade Code
```

The Payroll/ Personnel Master file has the employee number (6 bytes long) as its key.

The Description of the CLIST and the Program

Let us suppose that we decide to write the program in COBOL, because it is the most commonly used language for developing commercial applications all over the world. Now, if this CLIST is stored as member DISPEMP in a CLIST library allocated under DDname SYSPROC during a user's TSO session, it can be executed by issuing the following TSO command from any of the ISPF panels:

```
TSO %DISPEMP
```

This CLIST will then prompt the user for employee number which is to be inquired. If the employee number entered is not numeric, the following message will be displayed, and the user will be prompted for the employee number again:

```
THE EMPLOYEE NUMBER ENTERED IS NOT NUMERIC. IT IS REJECTED.
```

If the employee number entered is numeric but is not exactly six characters long, the following message will be displayed and the user will be prompted for the employee number again:

```
THE EMPLOYEE NUMBER ENTERED MUST BE EXACTLY SIX CHARACTERS LONG.
```

If the employee number entered is numeric, is six characters long but is zero, then the following message will be displayed on the terminal and the user will be prompted for another value for the employee number:

```
THE EMPLOYEE NUMBER ENTERED IS ZERO. IT IS REJECTED.
```

If the employee number entered passes all these tests, the CLIST will pass control via the CALL command of TSO to load module DISPEMP stored in Z2BKN.SPPS.LOAD, passing it the employee number entered by the user. Program DISPEMP will first open the Payroll/ Personnel Master file and if the OPEN is successful, it will issue a random READ for the record of the specified employee number from the file. If the record is not present on the master file, the following messages will be displayed on the terminal by program DISPEMP:

```
EMPLOYEE NUMBER nnnnnn IS NOT ON MASTER FILE
```

The COBOL program will then STOP RUN which will cause the operating system to pass control to the calling CLIST, which will then prompt the user for another employee number. However, if a record for the specified employee is successfully read from the master file, program DISPEMP will display the desired information on the terminal, and will then STOP RUN. This will transfer control to the CLIST that called this program. The CLIST will then prompt the user for another value for employee number. When the user enters the word QUIT when prompted for employee number, the CLIST will terminate execution, and the control will return to TSO. Figure 3.7 shows the man-machine dialog for displaying records of employee number 090156. In this figure note the headings <System:> and <Operator:>. The lines following the heading <System:> are displayed by the system and the line following the heading <Operator:> is keyed by the TSO user.

The Solution

Figure 3.8 shows the CLIST DISPEMP and the COBOL program DISPEMP is shown in Figure 3.9. The following points should be noted about these programs.

The user does not pass the employee number to the CLIST as a positional or a keyword parameter. Instead, the CLIST displays a number of lines of messages right in the beginning explaining how the employee number is to be entered. This way the operator is informed about the format of the input data to be entered. These messages are displayed only once at the time of initial execution of this CLIST. When the operator is prompted for another value of

```
<Operator:>

%DISPEMP

<System:>

=======================================================================
ENTER THE EMPLOYEE NUMBER WHOSE PERSONNEL INFORMATION YOU WISH
TO INQUIRE. NOTE THAT ALL SIX CHARACTERS OF EMPLOYEE NUMBER MUST
BE ENTERED, INCLUDING ANY LEADING ZEROS. EMPLOYEE NUMBER MUST BE
A NON-ZERO NUMERIC VALUE.
=======================================================================
PLEASE ENTER EMPLOYEE NUMBER BELOW ==>>
(OR ENTER QUIT TO TERMINATE THIS PROGRAM.)

<Operator:>

90156

<System:>

THE EMPLOYEE NUMBER ENTERED MUST BE EXACTLY SIX CHARACTERS LONG.
PLEASE ENTER EMPLOYEE NUMBER BELOW ==>>
(OR ENTER QUIT TO TERMINATE THIS PROGRAM.)

<Operator:>

090156

<System:>

NOW PROCESSING EMPLOYEE NUMBER: 090156
=======================================================
EMPLOYEE NAME IN ENGLISH   = HOLLINGER      RON   K.
EMPLOYEE(S) PERMANENT ADDRESS IS AS FOLLOWS:
123 WILSON BLVD. SUITE: 660, CHICAGO, ILLINOIS, U.S.A.
THE BASIC PAY OF EMPLOYEE  =  15,500.00
EMPLOYEE'S GRADE CODE      = 22
=======================================================

PLEASE ENTER EMPLOYEE NUMBER BELOW ==>>
(OR ENTER QUIT TO TERMINATE THIS PROGRAM.)

<Operator:>

QUIT
```

Figure 3.7. One example of man-mchine dialog when a user executes the CLIST in Figure 3.8 for inquiring about employee number 090156.

employee number, only two lines of messages (lines 15 and 16 in Figure 3.8) are displayed as the prompt. This method of explaining the type and format of input data to be entered by the user is being user-friendly. This spares the user from having to look up a separate documentation about the command and also eliminates errors caused by keying data incorrectly.

Also note how the user is given a way to terminate the dialog by entering QUIT when prompted for the employee

```
Line   CLIST Statement

1      PROC 0
2      CONTROL NOMSG END(ENDX)
3      /*========================================================================*
4      /* THIS CLIST IS USED TO DISPLAY SELECTED FIELDS FROM THE PAYROLL/    *
5      /* PERSONNEL MASTER FILE RECORD OF ANY SPECIFIED EMPLOYEE.            *
6      /*========================================================================*
7      FREE F(PAYMSTR)
8      ALLOC F(PAYMSTR) DA('PRPPA.PAYROLL.MASTER.FILE')   SHR
9      WRITE ==================================================================
10     WRITE ENTER THE EMPLOYEE NUMBER WHOSE PERSONNEL INFORMATION YOU WISH
11     WRITE TO INQUIRE. NOTE THAT ALL SIX CHARACTERS OF EMPLOYEE NUMBER MUST
12     WRITE BE ENTERED, INCLUDING ANY LEADING ZEROS. EMPLOYEE NUMBER MUST BE
13     WRITE A NON-ZERO NUMERIC VALUE.
14     WRITE ==================================================================
15     READEMP: WRITE PLEASE ENTER EMPLOYEE NUMBER BELOW ==>>
16     WRITE (OR ENTER QUIT TO TERMINATE THIS PROGRAM.)
17     READ &EMPLOYEE
18     IF &EMPLOYEE = QUIT THEN GOTO ENDCLIST
19     IF &DATATYPE(&EMPLOYEE) NE NUM THEN DO
20       WRITE THE EMPLOYEE NUMBER ENTERED IS NOT NUMERIC. IT IS REJECTED.
21       GOTO READEMP
22       ENDX
23     IF &LENGTH(&STR(&EMPLOYEE)) NE 6 THEN DO
24       WRITE THE EMPLOYEE NUMBER ENTERED MUST BE EXACTLY SIX CHARACTERS LONG.
25       GOTO READEMP
26       ENDX
27     IF &EMPLOYEE EQ 000000 THEN DO
28       WRITE THE EMPLOYEE NUMBER ENTERED IS ZERO. IT IS REJECTED.
29       GOTO READEMP
30       ENDX
31     CALL 'Z2BKN.SPPS.LOAD(DISPEMP)' '&EMPLOYEE.'
32     GOTO READEMP
33     ENDCLIST: EXIT
```

Figure 3.8.   A CLIST that will display selected fields from the Payroll/Personnel Master file record of any specified employee.

```
ID DIVISION.
PROGRAM-ID.          DISPEMP.
REMARKS.
     THIS PROGRAM DISPLAYS CERTAIN PERSONNEL DATA OF REQUESTED
     EMPLOYEES FROM THE PAYROLL/PERSONNEL MASTER FILE (VSAM).
DATE-COMPILED.
ENVIRONMENT DIVISION.
INPUT-OUTPUT SECTION.
FILE-CONTROL.
     SELECT PAYMSTR  ASSIGN TO PAYMSTR
        ACCESS MODE DYNAMIC
        ORGANIZATION INDEXED
        RECORD KEY MAST-EMP-NUM
        FILE STATUS STAT1.
DATA DIVISION.
FILE SECITON.
FD   PAYMSTR
     LABEL RECRODS STANDARD
     RECORD CONTAINS 1400 CHARACTERS.
01   PAYMSTR-REC.
     05 MAST-EMP-NUM     PIC 9(6).
     05 FILLER           PIC X(1394).
WORKING-STORAGE SECTION.
01   STATE 1                  PIC X(02) VALUE SPACES.
01   DISPLAY-FIELDS.
     05 WS-BASIC-PAY          PIC ZZZ,ZZ9.99-.
01   PAYROLL-PERSONNEL-MSTR-RECORD.
     05 EMP-NUM               PIC X(06).
     05 EMP-NAME              PIC X(40).
     05 FILLER                PIC X(196).
     05 EMP-ADDRESS           PIC X(60).
     05 FILLER                PIC X(52).
     05 EMP-GRADE-CODE        PIC X(02).
     05 FILLER                PIC X(44).
     05 EMP-BASIC-PAY         PIC 9(6)V99.
     05 FILLER                PIC X(992).

LINKAGE SECTION.
01   LINKAGE-PARM.
     05 FILLER                PIC X(02).
     05 LS-EMP-NUM            PIC X(06).

*********************************************************************
 PROCEDURE DIVISION USING LINKAGE-PARM.
*********************************************************************
     OPEN INPUT PAYMSTR.
     IF STAT1 NOT EQUAL TO ZEROS
```

Figure 3.9.   The COBOL program that is called by the CLIST of Figure 3.8 and which displays selected fields from Payroll/Personnel Master file for the specified employee.

```
        DISPLAY '==================================================='
        DISPLAY 'ERROR OPENING PAYROLL/PERSONNEL MASTER FILE'
        DISPLAY 'PROGRAM DISPEMP IS ABNORMALLY TERMINATING'
        DISPLAY 'PLEASE CORRECT THE PROBLEM AND RERUN THIS PROGRAM'
        DISPLAY '==================================================='
        STOP RUN.
    DISPLAY 'NOW PROCESSING EMPLOYEE NUMBER:  ' LS-EMP-NUM.
    MOVE LS-EMP-NUM TO MAST-EMP-NUM.
    READ PAYMSTR INTO PAYROLL-PERSONNEL-MSTR-RECORD INVALID KEY
        DISPLAY 'EMPLOYEE NUMBER ' MAST-EMP-NUM ' IS NOT ON MAST'
          'ER FILE'
        CLOSE PAYMSTR
        STOP RUN.
    DISPLAY '==================================================='.
    DISPLAY 'EMPLOYEE NAME IN ENGLISH   = ' EMP-NAME.
    DISPLAY 'EMPLOYEE(S) PERMANENT ADDRESS IS AS FOLLOWS:'
    DISPLAY EMP-ADDRESS.
    MOVE EMP-BASIC-PAY    TO WS-BASIC-PAY.
    DISPLAY 'THE BASIC PAY OF EMPLOYEE  = ' WS-BASIC-PAY.
    DISPLAY 'EMPLOYEE''S GRADE CODE      = ' EMP-GRADE-CODE
    DISPLAY '==================================================='.
    CLOSE PAYMSTR
    STOP RUN.
```

Figure 3.9.   The COBOL program that is called by the CLIST of Figure 3.8 and which displays selected fields from Payroll/Personnel Master file for the specified employee (continued).

number. And the user is reminded that QUIT can be used to terminate the dialog, every time he or she is prompted for another value for employee number. This is being supportive of the user and making it easy for him or her to use these programs. If we informed the user only once, at the beginning of the CLIST about the use of QUIT, he might forget about it and subsequently when he is prompted for input data, may panic, not knowing how to terminate the dialog. He can always press the PA1 key to terminate the dialog. But what if the user is not a programmer but a non-technical user who is not aware of the functions of various keys on the keyboard? Why not make it easy for the user to

```
//GEN09X   JOB  (645110,999W,99,99),'NIRMAL-X2398',MSGCLASS=X,CLASS=K,
//   NOTIFY=GEN09
//STEP01    EXEC PGM=DISPEMP,PARM='090144'
//STEPLIB   DD DSN=Z2BKN.SPPS.LOAD,DISP=SHR
//PAYMSTR   DD DSN=PRPPA.PAYROLL.MASTER.FILE,DISP=SHR
//SYSOUT    DD SYSOUT=*
```

Figure 3.10.   A batch job to execute COBOL program DISPEMP of
Figure 3.9.

use the programs by displaying one line of massage about
the use of QUIT every time he is prompted for input data?
Why save the time involved in sending one line of message
but lose the vital quality of interactive systems called user-
friendliness?

The COBOL program shown in Figure 3.9 is actually a
batch program in the sense that it can be executed in
batch. Figure 3.10 shows the JCL required to execute this
program for employee number 090144. As you will notice,
the employee number is passed to the program through the
PARM parameter on the EXEC card in the JCL. Before this
program gets control, the operating system does the
required dataset allocations: DDname PAYMSTR is allocated to VSAM dataset PRPPA.PAYROLL.MASTER.FILE,
DDname SYSOUT is allocated to SYSOUT class of X which
may be assigned at one MVS installation to TSO Held
Queue. When this program gets control, it opens the
dataset allocated under DDname PAYMSTR and issues a
random READ for the record with key equal to the employee number passed to it through the LINKAGE SECTION.
Note that the DISPLAY statement of COBOL results in messages being written to DDname SYSOUT. One example of
output written by the JCL in Figure 3.10 to DDname
SYSOUT is shown in Figure 3.11.

There are close similarities between the JCL in Figure
3.10 and the CLIST in Figure 3.8. When this batch COBOL
program is to be executed through a CLIST, we must make

```
NOW PROCESSING EMPLOYEE NUMBER: 090144
========================================================
EMPLOYEE NAME IN ENGLISH    = SIMON        GERRY         S
EMPLOYEE(S) PERMANENT ADDRESS IS AS FOLLOWS:
P.O. BOX- 998, POSTAL STATION 'B', TORONTO, ONT.  CANADA
THE BASIC PAY OF EMPLOYEE   = 13,000.00
EMPLOYEE'S GRADE CODE       = 21
```

Figure 3.11.   One example of output written by program DISPEMP of the job shown in Figure 3.10 onto DDname SYSOUT.

sure that all dataset allocations are properly done before this program gets control. The ALLOC statement on line 8 in this CLIST allocates the VSAM master file to DDname PAYMSTR. (Note how on line 7 we FREE up the DDname PAYMSTR, in case it was previously allocated to some other dataset. Also note that if DDname PAYMSTR is not pre-allocated, the FREE command will result in an error message; that is why we specified NOMSG option on the CONTROL statement on line 2. This way the user will not receive any messages caused by the execution of the FREE command.) As regards DDname SYSOUT, normally when a TSO user is logged on, DDname SYSIN and SYSOUT are both allocated to terminal. Hence when the COBOL program issues DISPLAY statements, the messages will appear on the terminal. To make sure that SYSIN and SYSOUT are properly allocated during your TSO session, issue the following TSO command which will display all dataset allocations that currently exist during your TSO session:

```
LISTA STAT H
```

You should see the following:

```
—DSORG—CREATED—EXPIRES—SECURITY—DDNAME—DISP—
TERMFILE  SYSOUT
TERMFILE  SYSIN
   - - - -
   - - - -
```

This indicates that DDnames SYSIN and SYSOUT are both assigned to terminal.

If SYSIN and SYSOUT are not allocated to terminal, they can be changed to this status by issuing the following three TSO commands from TSO or any of the ISPF panels:

```
FREE F(SYSIN, SYSOUT)
ALLOC F(SYSIN) DA(*)
ALLOC F(SYSOUT) DA(*)
```

The FREE command will free up DDnames SYSIN and SYSOUT, so that they can be allocated to some other output device. The ALLOC commands will then assign both SYSIN and SYSOUT to terminal. Note that if DDname SYSOUT is unallocated prior to executing this CLIST, messages will appear on the terminal to the effect that SYSOUT DD statement is missing and the COBOL program will abend.

The CALL statement on line 31 in Figure 3.8 is equivalent to the EXEC card in the batch job of Figure 3.10. In the batch job, the program comes from the dataset allocated under DDname STEPLIB; whereas with the CLIST, the CALL command specifies three things: the load library, the load module to be executed and the parameter to be passed to the program. The parameter passed to the COBOL program in both cases is the six character employee number. The COBOL program receives the parameter in the LINKAGE SECTION.

The CLIST and the COBOL program discussed here illustrate how a batch COBOL programmer can execute his batch programs interactively by means of CLISTs. This is to say that the mastering of CLISTs and TSO commands allows a batch COBOL programmer to quickly become an on-line programmer.

A CLIST TO BROWSE A DATASET BYPASSING THE BROWSE ENTRY PANEL

Suppose that the dataset 'SYS2.TSO.USERIDS' is a sequential dataset (DSORG=PS) that contains information about all TSO user IDs issued by the systems programming group. Both active and inactive IDs are stored there. There is one record in this dataset for one TSO user ID. The fields in the record are as listed below:

- User ID
- Name of the user
- His/her work telephone number
- His/her work telephone extension
- User's organization code
- Date user ID assigned
- Date user ID inactivated (if user ID is inactive)

This information allows the systems programming group to contact the user if his TSO session or batch job (which has the name starting with TSO user ID, followed by one, two or three characters) is creating a problem in the MVS system. The information stored in SYS2.TSO.USERIDS can also be useful to other personnel such as EDP security personnel in controlling, and preventing unauthorized access to the MVS system. Suppose that a systems programmer in charge of TSO has to look up this dataset on a frequent basis. He can, of course, select the browse option (normally option 1) of TSO/ISPF and, when the browse entry panel is displayed, he must enter the name of this dataset and then press the Enter key. The browse panel with the first few records from the dataset will then be displayed.

The other alternative is to write a CLIST that can be invoked from any of the TSO/ISPF panels as a TSO command. This CLIST consists of the following three lines:

```
CONTROL MSG
ISPEXEC BROWSE DATA SET('SYS2.TSO.USERIDS')
EXIT
```

This three-line CLIST can be of immense help to the user who has to browse this dataset many many times during the course of a working day. Assuming that this CLIST is stored as member USER in a CLIST library (PDS) allocated under DDname SYSPROC during a user's TSO session, all he must do is issue the TSO command %USER and the system will immediately display the browse panel containing the first few records from the dataset. When the user presses the END key (normally PF3) to terminate browse, he will be returned to the panel from where the command %USER was issued.

The above CLIST uses command ISPEXEC which is a part of ISPF (Interactive System Productivity Facility) which allows you to develop interactive applications using CLISTs, panels, messages and tables, etc. (We will not discuss in any detail the techniques of developing on-line applications using panels in this book because that is not a small topic and requires a separate volume to properly teach all the concepts and techniques involved.) The use of BROWSE on the ISPEXEC command requires that program product ISPF/PDF be installed. Of course most of the MVS installations have ISPF and ISPF/PDF installed.

If you or your user frequently browses a dataset, for example, one containing telephone extensions of all the employees of the EDP department or one containing information about all the IBM manuals available in the EDP library, you may set up a CLIST similar to the one given above and execute that CLIST, rather than going through the BROWSE panel of ISPF. The savings in time and effort will be significant, as you can easily verify yourself.

The ISPEXEC command with the BROWSE option can also be used to allow a TSO user who does not have access to the entire ISPF facility, or who does not have knowledge about using ISPF, (for example a data control clerk) to browse selected datasets. It should be noted that under TSO, an MVS installation can be running many applications such as ISPF, RMDS (Report Management and Distribution System). Not all TSO users will be able to access all the applications running under TSO, when they log-on to TSO. The technique of using CLISTs to restrict TSO users' access to applications running under TSO is discussed in a later chapter.

A CLIST TO EDIT A DATA SET BYPASSING THE EDIT ENTRY PANEL

Suppose that a user frequently needs to edit the dataset 'PAYROLL.PDS.FILE(USERS)' and he needs to edit it while working with any of the ISPF panels and then return to the original panel. Then this smart user can write the following CLIST:

```
CONTROL MSG
ISPEXEC EDIT DATA SET('PAYROLL.PDS.FILE(USERS)')
EXIT
```

This CLIST can be stored in any of the CLIST libraries allocated under DDname SYSPROC, for example under name EDIT1. Then from anywhere in ISPF, he can invoke this CLIST by executing the following command:

```
%EDIT1
```

This CLIST will display the edit panel for the dataset, bypassing the edit entry panel. After the user has finished editing this dataset and presses the END key, he will be returned to the panel from where he executed the EDIT1 command.

As you can see, the time saving obtained by using this CLIST is significant. The ISPEXEC command mentioned above is fully described in the following IBM manual:

Interactive System Productivity Facility (ISPF)
Dialog Management Services
(IBM Publication Number: SC34-2088)

A CLIST TO CALCULATE BLOCK SIZE AND SPACE REQUIREMENTS FOR A DATASET

This problem is to write a CLIST which can be used to automate the task of calculating block sizes and space requirements in tracks for datasets to be allocated by pro-grammer/analysts. This CLIST when invoked will prompt the user for the following input parameters:

- the logical record length of the dataset (dataset organi-zation is assumed to be Fixed Blocked.)
- initial choice of block size in terms of one-fifth track, one-sixth track, or one-seventh track blocking on an IBM 3380 DASD
- the estimated number of logical records the dataset will contain.

This CLIST will then calculate and display the following parameters:

- final block size value calculated based on the initial value for block size selected by the user
- the primary track requirements for the dataset
- the secondary track requirements for the dataset
- the number of logical records to be contained in one track of IBM 3380 DASD based on the final block size value calculated

- percentage of track capacity utilized based on the block size calculated.

How can this CLIST be useful in day-to-day work of programmer/analysts? This CLIST will be of immense help to the DP professionals who will no longer have to look up a manual or a textbook to calculate the best values for block sizes of their datasets. They can invoke this CLIST and obtain block sizes as well as space requirements which can be directly used in allocating the datasets either through TSO/ISPF (normally option 3.2 of ISPF) or through a batch job. Also, the track capacity utilization calculated by this CLIST will indicate whether efficient use is being made of track capacity. To determine if this is the case, the user can invoke this CLIST again entering some other value for the initial block size. The CLIST will then display another set of values for the parameters calculated. This way the programmer/analyst can compare various values of block size and track utilization and select the best value for the block size. It should be noted, however, that even if a lower value for block size results in a slightly better track utilization compared with a higher block size value, the higher block size value may be the best choice. This is due to the fact that a higher value for block size results in better utilization of CPU and channel, as stated earlier.

The Solution

The CLIST that solves this problem is shown in Figure 3.12. The reader is advised to study this CLIST thoroughly and be convinced that it will faithfully and accurately calculate the various parameters as stated above. Also to be noted is the technique of rounding up or down the value for track utilization percentage before it is displayed. For example, if track utilization percentage is less than 93.50 but greater than or equal to 93.00, then the value dis-

```
1     PROC 0
2     CONTROL MSG END(ENDX)
3     WRITE ===============================================================
4     WRITE THIS CLIST WILL ASK YOU TO ENTER THE RECORD LENGTH OF YOUR FIXED
5     WRITE BLOCKED FILE. IT WILL THEN ASK YOU WHETHER YOU WANT 1/5TH, 1/6TH
6     WRITE OR 1/7TH TRACK BLOCKING ON IBM 3380 DASD. IT WILL ALSO ASK YOU
7     WRITE FOR ESTIMATED NUMBER OF RECORDS THAT THE FILE WILL CONTAIN. IT
8     WRITE WILL THEN DO THE CALCULATIONS AND GIVE YOU THE FOLLOWING
9     WRITE PARAMETERS FOR USE IN ALLOCATING YOUR FILE THRU A BATCH JOB OR
10    WRITE THRU TSO/ISPF:
11    WRITE
12    WRITE THE BLOCK SIZE TO USE
13    WRITE THE PRIMARY ALLOCATION QUANTITY IN TRACKS
14    WRITE THE SECONDARY ALLOCATION QUANTITY IN TRACKS
15    WRITE THE NUMBER OF LOGICAL RECORDS CONTAINED IN ONE TRACK OF IBM 3380
16    WRITE ===============================================================
17    START: WRITE
18    WRITENR ENTER RECORD LENGTH PLEASE ==>>
19    READ &LRECL
20    IF &DATATYPE(&LRECL) NE NUM THEN DO
21       WRITE RECORD LENGTH ENTERED IS NOT NUMERIC. IT IS REJECTED.
22       GOTO START
23       ENDX
24    WRITE
25    WRITE ENTER YOUR CHOICE OF BLOCKING FROM THE LIST BELOW:
26    WRITE
27    WRITE 5 = ONE FIFTH TRACK BLOCKING   (MAXIMUM BLOCKSIZE = 9,076)
28    WRITE 6 = ONE SIXTH TRACK BLOCKING   (MAXIMUM BLOCKSIZE = 7,476)
29    WRITE 7 = ONE SEVENTH TRACK BLOCKING (MAXIMUM BLOCKSIZE = 6,356)
30    READFAC: WRITE
31    WRITENR YOUR CHOICE FOR BLOCKING PLEASE (5,6 OR 7) ==>>
32    READ &FACTOR
33    IF &FACTOR = 5 OR &FACTOR = 6 OR &FACTOR = 7 THEN GOTO VALIDFAC
34       ELSE DO
35          WRITE
36          WRITE ACCEPTABLE ANSWER IS 5,6 OR 7 ONLY. YOUR ANSWER IS REJECTED.
37          GOTO READFAC
38          ENDX
39    VALIDFAC: +
40    IF &FACTOR = 5 THEN SET &MAXBLKSIZE = 9076
41       ELSE IF &FACTOR = 6 THEN SET &MAXBLKSIZE = 7476
42          ELSE IF &FACTOR = 7 THEN SET &MAXBLKSIZE = 6356
43    IF &LRECL GT &MAXBLKSIZE THEN DO
44       WRITE
45       WRITE THE LOGICAL RECORD LENGTH YOU ENTERED IS GREATER THAN THE
46       WRITE BLOCKSIZE CALCULATED BASED ON YOUR CHOICE OF BLOCKING.
47       WRITE DUE TO THIS ERROR, CLIST EXECUTION IS ABNORMALLY TERMINATING.
```

Figure 3.12. A CLIST to calculate blocksize, primary and secondary track requirements and number of records to be contained in a track of IBM 3380 DASD for a fixed blocked data set, based on parameters supplied by the user.

```
48         GOTO ENDCLIST
49         ENDX
50      READEST: +
51      WRITE
52      WRITENR ENTER ESTIMATED NUMBER OF RECORDS FOR THIS DATA SET ==>>
53      READ &NUMREC
54      IF &DATATYPE(&NUMREC) NE NUM THEN DO
55         WRITE YOUR ANSWER IS NOT NUMERIC. IT HAS BEEN REJECTED.
56         GOTO READEST
57         ENDX
58      SET &BLKFACT = &MAXBLKSIZE / &LRECL
59      SET &BLKSIZE = &BLKFACT * &LRECL
60      SET &TRACKS = (&NUMREC / &BLKFACT ) / &FACTOR
61      SET &PRIMTRKS = &TRACKS + 1
62      SET &SECTRKS  = (&PRIMTRKS / 10) + 1
63      SET &RECPERTRK = &BLKFACT * &FACTOR
64      SET &TRKUTIL = (&RECPERTRK * &LRECL * 100) / 47476
65      SET &REMAINDER = (&RECPERTRK * &LRECL * 100) // 47476
66      IF &REMAINDER GE 23738 THEN SET &TRKUTIL = &TRKUTIL + 1
67      WRITE
68      WRITE *++++++++++++++++++++++++++++++++++++++++++++++++++++++++++++++*
69      WRITE
70      WRITE         RECORD FORMAT        = FIXED BLOCKED
71      WRITE         LOGICAL RECORD LENGTH  = &LRECL
72      WRITE         BLOCKSIZE            = &BLKSIZE
73      WRITE
74      WRITE         PRIMARY NUMBER OF TRACKS REQUIRED   = &PRIMTRKS
75      WRITE         SECONDARY NUMBER OF TRACKS REQUIRED = &SECTRKS
76      WRITE
77      WRITE ONE TRACK WILL ACCOMODATE &RECPERTRK NUMBER OF LOGICAL RECORDS.
78      WRITE TRACK CAPACITY UTILIZATION = &TRKUTIL.  PERCENT.
79      WRITE *++++++++++++++++++++++++++++++++++++++++++++++++++++++++++++++*
80      WRITE
81      WRITE IF YOU ARE CREATING THIS DATA SET IN A BATCH JOB, USE THE
82      WRITE FOLLOWING ALONG WITH   DISP=(NEW,CATLG,DELETE):
83      WRITE
84      WRITE         DCB=(RECFM=FB,LRECL=&LRECL.,BLKSIZE=&BLKSIZE.),
85      WRITE         SPACE=(TRK,(&PRIMTRKS.,&SECTRKS.),RLSE)
86      WRITE
87      WRITE *++++++++++++++++++++++++++++++++++++++++++++++++++++++++++++++*
88      WRITE
89      WRITENR DO YOU WISH TO EXECUTE THIS CLIST AGAIN (Y/N) ==>>
90      READ &WISH
91      IF &WISH = Y THEN GOTO START
92      ENDCLIST: EXIT
```

Figure 3.12. A CLIST to calculate blocksize, primary and secondary track requirements and number of records to be contained in a track of IBM 3380 DASD for a fixed blocked data set, based on parameters supplied by the user (continued).

```
<<--------- User Supplied -------->>><<------ CLIST Calculated Results ------>>>

Logical  Blocking      Estimated        Blocksize   Primary    Secondary  Track
Record   Chosen        Num. of Records  Calculated  Number of  Number of  Capacity
Length   by User       in File          by CLIST    Tracks     Tracks     Utilization
-------  ------------  ---------------- ----------  ---------  ---------- -----------
  254    1/5th Track       2,000           8890         12          2     94 Percent
   75    1/5th Track       4,000           9075          7          1     96 Percent
   75    1/6th Track       4,000           7425          7          1     94 Percent
   75    1/7th Track       4,000           6300          7          1     93 Percent
```

Figure 3.13.   Some examples of parameters calculated by the CLIST of Figure 3.12.

played is 93 percent. However, if the track utilization is greater than or equal to 93.50 but less than or equal to 94.00, then the value displayed is 94 percent. This rounding is done by statements on lines 65 and 66 in this CLIST.

Figure 3.13 displays some results returned by this CLIST based on the parameters supplied by the user.

EXERCISES

1. Write a CLIST that will prompt the user for a word, any word. It will then create another word which is the reverse of the original word. The CLIST will print the reversed word. It will then decide if the original word is a palindrome; that is, if it reads the same forwards and backwards. One dialog with this CLIST may be as follows:

```
ENTER A WORD PLEASE.
MADAM
THE REVERSE OF MADAM IS MADAM
MADAM IS PALINDROMIC.
DO YOU WISH TO PLAY THIS GAME AGAIN (Y/N) ?
Y
```

```
ENTER A WORD PLEASE.
RICHARD
THE REVERSE OF RICHARD IS DRAHCIR
RICHARD IS NOT PALINDROMIC.
- - -
- - -
```

2. Write a CLIST that will accept a hexadecimal number as a positional parameter and will calculate and display its decimal equivalent. Some examples of the message displayed by this CLIST are as follows:

```
DECIMAL EQUIVALENT OF HEXADECIMAL NUMBER 12F9 = 4857
DECIMAL EQUIVALENT OF HEXADECIMAL NUMBER 123456 = 1193046
DECIMAL EQUIVALENT OF HEXADECIMAL NUMBER 52B7BC = 5420988
```

Chapter 4
APPLICATION OF CLISTs IN TWO IMPORTANT AREAS

In this chapter we will discuss the application of CLISTs in two important areas:

- Using CLISTs in TSO log-on processing, to control users, access to applications running under TSO
- Using CLISTs in conjunction with ISPF panels and programs written in COBOL, PL/I or Assembler to build on-line applications that display full-screen panels.

CLISTs IN TSO LOG-ON PROCESSING

In this section we discuss and explain the processing that takes place when a TSO user logs on to TSO. This topic is of paramount importance since an understanding of this topic will enable you to solve many problems that users encounter when trying to log on to TSO and also to modify the software elements involved in TSO log-on processing so as to achieve the desired results.

The Crucial Role of the TSO Log-on Procedure

The discussion presented below will highlight the crucial role of the TSO log-on procedure in TSO log-on processing.

The TSO log-on procedure resides in a member of a system procedure library and has the same syntax as that of a catalogued procedure used in a batch job. However, a log-on procedure executes IBM's program IKJEFT01.

Using CLISTS to Control TSO User's Access to Applications

The discussion below will show how CLISTs can be used to control a TSO user's access to various application systems running under TSO.

Case Study of One Company's TSO Log-On Environment

The best approach to understanding the very important concepts and techniques involved in TSO log-on processing is to take a real-life situation as a case study. Let us suppose that we want to assign TSO user IDs to computer operators and programmers. When an operator logs on to TSO, he should be able to access only the Spool Display and Search Facility (SDSF) and no other application, and when the operator exits from SDSF, he is logged off TSO completely. And, in case of programmers, we want them to be presented with the main menu of ISPF when they log on. When they exit from ISPF, they should get the native TSO screen, so that they can execute any of the TSO commands or type ISPF and press the Enter key to reenter ISPF.

To make things simpler, let us suppose that operators will have their TSO user IDs start with the string 'OPR' and the programmers will have theirs start with the string 'PRG'. To understand how this works, let us trace the flow when user PRG01 logs on to TSO.

Tracing the execution flow for TSO USER PRG01. Figure 4.1 is the log-on procedure stored in a procedure library

```
//$LOGON1    PROC
//*=======================================================================
//* LOG-ON PROCEDURE FOR COMPUTER OPERATORS (USER ID = OPRXX)  AND
//* APPLICATIONS PROGRAMMERS (USER ID = PRGXX) WHERE XX= 01 TO 99
//*=======================================================================
//$LOGON1    EXEC PGM=IKJEFT01,PARM='%START0',DYNAMNBR=50,
//           TIME=15
//SYSPROC    DD DSN=Z2BKN.CLIST,DISP=SHR,DCB=BUFNO=1
//SYSPRINT   DD TERM=TS
//SYSOUT     DD TERM=TS
//SYSIN      DD TERM=TS
```

Figure 4.1. Log-on procedure $LOGON1 stored in SYS2.PROCLIB.

(SYS2.PROCLIB or SYS1.PROCLIB, for example) which comes into play anytime an operator or a programmer logs on to TSO. This is because, for each of these users, the content of an appropriate member in the partitioned dataset SYS1.UADS (or an ACF/2 or RACF dataset) specifies that for this user member $LOGON1 in a procedure library (e.g. SYS2.PROCLIB or SYS1.PROCLIB) will be used as the log-on procedure. In this procedure shown in Figure 4.1 the presence of PARM='%START0' on the EXEC statement means that after all the file allocations indicated in the procedure have been made and program IKJEFT01 has received control, it causes the control to be transferred to the CLIST member START0 of one of the datasets allocated to DDname SYSPROC. In this example, since DDname SYSPROC is allocated to the single partitioned dataset, Z2BKN.CLIST, control would go to member START0 of Z2BKN.CLIST. Figure 4.2 shows the content of CLIST START0.

In this CLIST, the statement on line 10 indicates to the system that CLIST ALLOCALL is to be executed. (You will recall that the character % indicates that the system is to search only the CLIST libraries for member ALLOCALL.) The system searches Z2BKN.CLIST and finding member ALLOCALL in it, executes it. This CLIST is shown in Figure

```
LINE   STATEMENT

1      PROC 0
2      CONTROL MAIN,NOMSG
3      ERROR DO
4        IF &SYSPCMD = EXEC THEN EXIT
5        RETURN
6        END
7      ATTN DO
8        LOGOFF
9        END
10     %ALLOCALL
11     SET &GROUP = &SUBSTR(1:3,&SYSUID)
12     IF &GROUP = OPR  THEN  GOTO OPERATE
13     IF &GROUP = PRG  THEN  GOTO PROGRAM
14     GOTO INVALID
15     OPERATE: ISPSTART PANEL(ZSDSFOP2) NEWAPPL(ISF)
16     LOGOFF
17     PROGRAM: ISPF
18     WRITE YOU ARE NOW IN NATIVE MODE OF TSO. IF YOU WANT TO GO TO ISPF,
19     WRITE TYPE ISPF AND PRESS ENTER. IF YOU WANT TO GO TO SDSF, TYPE SDSF
20     WRITE AND PRESS ENTER. FROM NATIVE MODE OF TSO, YOU CAN EXECUTE ANY OF
21     WRITE THE TSO COMMANDS, SUCH AS LISTC, LISTA, STATUS, LOGOFF, ETC.
22     GOTO X001
23     INVALID: WRITE CLIST START0 REFUSES TO RECOGNIZE THIS USER ID
24     WRITE CONTACT YOUR TSO SUPPORT SPECIALIST FOR HELP IN LOGGING ON TO TSO
25     WRITE PRESS ENTER KEY NOW TO LOG OFF TSO. THANK YOU VERY MUCH.
26     READ
27     LOGOFF
28     X001: EXIT
```

Figure 4.2.   CLIST Member START0 of Z2BKN.CLIST.

4.3. In this CLIST, file SYSPROC is freed and then it is reallocated to a concatenation of SYS1.CLIST and SYS1.ISRCLIB. This is followed by allocation of DDname ISPPROF to the ISPF profile dataset. This is followed by the allocations of DDnames ISPPLIB (ISPF panel library), ISPSLIB (ISPF source library), ISPMLIB (ISPF message library), and ISPTLIB (ISPF table library) to appropriate datasets. Please consult an appropriate IBM manual on ISPF for explanation and significance of these DDnames. Note that all datasets necessary for ISPF and SDSF to function properly must be allocated in the CLIST of Figure 4.3. The last line in this CLIST causes control to be transferred to the caller. So, control comes to line 11 in the command procedure START0 of Figure 4.2.

```
PROC 0
/*----------------------------------------------
/* THIS CLIST ALLOCATES THE DATA SETS NECESSARY TO EXECUTE SDSF FOR
/* OPERATORS AND ISPF OR SDSF FOR PROGRAMMERS. THIS CLIST IS INVOKED BY
/* CLIST 'START0' IN Z2BKN.CLIST.
/*----------------------------------------------
CONTROL MAIN,NOMSG
ERROR DO
  IF &SYSPCMD = EXEC THEN EXIT
  IF &SYSPCMD = FREE THEN RETURN
  WRITE ERROR TRACED FROM LOGON CLIST = ALLOCALL +
    SYSPCMD= &SYSPCMD  LASTCC = &LASTCC
  EXIT
  END
ATTN OFF
FREE F(SYSPROC)
ALLOC F(SYSPROC) DA('SYS1.CLIST' +
                    'SYS1.ISRCLIB') SHR
ATTR S1 BUFNO(1)
ATTR S2 BUFNO(2)
ALLOC F(ISPPROF) DSN('&SYSUID..ISPF.PROFILE') SHR
ALLOC F(ISPPLIB) DA('SYS1.ISRPLIB' +
                    'SYS1.ISPPLIB' +
                    'SYS1.ISFPLIB') SHR USING(S2)
ALLOC F(ISPSLIB) DA('SYS1.ISPSLIB'    +
                    'SYS1.ISRSLIB) SHR USING(S2)
ALLOC F(ISPMLIB) DA('SYS1.ISPMLIB' +
                    'SYS1.ISRMLIB') SHR USING(S2)
ALLOC F(ISPTLIB) DA('SYS1.ISPTLIB' +
                    'SYS1.ISRTLIB' +
                    'SYS1.ISFTLIB') SHR USING(S2)
EXIT CODE(0)
```

Figure 4.3. CLIST ALLOCALL stored in Z2BKN.CLIST.

In this CLIST, the statement on line 12 specifies that if the user ID starts with the string OPR, then the control is to be transferred to the line with the label OPERATE. And line 13 specifies that if the user ID starts with the string PRG, then the control is to be transferred to the line with the label PROGRAM. In the case of user PRG01, control goes to line 17. Here the command ISPF is executed. This command causes the system to search for member ISR@PRIM in the partitioned datasets allocated under DDname ISPPLIB. Panel ISR@PRIM is supposed to be for the main menu of ISPF. In this case, the system would first search SYS1.ISRPLIB, and, if this member is not present in this PDS, it would next search SYS1.ISPPLIB. It will find member ISR@PRIM in one of these two libraries (because SYS1.ISFPLIB which is the last dataset assigned to DDname ISPPLIB is supposed to contain panels for SDSF), and will display that panel. So TSO user PRG01 would be presented with the main menu of ISPF.

The user can select any option on the main menu of ISPF. When he or she terminates ISPF, the control is transferred to line 18 in CLIST START0 of Figure 4.2. At this point we are in TSO, and the WRITE statements on lines 18 thru 21 cause a number of message lines to be written to the terminal. Control then is transferred to line 28, where the EXIT statement causes the CLIST START0 to terminate. The user is now sitting with the terminal freed and a number of lines of message lines (written by lines 18 thru 21 of Figure 4.2) followed by TSO READY sign appearing on it. As these messages indicate, the user can type in any of the TSO commands or he can type ISPF and press the Enter key to receive the main menu of ISPF. At any point the user can type LOGOFF and press the Enter key to exit from TSO and obtain the initial logo, which usually has the company's name on it. From this initial logo, the user can access any of the of the various applications running under MVS, such as TSO, CICSTEST, CICSPROD, etc.

Tracing the execution flow for USER OPR05.   Let us suppose that an appropriate member of dataset SYS1.UADS (or an ACF2 or RACF dataset) specifies $LOGON1 as the log-on procedure name for TSO user OPR05. When user OPR05 logs on to TSO, the system searches the procedure libraries set up by the systems programmer and finds member $LOGON1 in a procedure library (SYS2.PROCLIB or SYS1.PROCLIB, for example). The log-on procedure shown in Figure 4.1 is executed. From this point on, the processing is similar to that described above for user PRG01.

Eventually the control will be transferred to the CLIST START0 shown in Figure 4.2. Here on line 12, the test will be satisfied and control will flow to line 15, where the ISP-START command of ISPF will cause the panel libraries allocated under DDname ISPPLIB to be searched for member ZSDSFOP2. This is the panel for the main menu of SDSF and will be found in SYS1.ISFPLIB. The main menu of SDSF will thus be displayed. On this menu, the user can select one of several options and the processing that takes place will depend on how SDSF is designed. But the important point to note here is that once the user exits from SDSF, control will flow to line 16 in the CLIST of Figure 4.2. On this line, we find the LOGOFF command of TSO, which will cause the TSO user OPR05 to be logged off TSO.

CLISTs AND ISPF PANELS

CLISTs used in conjunction with ISPF panels, and COBOL, PL/I or Assembler programs are widely used for building on-line applications running under TSO that display full-screen panels. The best way to understand how this is done is to take a real example. The case study presented below will illustrate the techniques involved.

Case Study of an On-line System Using CLISTs, Panels and COBOL Program

Let us examine an on-line system based on TSO that has been built for the users of the Finance Department. All users of this department have their TSO user ID in the form A2xxx where xxx represents the initials of the user. In fact, all users of the installation have their TSO user IDs in the form aaxxx where aa represents the department or group of the user and xxx represents the initials of the user. For example, all systems programmers have their

```
1    //@LOGA2     PROC
2    //*--- LOGON PROCEDURE FOR USERS USING FINANCIAL SYSTEMS
3    //*--------------------------------------------------------
4    //LOGA2       EXEC PGM=IKJEFT01,PARM='%SYSALL',
5    //             DYNAMNBR=40,TIME=1439
6    //SYSOUT      DD TERM=TS
7    //SYSPRINT    DD TERM=TS
8    //SYSIN       DD TERM=TS
9    //SYSPROC     DD DISP=SHR,DSN=SYS1.CLIST
10   //           DD DISP=SHR,DSN=SYS1.ISRCLIB
11   //ISPPLIB    DD DISP=SHR,DSN=SYS1.ISPPLIB
12   //           DD DISP=SHR,DSN=SYS1.ISRPLIB
13   //           DD DISP=SHR,DSN=SYS1.ISFPLIB
14   //ISPTLIB    DD DISP=SHR,DSN=SYS1.ISPTLIB
15   //           DD DISP=SHR,DSN=SYS1.ISRTLIB
16   //           DD DISP=SHR,DSN=SYS1.ISFTLIB
17   //ISPSLIB    DD DISP=SHR,DSN=SYS1.ISPSLIB
18   //           DD DISP=SHR,DSN=SYS1.ISRSLIB
19   //ISPMLIB    DD DISP=SHR,DSN=SYS1.ISPMLIB
20   //           DD DISP=SHR,DSN=SYS1.ISRMLIB
21   //FT05F001   DD TERM=TS
22   //FT06F001   DD TERM=TS
```

Figure 4.4.   TSO log-on procedure @LOGA2 stored in a procedure library.

TSO user ID in the form A1xxx, and all applications programmers have their IDs in the form A3xxx. This scheme allows us to figure out from a TSO user ID, the department or group as well as the initials of the person assigned that user ID. For example, from user ID A2DBD we can immediately figure out that this user is in the Finance Department (A2 represents Finance Department) and his initials are DBD (Dan B. Denver).

Now, let us suppose that the log-on procedure of each TSO user of the Finance Department is @LOGA2, which is shown in Figure 4.4. In this procedure, all datasets necessary for ISPF, ISPF/PDF and SDSF (Spool Display and Search Facility) to function have been allocated. The string PARM='%SYSALL' on the EXEC statement on line 4 indicates that after all dataset allocations in this procedure have been made and program IKJEFT01 has been given control, TSO will invoke CLIST SYSALL present in a dataset allocated under DDname SYSPROC. Let us suppose that SYS1.CLIST, which is the first dataset allocated under DDname SYSPROC contains member SYSALL. In fact, all log-on procedures for all users at the installation have PARM='%SYSALL' on the EXEC statement. This means that member SYSALL of SYS1.CLIST is executed for each and every user of the installation. A partial listing of this CLIST is shown in Figure 4.5. We have shown all statements necessary for users of the Finance Department but have omitted some other statements required for other users.

Let us now examine this CLIST from the top. In the beginning, an attention exit is set up, but only for users whose user ID is not of the form A1xxx. Next, the user's ISPF/PDF profile dataset is allocated. The &SYSDSN built-in function is used to check whether this dataset is already present. If it is present, it is allocated under DDname ISPPROF with the disposition of OLD; otherwise, it is allocated as a new dataset with the following attributes:

Logical Record Length:	80
Block Size:	3200
Record Format:	Fixed Blocked
Primary Space:	1 Track
Secondary Space:	1 Track
Volume Where Allocated:	Any DASD Belonging to Group SYSTSO
Directory Blocks:	2

Next, a check is made whether the log-on procedure name is @LOGA2. If this is not true, control will flow to the line with label NEXT02; otherwise, DDname SYSPROC is freed and is reallocated to a concatenation of three datasets. DDname SYSHELP is also allocated. Control then flows to the line with label NEXT03, where the CLEAR command is used to clear the screen. Attention exit is then deactivated. Next a check is made to determine if the user's prefix is null. If so, variable &PREFIX is set to the user ID; other-

```
PROC 0
CONTROL NOLIST NOMSG
/*──────────────────────────────────────────*/
/* THIS CLIST IS INVOKED BY EACH LOG-ON PROCEDURE AT OUR INSTALLATION.   */
/* AFTER DOING INITIAL WORK SUCH AS ALLOCATING DATA SETS ETC. THIS       */
/* CLIST WILL INVOKE MEMBER MYCLIST IN DATA SET userid.CLIST             */
/*──────────────────────────────────────────*/
SET &PREF1 = &SUBSTR(1:2,&SYSUID)
ALLOC F(SYSUDUMP) SYSOUT(X)
IF &PREF1 = A1 THEN GOTO NEXT01
ATTN DO
  WRITE SIR/MADAM, PRESSING ATTN KEY WILL NOT HELP YOU DURING INITIAL
  WRITE TSO LOG-ON PROCESSING. YOU ARE BEING LOGGED OFF. PRESS ENTER
  WRITE KEY NOW AND TRY LOGGING ON TO TSO AGAIN.
  READ
  LOGOFF
END
/*─────────────────────────────────────
/*    NOW ALLOCATE THE USER'S ISPF/PDF PROFILE DATA SET.
/*─────────────────────────────────────
NEXT01: IF &SYSDSN('&SYSUID..ISPF.PROFILE') = OK THEN +
           ALLOC F(ISPPROF) DA('&SYSUID..ISPF.PROFILE') OLD
        ELSE DO
           ATTR ATTR1 LRECL(80) BLKSIZE(3200) RECFM(F B)
           ALLOC F(ISPPROF) DA('&SYSUID..ISPF.PROFILE') NEW SPACE(1 1) +
             DIR(2) TR USING(ATTR1) UNIT(SYSTSO)
           END
/*─────────────────────────────────────
/* NOW ALLOCATE OTHER DATA SETS NEEDED BY LOG-ON PROCEDURE @LOGA2
/*─────────────────────────────────────
IF &SYSPROC NE &STR(@LOGA2) THEN GOTO NEXT02
FREE F(SYSPROC)
ALLOC F(SYSPROC) DA('SYS4.CLIST' 'SYS1.CLIST' 'SYS1.ISRCLIB') SHR
ALLOC F(SYSHELP) DA('SYS4.ISPFHELP' 'SYS1.HELP'  'SYS2.HELP') SHR
GOTO NEXT03
NEXT02: +
- - - - - -
- - - - - -
NEXT03: CLEAR
        ATTN OFF
        IF A&SYSPREF = A  THEN +
          SET &PREFIX = &SYSUID
        ELSE SET &PRERFIX = &SYSPREF
        EXECUTE '&PREFIX..CLIST(MYCLIST)'
EXIT
```

Figure 4.5.   Partial listing of CLIST SYSALL invoked by the procedure in Figure 4.4.

```
1    PROC 0
2    CONTROL NOMSG NOLIST NOFLUSH
3    PROFILE MSGID WTPMSG
4    CLEAR
5    FREE F(SYSPROC)
6    ALLOC F(SYSPROC) DA(CLIST 'SYS1.ISRCLIB' 'SYS1.CLIST' +
7      'SYS4.CLIST' 'SYS3.CLIST') SHR
8    %ALLOCDSN
9    ISPSTART PANEL(FIN@PRIM)
```

Figure 4.6.   CLIST MYCLIST stored in data set A2BKN.CLIST of TSO
user A2BKN.

wise, it is equated to the user's prefix. Next member
MYCLIST of dataset prefix.CLIST is executed. So, if user
A2BKN is logging on to TSO and his TSO prefix is A2BKN,
then member MYCLIST of dataset A2BKN.CLIST would get
executed. This CLIST is shown in Figure 4.6. The point to
remember is that since the CLIST in Figure 4.5 is executed
for all users, this CLIST will finally end up executing member MYCLIST of the user's private CLIST library which is
named userid.CLIST. In the user's private CLIST library,
member MYCLIST can contain commands to customize the
TSO environment for the user. For example, for user
A2BKN of the Finance Department, CLIST MYCLIST shown
in Figure 4.6 frees DDname SYSPROC, then reallocates it
to a concatenation of five CLIST libraries, with
A2BKN.CLIST being the first in the concatenation. This way
TSO user A2BKN can place a CLIST in his private CLIST
library and execute it implicitly, even though a CLIST with
the same name may exist in another library allocated
under SYSPROC.

So, in the CLIST of Figure 4.6, after reallocating
SYSPROC, on line 8 the command %ALLOCDSN is issued.
This causes the system to search the datasets allocated
under DDname SYSPROC and execute member ALLOCD-
SN. Supposing that SYS4.CLIST is the first CLIST library in
the concatenation that contains member ALLOCDSN. This

```
1     PROC 0
2     CONTROL NOMSG NOLIST
3     FREE F(ISPPLIB ISPMLIB ISPTABL ISPTLIB ISPSLIB ISPFILE ISPLLIB)
4     FREE F(SYSOUT)
5     ALLOC F(ISPMLIB) DA('SYS4.ISPMLIB' 'SYS1.ISRMLIB' +
6            'SYS1.ISPMLIB') SHR
7     ALLOC F(ISPPLIB) DA('SYS4.ISPPLIB' 'SYS1.ISRPLIB' +
8            'SYS1.ISPPLIB' 'SYS1.ISFPLIB') SHR
9     ALLOC F(ISPSLIB) DA('SYS4.ISPSLIB' 'SYS1.ISRSLIB' +
10           'SYS1.ISPSLIB') SHR
11    ALLOC F(ISPTLIB) DA('SYS1.ISRTLIB' 'SYS1.ISPTLIB' +
12           'SYS1.ISFTLIB' 'SYS4.ISPTLIB') SHR
13    ALLOC F(ISPLLIB) DA('SYS4.LOADLIB' 'SYS1.VFORTLIB') SHR
14    ALLOC F(ISPTABL) DA('SYS4.ISPTABL') SHR
15    ALLOC F(ISPFILE) DA('SYS4.INPUT') SHR
16    EXIT
```

Figure 4.7.   Member ALLOCDSN stored in SYS4.CLIST which is used for all TSO users of the Finance Department.

means that datasets A2BKN.CLIST, SYS1.ISRCLIB and SYS1.CLIST do not contain member ALLOCDSN. Member ALLOCDSN of SYS4.CLIST will get executed as a result of executing command %ALLOCDSN on line 8 in Figure 4.6. This CLIST is shown in Figure 4.7. The purpose of this CLIST is to perform dataset allocations required for all users of the Finance department. For each user of the Finance Department, his private CLIST library's member MYCLIST will contain command %ALLOCDSN. The important point is that functions to be performed for all users of a group are placed in a common CLIST member, rather than in member MYCLIST of each user's private CLIST library. This eases the task of software maintenance and debugging.

The CLIST in Figure 4.7 frees a number of DDnames and then reallocates them to a new concatenation of libraries. The important point here is that SYS4 datasets are included in the concatenations, which were not present before. The SYS4 datasets contain members for use of financial applications. In our example, after ALLOCDSN has executed, control flows to line 9 in the CLIST of Figure

```
01   %───────── FINANCIAL APPLICATIONS ──────────
02   %SELECT OPTION ==> _OPT %                            USERID - &ZUSER
03   %                                                    TIME   - &ZTIME
04   %
05   %   0   + DISPLAY USER COMMENTS SCREEN
06   %   1   + LIST BANK CODES
07   %   2   + PAYROLL SUBSYSTEM
08   %   3   + PERSONNEL INFORMATION SUBSYSTEM
09   %   4   + FINANCIAL MODELLING
10   %   5   + TABLES MAINTENANCE SUBSYSTEM
11   %   X   + EXIT FROM ISPF
12   +
13   +PRESS %END KEY (PF3/PF15) TO+TERMINATE ISPF
14   +PRESS %PF1/PF13 KEY+FOR HELP
15   ) INIT
16    &ZPRIM = YES
17    .CURSOR = OPT
18    &OPT = ' '
19   ) PROC
20    &SEL = TRANS( TRUNC (&OPT,'.')
21                    0,'CMD(COMMENTS) NEWAPPL'
22                    1,'CMD(BANK) NEWAPPL'
23                    2,'CMD(PAYROLL) NEWAPPL'
24                    3,'CMD(PERSONNEL) NEWAPPL'
25                    4,'PANEL(FIMODEL)'
26                    5,'CMD(TABLES) NEWAPPL'
27                    ' ','*?'
28                    X,'EXIT'
29                    *,'?')
30   ) END
```

Figure 4.8.   Member FIN@PRIM stored in SYS4.ISPPLIB as an ISPF panel.

4.6. Here we find the ISPSTART command which displays member FIN@PRIM present in the first dataset allocated under DDname ISPPLIB. Since SYS4.ISPPLIB is the first dataset allocated to ISPPLIB, its member FIN@PRIM, shown in Figure 4.8 is displayed.

Understanding the panels of Figure 4.8 and 4.10 and the CLIST of Figure 2.9.   Now let use understand how the panel shown in Figure 4.8 works. In this figure, line numbers shown on the left are not part of the panel. The % sign shown on line 1 is in column 1 and all 80 characters of each record can be used. The attribute characters are as

```
1    PROC 0
2    CONTROL LIST MSG
3    SET M = &SUBSTR(1:2,&SYSDATE)
4    SET D = &SUBSTR(4:5,&SYSDATE)
5    SET Y = &SUBSTR(7:8,&SYSDATE)
6    SENDMAP: ISPEXEC DISPLAY PANEL(PERSMENU)
7    IF &OPT = X THEN DO
8      GOTO FINITO
9      END
10   IF &OPT = 1 THEN DO
11     FREE F(PERMAST)
12     FREE F(SYSDBOUT)
13     ALLOC F(PERSMAST) DA('PRPPY.PAYROLL.MASTER') SHR
14     ALLOC F(SYSDBOUT) DA(*)
15     ISPEXEC SELECT PGM(PERSPROG)
16     FREE F(PERSMAST)
17     FREE F(SYSDBOUT)
18     GOTO SENDMAP
19     END
20   IF &OPT = 2 THEN DO
21   SUBMIT * END($$)
22   //&SYSUID.R2 JOB PRPPY,'FINANCE DEPT',MSGCLASS=0,
23   //    NOTIFY=&SYSUID
24   //STEP01   EXEC SAS
25   //SYSUT1    DD DISP=SHR,DSN=PRPPY.PAYROLL.MASTER
26   //SYSPRINT DD SYSOUT=A,COPIES=&C
27   //SYSIN     DD DISP=SHR,DSN=SYS4.INPUT(PERSREP2)
28   $$
29   GOTO SENDMAP
30   END
31   IF &OPT = 3 THEN DO
32   SUBMIT * END($$)
33   //&SYSUID.R3 JOB PRPPY,'FINANCE DEPT',MSGCLASS=0,
34   //    NOTIFY=&SYSUID
35   //STEP01   EXEC SAS
36   //SYSUT1    DD DISP=SHR,DSN=PRPPY.PAYROLL.MASTER
37   //SYSPRINT DD SYSOUT=A,COPIES=&C
38   //SYSIN     DD DISP=SHR,DSN=SYS4.INPUT(PERSREP2)
39   $$
40   GOTO SENDMAP
41   END
42   IF &OPT = 4 THEN DO
43   SUBMIT * END($$)
44   //&SYSUID.R4 JOB PRPPY,'FINANCE DEPT',MSGCLASS=0,
45   //    NOTIFY=&SYSUID
46   //STEP01   EXEC SAS
47   //SYSUT1    DD DISP=SHR,DSN=PRPPY.PAYROLL.MASTER
48   //SYSPRINT DD SYSOUT=A,COPIES=&C
49   //SYSIN     DD DISP=SHR,DSN=SYS4.INPUT(PERSREP2)
50   $$
51   GOTO SENDMAP
52   END
53   FINITO: +
54   EXIT
```

Figure 4.9.   CLIST PERSONNEL stored in SYS4.CLIST that is invoked when user selects option 3 on the panel of Figure 4.8.

follows:

% (percent sign)	-	text (protected) field, high intensity
+ (plus sign)	-	text (protected) field, low intensity
_ (underscore)	-	input (unprotected) field, high intensity

Lines 1 thru 14 are part of the body section of the panel, lines 15 thru 18 are part of the initialization section, and lines 19 thru 29 are part of the processing section. So, on this panel the only field that is unprotected is on line 2, where the user can type a value for variable OPT.

In the initialization section, &ZPRIM=YES indicates that this is the primary panel. (&ZPRIM is a system variable.) CURSOR=OPT indicates that when the panel is displayed, the cursor is to be positioned in the field associated with variable OPT, and the statement on line 18 indicates that, prior to displaying the panel, variable &OPT is to be initialized to spaces.

Now, let us turn our attention to the processing section. After the panel is displayed and the user enters some data on the screen and presses the Enter key, the system follows the directives given in the processing section. If the user entered 1 in the option field, then system would invoke CLIST BANK. Note: In CMD(BANK) on line 22, CMD stands for CLIST and should not be confused with the term TSO command, or anything else.

So, on this panel if the user selected option 3, the system would invoke CLIST PERSONNEL stored in a library allocated under DDname SYSPROC. This CLIST is shown in Figure 4.9. In this CLIST, the first of all variables M, D, and Y are set to the current month, day, and year. On line 6 panel PERSMENU is displayed. This causes the system to search the libraries allocated under DDname ISPPLIB for panel PERSMENU and display it. This panel is shown in Figure 4.10

Only two fields on this panel (on lines 5 and 7) are unprotected. The initialization section indicates that prior to displaying the panel, variable &C is to be set to 1 and

```
1      %───────── PERSONNEL SUBSYSTEM MENU ──────────
2      %
3      %                        DATE: &M/&D/&Y
4      %
5      %SELECT OPTION ===>_OPT %                    USERID:  &ZUSER
6      %                                            TIME:    &ZTIME
7      +NUMBER OF COPIES REQUIRED: _C
8      %
9      %  1 + ENTER ONLINE FACILITY TO ADD/UPDATE/DELETE PERSONNEL RECORDS
10     %  2 + PRINT REPORT ON ALL EMPLOYEES SORTED BY EMPLOYEE NUMBER
11     %  3 + PRINT REPORT ON ALL EMPLOYEES BY ORGANIZATION CODE
12     %  4 + PRINT REPORT ON ALL EMPLOYEES BY JOB CODE
13     %  X + END
14     )INIT
15       &OPT = ' '
16       &C = '1'
17     )PROC
18       VER (&C,PICT,'N')
19     )END
```

Figure 4.10. Panel PERSMENU stored in SYS4.ISPPLIB and displayed by the CLIST in Figure 4.9.

&OPT is to be set to spaces. When the user has entered values in these two unprotected fields, the processing section comes into play. In this section we have only specified that the system is to verify that variable C is numeric. If it is not, the system would display a message to this effect before proceeding. If the value of variable C entered by the user is numeric, control would flow to line 7 in the CLIST of Figure 4.9. Here a check is made to determine if the value of OPT entered by the user is X. If so, control flows to line 53 where the EXIT statement is executed causing the CLIST execution to terminate. This causes the system to display the panel of Figure 4.8, because it was from this panel that the CLIST of Figure 4.9 was invoked. However, if on the panel of Figure 4.10, the user entered 1 for variable OPT, the CLIST would free two DDnames, reallocate them, and on line 15 invoke program PERSPROG. The system would search the load libraries allocated under ISPLLIB and finding program PERSPROG, execute it. This program would then display another panel and process the data entered by the user on that panel. The source code of program PERSPROG is not shown here nor is the panel that this program displays. But you can learn to write such a program by reading the following IBM manual:

Interactive System Productivity Facility (ISPF)
Dialog Management Services

After this program has terminated, control flows to line 6 where panel PERSMENU is displayed again. If the user enters 2 for OPT on panel PERSMENU, then CLIST PERSONNEL on lines 20 thru 28 submits a batch job for execution. This batch job has correct value for job name and number of copies of the report to be printed. Control then flows to line 6 where panel PERSMENU is displayed again. You will notice that this CLIST does not explicitly inform the user that a batch job was submitted which would print the desired report. This would be a desirable thing to do. However, if the MSG option on CONTROL statement is turned on in this CLIST, the system would display a message informing about the submission of the job and indicating the job name and job number.

Now, what happens if the value of OPT entered by the user is neither X, nor 1,2,3, or 4? You will agree that control would reach line 53 in CLIST PERSONNEL where the EXIT statement would terminate the CLIST execution. Control would then flow to the point where this CLIST was invoked. Since this CLIST was invoked on panel FIN@PRIM, this panel would be displayed.

The discussion above has sought to clarify the processing that takes place in the on-line system under study. You have learned how CLISTs, panels, and programs are interrelated and are used in conjunction with one another to build user-friendly on-line systems based on TSO and ISPF. The information presented above is by no means exhaustive. For more details, read the IBM manual mentioned above or a suitable textbook on the subject.

Chapter 5
FILE INPUT/OUTPUT AND OTHER ADVANCED CLIST TOPICS

In this chapter we will cover the file input/output statements as well as a number of other important CLIST statements. In CLISTs, terminal input/output statements such as READ, WRITE, and WRITENR are very important because they provide one of the means by which data can be input to a CLIST and results of computation performed by the CLIST displayed on the terminal. But what if you want to read records from sequential files and write records to them? You do this by using the statements OPENFILE, GETFILE, PUTFILE and CLOSFILE. These statements have the following similarities to COBOL verbs:

Function	COBOL VERB	CLIST Statement
Open a file	OPEN	OPENFILE
Read the next sequential record from an already opened file	READ file-name	GETFILE
Write a record to an already opened file	WRITE record-name	PUTFILE
Close an already opened file	CLOSE	CLOSFILE

OPENING A FILE

As with COBOL, a sequential (QSAM) file must be opened before file I/O can be performed on it. For example, let us consider a payroll/ personnel master file named PRPPY.PAYROLL.PSNL.MASTER. Suppose we want to write a CLIST in which we will read records from it sequentially beginning with the first record until the end of file. This CLIST will display each record on the terminal.

First, we must allocate this sequential file under a DDname of our choosing. Let us do this by using the following command in our CLIST:

```
ALLOC F(EMPMAST) DA('PRPPY.PAYROLL.PSNL.MASTER') SHR
```

To open this file for input, we can issue this statement in the CLIST:

```
OPENFILE EMPMAST INPUT /* REMEMBER "INPUT" IS OPTIONAL BUT RECOMMENDED */
```

Here is the syntax of this statement:

```
[label:]   OPENFILE   ddname
```
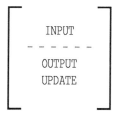

ddname. This specifies the ddname under which the file has been previously allocated either thru the TSO ALLOCATE command or by virtue of being present in the JCL, e.g. log-on procedure. This ddname will become a symbolic variable which will contain either a record read through the GETFILE statement, or a record that can be set prior to issuing the PUTFILE statement.

INPUT. This specifies that the file is to be opened for read operation. This is the default when neither INPUT, OUTPUT, nor UPDATE is specified.

OUTPUT. This specifies that the file is to be opened for write operation.

UPDATE. This specifies that the file will be opened for *updating in place.* This means that you can read a record thru the GETFILE statement and then rewrite it to the file by issuing the PUTFILE statement.

READING A RECORD FROM A FILE

Once a sequential (QSAM) file has been opened, you can read records from it sequentially. The statement you use for this purpose is GETFILE.

```
[label:]     GETFILE     &ddname
```

&ddname. This is the ddname under which the file was allocated and that was used on the OPENFILE statement. Note that the ampersand (&) is optional.

One execution of GETFILE makes one record from the file available in the symbolic variable &ddname. To read a record in the case of our payroll/personnel file that was opened under DDname EMPMAST, we would issue this command:

```
GETFILE EMPMAST
```

And, to display this record on the terminal, we could use the following statement:

```
WRITE THE PAYROLL/ PERSONNEL RECORD READ FROM THE FILE FOLLOWS:
WRITE &EMPMAST
```

USING READDVAL TO STORE FIELDS OF A RECORD INTO SEPARATE VARIABLES

Here is an example of using system control variable &SYS-DVAL and the READDVAL statement to fetch various data items from a record read from a file and place them in separate symbolic variables.

```
ALLOC F(SYSDVAL) DA(TEST.FILE1) SHR
OPENFILE SYSDVAL INPUT
GETFILE SYSDVAL
READDVAL &VAR1 &VAR2 &VAR3
```

Suppose that your TSO prefix is Z2HSM, the ALLOC command will allocate Z2HSM.TEST.FILE1 under DDname SYSDVAL. The OPENFILE statement will open it for read operation. The GETFILE statement will read the first record from this file into symbolic variable &SYSDVAL. Let us suppose that this record looks like this:

```
090145    HARRY SMITH
```

After the READDVAL statement has executed, the content of &VAR1 will be 090145, the content of &VAR2 will be HARRY and the content of &VAR3 will be SMITH.

TESTING FOR END-OF-FILE CONDITION

How do we test that the end of file has been reached, when reading records from it? We do so by using the TSO control variable &LASTCC. When this variable assumes a value of 400, this means that the end of file has been reached. In the case of the payroll/personnel master file that we have been using as a running example, we could use the CLIST shown in Figure 5.1 to read each record from the file and display it on the terminal.

```
1     PROC 0
2     CONTROL NOLIST NOMSG
3     ERROR DO
4       IF &LASTCC = 400 THEN GOTO EOFILE
5     END
6     FREE F(EMPMAST)
7     ALLOC F(EMPMAST) DA('PRPPY.PAYROLL.PSNL.MASTER') SHR
8     OPENFILE EMPMAST INPUT
9     DO WHILE  1 = 1     /* EXIT ONLY WHEN END OF FILE OCCURS */
10      GETFILE &EMPMAST
11       WRITE &EMPMAST
12    END
13    EOFILE: WRITE GETTING OUT OF THIS CLIST
14    CLOSFILE EMPMAST
15    EXIT
```

Figure 5.1.   A CLIST to read a sequential file until end of file is reached.

Note the technique of testing for end of file shown in Figure 5.1. The GETFILE inside the DO-WHILE loop is executed repeatedly. At last end of file condition would be raised on GETFILE which would mean that the GETFILE would end with return code of 400. This is considered an error condition, and control would be transferred to line 3 where a test is made, if the last return code is 400. If so, control is transferred to line 14. This is a very good technique for testing for end of file and getting out of a loop as shown in this figure.

WRITING A RECORD TO A FILE

To write a record to a file, the file must have been previously allocated under a DDname and must have been opened using the OPENFILE statement. The PUTFILE statement is then used to write one record to the file. Only one record can be written through one PUTFILE statement. The record to be written must be stored in the symbolic variable whose name is the same as the DDname under which the file was opened. This storing is done thru the SET statement, just before issuing the PUTFILE unless, of course, the same record is to be written to the file more than once.

```
[label:]  PUTFILE   ddname
```

Note: PUTFILE &ddname will not work. This is to say that ampersand should not be used in the ddname on PUTFILE.

Example.   This example shows how to write a few records to dataset 'Z3AUM.TEST.FILE1' which has been already created thru option 3.2 of ISPF with the following characteristics:

Dataset Organization: PS (Physical Sequential)
Record Format: Fixed Blocked
Record Length: 80
Block Size: Any Multiple of Record Length

The following records are to be written to the file:

```
01/09/88 SYSTEM STATE: COLD START
SYSTEM PROGRAMMER: BARRY NIRMAL
SYSTEM PROGRAMMER: BARRY NIRMAL
START TIME: 09.30.40
```

Note: The second and the third records are identical. The following CLIST can be used for this purpose:

```
PROC 0
CONTROL NOMSG NOLIST
FREE F(SYSDATA)
ALLOC F(SYSDATA) DA('Z3AUM.TEST.FILE1') SHR
OPENFILE SYSDATA OUTPUT
SET  &SYSDATA = &STR(01/09/88 SYSTEM STATE: COLD START)
PUTFILE SYSDATA
SET &SYSDATA = &STR(SYSTEM PROGRAMMER: BARRY NIRMAL)
PUTFILE SYSDATA
PUTFILE SYSDATA
```

```
SET &SYSDATA = &STR(START TIME: 09.30.40)
PUTFILE SYSDATA
CLOSFILE SYSDATA
EXIT
```

CLOSING A FILE

As you may have guessed from the code given above, the CLOSFILE statement is used to close a file that was previously opened. Only one file can be closed thru one CLOSFILE statement.

```
[label:]    CLOSFILE   ddname
```

ddname. This specifies the DDname under which the file was allocated and under which it was previously opened through the OPENFILE statement.

Before closing the discussion of file I/O statements, it must be pointed out that whenever you are using file I/O statements in a CLIST, make sure NOFLUSH is present on the CONTROL statement in the beginning of your CLIST. If your CONTROL statement has option MAIN, then you need not specify NOFLUSH.

THE DATA-ENDDATA STATEMENT SEQUENCE

If you looked closely at some of the CLISTs in this book that use the EDIT command, you have probably noticed that the lines starting with the EDIT command and ending with the END SAVE or END NOSAVE subcommand were enclosed within the DATA-ENDDATA sequence. This was done for a very good reason, which will become clear after you have finished with this section. But this does not mean that every time you use the EDIT command, you must enclose the lines within the EDIT command and the END subcommand of EDIT within DATA-ENDDATA sequence.

A group of TSO commands and subcommands, when enclosed within DATA-ENDDATA sequence, are looked at as data by the CLIST but as commands and subcommands by TSO. This has the following implications:

- IF DATA-ENDDATA sequence is included within a DO-group, the DO-group ignores an END in the DATA-END-DATA sequence, rather than terminating the DO-group. This is the main reason why DATA-ENDDATA is used.
- Before executing the statements within the DATA-END-DATA sequence, symbolic substitution is performed.
- No CLIST statements such as GOTO should be present within a DATA-ENDDATA group because TSO will attempt to execute them as TSO commands or subcommands and this will definitely result in an error.

```
[label:]    .       DATA
                    - - - -
                    - - - -
                    - - - -
                    ENDDATA
```

Note that a label may be present for DATA but it must not be present for ENDDATA.

Example.   Let us suppose that an edit operation is to be performed within a DO-group. This necessitates the use of DATA-ENDDATA sequence as shown by the following code:

```
- - - - -
- - - - -
IF &EMPNUM  GE 90100 THEN +
   DO
      WRITE PLEASE SUPPLY THE BIRTH DATE OF EMPLOYEE'S SPOUSE
      READ &BDATE
      DATA
         EDIT 'SYS3.PANVALET.JCL(SPECIAL1)' OLD CNTL
         BOTTOM
         INSERT  &EMPNUM &EMPNAME BIRTH-DATE= &BDATE
```

```
        END SAVE
    ENDDATA
    - - -
    - - -
END
    - - -
    - - -
```

In this code, if you put a GOTO statement after the EDIT command and execute the CLIST containing this code, you will receive a message saying that GOTO is not a valid sub-command. Once you have executed the EDIT command, you are in the edit mode and only subcommands of EDIT are allowed until the edit operation has been ended by executing END SAVE or END NOSAVE.

Another point is that if the dataset being edited has proper line numbers in columns 73-80, the line inserted at the bottom of the dataset will have proper line number in columns 73-80.

THE ATTN STATEMENT

You are probably familiar with the use of the ATTN or the PA1 (Attention) key on your 3270-type terminal. Suppose you issue the following command from option 6 of ISPF to print the contents of the indicated VSAM dataset in character format:

```
PRINT IDS('PRPPA.VPPA700A.CLUSTER') CHAR
```

The system will display the first few records from this file on your terminal, and at the bottom of the screen you will see three asterisks (***) indicating that more data is to follow. At this point, if you want to view subsequent records, press the Enter key. However, the file may have large number of records and you may not want to view all the records. In this case, press the PA1 or the ATTN key to terminate the PRINT command prematurely and take you to the panel where you issued the command.

The same concept applies when executing a CLIST. Suppose a CLIST reads a sequential file with large number of records and displays each record on the terminal. You may stop the CLIST from displaying any more records once you have viewed the records of interest to you. How do you make sure that when you press the ATTN or the PA1 key, the CLIST will stop reading any more records from the file and displaying them, and the control will go to label NEXTWORK in the CLIST? You do this by using the ATTN statement.

```
[label:]      ATTN        ⎡         OFF          ⎤
                          ⎢      - - - - -       ⎥
                          ⎣    desired-action    ⎦
```

As the syntax indicates, after the optional label, you code the word ATTN, which is followed by one statement, a number of statements enclosed within a DO-group, a null or OFF. The attention exit can only handle one TSO command per execution.

Example of coding a null on ATTN
    ATTN
Example of coding OFF on ATTN
    ATTN OFF

Note that OFF is the default. If you code ATTN with no other action specified, TSO assumes that you want any attention exit that might be active to be cancelled. This is to say that both null and OFF cause any previously active ATTN routine to be deactivated. This brings us to another concept, which is that a CLIST may have none, one, or more than one ATTN routine; but, at any one time, only one will be active.

The ATTN statement is different from the other CLIST statements. It does not get executed when it is encountered in the course of executing the CLIST logic. Rather, when it is reached either in the course of normal flow or due to a GOTO statement, it is said to have been activated. Once activated, the attention routine will be executed when an attention interrupt (e.g., the user pressing the ATTN or PA1 key on the keyboard) occurs.

There is a difference between the functions of the ATTN key and the PA1 key. The PA1 key on an IBM 3270-type terminal is used to create a *simulated interrupt*. TSO will only recognize the interrupt caused by the PA1 key if it is waiting for terminal input or the screen is full with three asterisks at the bottom and the user is expected to press a key. This means that if your CLIST goes into an endless loop and the three asterisks do not appear on the 3270 screen, the PA1 key will not get you out of the loop but the ATTN key will cause an attention interrupt; and, if the CLIST has no ATTN statement or has null ATTN or has ATTN OFF, the CLIST will be terminated. However, even if the CLIST goes into an endless loop but the screen has three asterisks at the bottom, pressing PA1 key will also cause attention interrupt and the CLIST will terminate if it has no ATTN statement or has null ATTN or ATTN OFF.

Example 1. In this example, the CLIST will read and display records from a sequential file. When the user presses the ATTN key or the PA1 key and causes attention interrupt, the ATTN routine causes one line to be written to the terminal, file JCLFILE to be closed, and control to flow to the line with the label NEXTWORK in the CLIST.

```
PROC 0
CONTROL MAIN END(ENDX) LIST MSG
ATTN DO
   WRITE ** NOW EXECUTING ATTENTION INTERRUPT ROUTINE **
   CLOSFILE JCLFILE
```

```
     GOTO NEXTWORK
   ENDX
   FREE F(JCLFILE)
   ALLOC F(JCLFILE) DA('Z2BKN.PAY.CNTL(AMSPRINT)') SHR
   OPENFILE JCLFILE
   DO WHILE 1 = 1
     GETFILE JCLFILE
     WRITE &JCLFILE
   ENDX
   CLOSFILE JCLFILE
   NEXTWORK: WRITE READING AND DISPLAYING FILE RECORDS FINISHED.
   EXIT
```

Note: If the file being read consists of a small number of records, by the time you press the ATTN or the PA1 key, all records would probably have been read and the CLIST would have terminated even though you have three asterisks at the bottom of the screen, which only means that more data remains to be displayed on the terminal. In this case, pressing ATTN or PA1 key would not execute the attention routine, but the remaining data would not be displayed and you would return to TSO or ISPF, depending on the position at which you executed the CLIST. However, if the file consists of a large number of records, at the time the ATTN or PA1 key is pressed, the CLIST would probably be still executing, in which case the attention interrupt would cause the attention routine to be executed.

It should be noted that in some situations when attention interrupt occurs, you may receive TSO READY message and be placed in native TSO mode even though you executed the CLIST from one of the ISPF panels. This is because if you do not have MVS version 2.2.0, ISPF 2.3 and TSO/E Release 4 or higher, you are advised not to use attention routines in CLISTs that are to be executed from ISPF or that contain ISPF commands. Without these levels of software, if an attention interrupt occurs, the results are unpredictable.

Example 2. Let us suppose we are writing a CLIST that is invoked for every TSO user every morning when he logs on for the first time. This CLIST calculates the DASD space occupied by all the datasets under that user ID, and stores the information in a dataset. If the user has exceeded his allowed limit, this information is also stored so that the next time the user logs on to TSO, he will be automatically logged off. Suppose we want to write an attention routine so that the user cannot bypass space check calculation by pressing the attention (PA1) key. However if the user ID is GEN09 (your own user ID for example), this attention routine is not to be activated. The following code can be used:

```
IF &SYSUID = GEN09 THEN GOTO PROCEED
ATTN DO
  WRITE YOU HAVE PRESSED ATTENTION KEY DURING INITIAL PROCESSING.
  WRITE THIS WILL NOT WORK. YOU ARE BEING LOGGED OFF. PLEASE DO
  WRITE NOT DO SO THE NEXT TIME YOU LOG ON. THANK YOU FOR YOUR PATIENCE.
  WRITE ***
  READ
  LOGOFF
END
  PROCEED: +
  - - - -
  - - - -
```

The attention interruption is also helpful when, for example, you are developing and testing a program and it gets into an endless loop. It allows you to halt program execution by pressing the Attention or the PA1 key. This way it allows you to end an 'endless' loop.

THE RETURN STATEMENT

This statement is used in an attention routine or an error routine to return control to the statement following the one that was interrupted by the attention mechanism or following the one that ended in error. (Error routine will be discussed in the next section.) This statement is valid only when issued from an error routine that had been activated or an attention routine that had been activated in this CLIST. If RETURN is issued in any other situation, it results in null action.

Normally after doing some analysis in an error routine or an attention routine, you terminate the CLIST by using the EXIT statement, or you return to the next statement by using the RETURN statement, or you explicitly branch to another point in the CLIST thru a GOTO statement.

```
[label:]      RETURN
```

Example 1. Let us consider a CLIST that copies one sequential file to another. The input file has large number of records. While the copying is being done, the user may get bored and may want to terminate CLIST execution by pressing the PA1 key. The CLIST should provide for an attention exit which would prompt the user as to his choice. Such a CLIST is shown in Figure 5.2.

Note: In response to the first question asked in the attention routine, if you answered Y, both files would be closed and the CLIST would terminate. However, if you answered N followed by NEXT, control would go to the statement following the one that was interrupted, and the the CLIST will end up in copying the entire input file to the output file. However, if you answered N followed by TAX, control would flow to the statement with label TAXCALC. At this label, even if you did not close the files, this would cause no problem. This is because the MVS system automatically closes sequential files when a program or CLIST terminates, if they were not explicitly closed by the program or the CLIST.

```
PROC 0
CONTROL MAIN MSG LIST END(ENDX)
ERROR DO
  IF &LASTCC = 400 THEN DO
    CLOSFILE INFILE
    CLOSFILE OUTFILE
    GOTO TERMIN
    ENDX
  ELSE RETURN
ENDX
ATTN DO
  WRITE ** NOW EXECUTING THE ATTENTION ROUTINE **
  WRITENR DO YOU WISH TO TERMINATE THE CLIST (Y/N) ?
  READ &ANS
  IF &ANS = Y THEN DO
    CLOSFILE INFILE
    CLOSFILE OUTFILE
    WRITE ** BOTH FILES NOW CLOSED. WILL TERMINATE CLIST NOW **
    EXIT  /* TERMINATE CLIST */
    ENDX
  ELSE DO
    WRITE DO YOU WISH TO RETURN TO THE NEXT STATEMENT OR YOU
    WRITE WISH TO GO TO LABEL TAXCALC FOR TAX CALCULATION (NEXT/TAX) ?
    READ &ANS
    IF &ANS = NEXT THEN RETURN
    GOTO TAXCALC
    ENDX
ENDX
FREE F(INFILE OUTFILE)
ALLOC F(INFILE) DA('Z3SSX.TEMP1') SHR
ALLOC F(OUTFILE) DA('Z3SSX.TEMP2') SHR
OPENFILE INFILE INPUT
OPENFILE OUTFILE OUTPUT
DO WHILE 1 = 1
  GETFILE INFILE
  SET &OUTFILE = &INFILE
  PUTFILE OUTFILE
ENDX
TAXCALC: WRITE SIR/MADAM, I AM AT TAXCALC NOW
- - - - -
- - - - -
TERMIN: WRITE SIR/MADAM, THIS CLIST NOW TERMINATES
FREE F(INFILE OUTFILE)
EXIT
```

Figure 5.2.   A CLIST that illustrates the use of ATTN and ERROR statements.

THE ERROR STATEMENT

The behavior of ERROR statement is quite similar to that of the ATTN statement. When any command, subcommand, or a CLIST statement results in a non-zero return code, an error is said to have occurred, and, if an error routine is active, it gets invoked.

In any CLIST that uses the ERROR statement, the MAIN or the NOFLUSH operand must be coded on the CONTROL statement so as to prevent flushing of the input stack. If any of these two operands is not present on the CONTROL statement, the ERROR routine is ignored and the return code of the statement in error will not be available for interrogation.

If ERROR is coded without any operands, the system will display the command, subcommand or the CLIST statement that ended in error. It will then try to continue execution with the next sequential statement.

```
[label:]    ERROR    ⎡                OFF                ⎤
                     ⎢                                   ⎥
                     ⎣    user-defined-action            ⎦
```

OFF.   This specifies that any ERROR routine previously activated is nullified. Note that OFF is not the default.

User-defined-action.   This consists of any routine, commonly a DO-group, that defines the action to be taken in the event of an error.

Note: If only the TIME command or a null statement is executed in the DO-group belonging to the ERROR routine, this may cause a recursive (repetitive) error condition and the system will display an error message. The reason is that neither the TIME command nor a null error statement resets the last condition code (&LASTCC) which is the basis for invoking the error routine.

The following additional points are worth noting regarding the ERROR statement:

1. When no ERROR routine is active, the default action depends on whether it is a CLIST statement or a TSO command that ended in non-zero return code. If it was a CLIST statement, the default action is to display the CLIST statement in error, display an error message, and terminate CLIST execution. However, if it was a TSO command (e.g., FREE or ALLOC) that ended in error, the default action is display an error message, if MSG option is in effect on CONTROL statement and then pass control to the next sequential CLIST statement. Here the programmer may test &LASTCC and save it (e.g. SET &RETSAVE = &LASTCC). A common mistake is to not save the value of &LASTCC immediately. &LASTCC becomes zero right after executing the next CLIST statement.

2. The EXIT statement can be used in ERROR routine to terminate the CLIST and transfer control to the calling CLIST, if this CLIST was called by another CLIST, or to return to TSO or EDIT. The effect of EXIT can be modified by using the CODE and QUIT operand as described in Chapter 8.

3. RETURN can be used in the ERROR routine to pass control to the statement following the one that ended in error.

4. If you code an ERROR routine which ends without executing an EXIT, RETURN, or GOTO, control will return to the statement that ended in error. This will mean that the error routine will be re-entered immediately, causing a recursive error situation. The best solution in this situation is to end the ERROR routine with ERROR OFF statement. The effect of this will be that the failing statement will be reexecuted, and it will be displayed

```
Line
Number  CLIST Statement
───     ──────────
1        PROC 0 CLISTLIB() PANEL()
2        CONTROL MAIN,MSG,LIST,END(ENDX)
3        SET &FILE =
4        ERROR DO
5          IF &SYSPCMD = EXEC THEN EXIT
6          IF &SYSPCMD = FREE THEN RETURN
7          IF &SYSPCMD = ALLOC && &FILE = SYSPROC THEN GOTO A002
8          IF &SYSPCMD = ALLOC && &FILE = ISPPLIB THEN GOTO B002
9          WRITE ERROR ENCOUNTERED IN CLIST PANELSET
10         WRITE COMMAND = &SYSPCMD  LASTCC = &LASTCC
11         LOGOFF
12       ENDX
13       /*================================================================*
14       /* ALLOCATE ISPF PROFILE LIBRARY AND OVERRIDE DEFAULT BUFFERS    *
15       /*================================================================*
16       ATTN OFF
17       FREE ATTR(X1 X2)
18       ATTR X1 BUFNO(1)
19       ATTR X2 BUFNO(2)
20       ALLOC F(ISPPROF) DSN('&SYSUID..ISPF.PROFILE') SHR
21       /*================================================================*
22       /* ALLOCATE CLIST LIBRARIES NOW                                 *
23       /*================================================================*
24       A001: SET &FILE = SYSPROC
25            ALLOC F(SYSPROC) DA(&CLISTLIB +
26                              'SYS2.CLIST' +
27                              'SYS1.ISRCLIB') SHR USING(X1)
28            GOTO B001
29       /*
30       A002: SET &FILE =
31            ALLOC F(SYSPROC) DA('SYS2.CLIST' +
32                              'SYS1.ISRCLIB') SHR USING(X1)
33       /*================================================================*
34       /* ALLOCATE PANEL LIBRARIES NOW                                 *
35       /*================================================================*
36       B001: SET &FILE = ISPPLIB
37            ALLOC F(ISPPLIB) DA(&PANEL +
38                              'SYS2.ISPPLIB' +
39                              'SYS1.ISPPLIB' +
40                              'SYS1.ISRPLIB' +
41                              'SYS1.DBNISPP') SHR USING(X2)
42            GOTO THATSIT
43       /*
44       B002: SET &FILE =
45            ALLOC F(ISPPLIB) DA('SYS2.ISPPLIB' +
46                              'SYS1.ISPPLIB' +
47                              'SYS1.ISRPLIB' +
48                              'SYS1.DBNISPP') SHR USING(X2)
49       THATSIT: EXIT
```

Figure 5.3.   A CLIST that allocates DDnames ISPPROF, SYSPROC and ISPPLIB.

along with an error message and the CLIST will be terminated.

5. Just like the ATTN statement, the ERROR statement must be executed before any action coded in ERROR routine can take place. Once executed, the ERROR routine is said to have been activated. Any ERROR routine activated replaces any previous ERROR routine that might be active at the time of the execution of this ERROR statement.

Example 1. Let us consider a CLIST that is executed when every TSO user at an installation logs on to TSO. This CLIST, shown in Figure 5.3, allocates three files, ISPPROF, SYSPROC, and ISPPLIB which are required for ISPF to function. It has an ERROR routine at the beginning. The following is a discussion of the statements in the ERROR routine.

Line 5 indicates that if the error was caused on an EXEC command, the EXIT statement is to be executed, which would terminate this CLIST. Line 6 indicates that if the error was caused by executing a FREE command, the control is to be transferred to the next sequential statement following the FREE command. This is because if a file did not get freed, it is most likely because that file was not allocated. So, this is not an error condition as such.

Line 7 indicates that if the error occurred with an ALLOC command and the value of symbolic variable &FILE was SYSPROC, control is to flow to the line with the label A002. You will notice that it is only on line 24 that we set &FILE to SYSPROC. So, line 7 is catering to the ALLOC on line 25 failing. The reasoning of the CLIST writer is as follows. It is thought that SYS2.CLIST and SYS1.ISRCLIB are always there, but the value of &CLISTLIB passed to this CLIST by the caller may represent a dataset name which may not be cataloged. Normally the caller would pass in &CLISTLIB, the user's private CLIST library, which may or may not be cataloged. In case the caller does not use the optional keyword parameter &CLISTLIB when invoking this CLIST, or, if the caller passes a dataset name as the value of &CLISTLIB that is cataloged and is present on the DASD, there is no problem. But if the dataset name passed as the value of &CLISTLIB is not cataloged or is not present on the DASD, then the ALLOC on line 25 would fail and this would cause the ERROR routine to be executed. In the ERROR routine, the statement on line 7 would transfer control to line 30 where &FILE is set to null, followed by allocation of SYSPROC to just two datasets, which are assumed to be always present.

In a similar manner, line 8 in the error routine is catering to the situation in which the ALLOC command on line 37 fails. In this case, the reasoning is that this is most likely due to an uncataloged dataset name passed as the value of &PANEL. In this case line 8 in the error routine would cause control to flow to line 44 where &FILE is set to null, followed by allocation of ISPPLIB to just the four panel libraries which are assumed to be always present. Line 9 thru 11 in the error routine are executed only when none of the preceding conditions are true. In this case, two lines of messages are written to the terminal and then the LOGOFF command is executed, which logs off the user.

THE READDVAL STATEMENT

This statement is used to take the current value of system control variable &SYSDVAL, parse it into syntactical words, and store these words in the symbolic variables specified on the READDVAL statement.

```
[label:]   READDVAL   [var1 [var2 ...varN]]
```

var1 - varN. These are the names of symbolic variables. The ampersand is optional. These symbolic variables need not have been defined previously and are positional in the sense that the first syntactical word in &SYSDVAL is stored in var1; the second syntactical word, in var2, and so on. If there are more variables specified on READDVAL than there are words for, the extra variables are assigned null values. If there are fewer variables than there are words in &SYSDVAL, the extra words are not assigned. The value of &SYSDVAL remains unchanged as a result of this statement.

Note: If READDVAL statement is entered without any operands, this statement is ignored.

THE TERMIN STATEMENT

This statement causes CLIST execution to be suspended and control to be given to the user in the TSO command mode. On the TERMIN statement, you can specify one or more character strings. Only when the user keys in any of these strings, is control transferred back to the CLIST at the next sequential statement following TERMIN.

When control returns to the CLIST, control variables &SYSDLM and &SYSDVAL are set. This will be explained in the examples that follow. If CLIST is executed from one of the ISPF panels (including TSO within ISPF), TERMIN causes termination of the CLIST and control returns to ISPF. So, instead of receiving READY message (which would be the case if the CLIST was executed from native TSO) user receives three asterisks, and when he presses the Enter key, control is transferred to the panel from where the CLIST was executed.

```
[label:]  TERMIN ⌈string1⌉ [string2..stringN]
                 ⌊      ⌋
```

(Note: the strings are delimited by a space or a comma.) The TERMIN statement should be immediately preceded by a number of WRITE statements explaining that the user now will be promoted for input and mentioning the strings that he can enter to return control back to the CLIST. The user should also be guided as to the meaning of each string that he can enter. This kind of explanatory messages written to the user prior to prompting for input is a highly desirable feature that makes a CLIST user-friendly. Without such messages, the CLIST becomes difficult to use and, at the worst, can be appropriately called user-hostile.

Example 1.

```
WRITE YOU CAN ENTER <FINISH>, <CONTINUE> OR <ABORT>
WRITE FINISH WILL BYPASS REST OF CLIST AND THE TERMINATION ROUTINE
WRITE WILL BE EXECUTED.
WRITE <CONTINUE> WILL CAUSE NORMAL CLIST EXECUTION.
WRITE <ABORT> WILL ABORT THE CLIST EXECUTION IMMEDIATELY.
TERMIN FINISH, CONTINUE, ABORT
- - - -
```

The TERMIN statement here causes the CLIST execution to be suspended and control to be given to the user. Here FINISH, CONTINUE, and ABORT are specified as the character strings that the user keys in. He then presses the ENTER key to return control back to the CLIST. Only one of these strings can be used to return control to the CLIST.

When control comes back to the CLIST, the control variable &SYSDLM contains the position number of the string that was keyed by the user. For example, if the user keyed in ABORT, &SYSDLM would contain 3, since ABORT is the third string on the TERMIN statement.

It should be noted that when TERMIN is executed, TSO displays the READY message. At this point, if the user enters a string not specified on the TERMIN, (e.g., TIME) TSO would attempt to execute it as a TSO command or CLIST. If that string represents a valid command or CLIST, it would be executed and then TSO would display the

READY sign. If that string does not represent a valid command or CLIST (e.g. XWQ2HY), TSO would display 'COMMAND NOT FOUND' message. At this point the user can enter another string which again may or may not be identical to one of the strings specified on the TERMIN statement. If the string entered is same as one of the strings specified on TERMIN, TSO would transfer control back to the CLIST.

This brings us to another question – what if the name of a TSO command (e.g., TIME or LISTDS) is specified on the TERMIN statement? In this case, when the user enters his string, TSO does not interpret it as a TSO command or CLIST name; rather, as one of the strings specified on TERMIN and transfers control to the CLIST at the statement following the TERMIN.

Example 2.

```
WRITE NOW YOU WILL BE PROMPTED FOR INPUT. YOU CAN EITHER SIMPLY PRESS
WRITE THE ENTER KEY WITHOUT KEYING ANYTHING, OR YOU CAN KEY IN DATA
WRITE BEFORE PRESSING THE ENTER KEY.
TERMIN
```

In this example, since no strings are specified on the TERMIN statement, the user can simply press the ENTER key to return control. If the user does so, &SYSDVAL is set to null and &SYSDLM is set to 1. However, if the user typed a string (e.g., TIME), that string is interpreted as a TSO command (or the name of a CLIST) and TSO executes that command, and then displays the READY sign indicating that TSO is waiting for user response again.

Example 3.

```
WRITE YOU WILL NOW BE PROMPTED FOR INPUT. YOU CAN SIMPLY PRESS THE
WRITE ENTER KEY OR YOU CAN KEY IN ALL, PARTIAL OR NONE AND THEN PRESS
WRITE THE ENTER KEY TO RETURN CONTROL TO THE CLIST.
TERMIN ,ALL,PARTIAL,NONE
```

In this example, as explained in the text on the WRITE statements, the user can either simply press the Enter key, or key in one of the three strings specified on the TERMIN statement to return control to the CLIST.

Note: The user has the option of entering additional data following the string used to return control to the CLIST. If this is done, the additional data is stored in the control variable &SYSDVAL. The CLIST can then use this data. For example, if ALL causes control to be transferred to the CLIST, and, if the user typed ALL 90143, &SYSDVAL would contain 90143 when control is transferred back to the CLIST. If the user did not enter any additional data, &SYSDVAL would be set to null when control returns to CLIST.

Example 4.

```
SET &CMD1 = PRINT
SET &CMD2 = COMPILE
SET &CMD3 = SETUP
SET &CMD4 =
SET &CMD5 =
TERMIN &CMD1 &CMD2 &CMD3 &CMD4 &CMD5
```

Here the user can enter PRINT, COMPILE or SETUP to return control to the CLIST. Any other response including simply pressing the Enter key would not return control to the CLIST. Only when the user enters one of the three specified strings, control is transferred back to the CLIST.

EXERCISES

1. Write a CLIST that will read the first 20 records from dataset 'TRPPA.EPPA900A' and will display them on the terminal. Each record displayed is to be preceded by record number. If the file contains 20 or fewer than 20

records, the program should write the following as the last line on the terminal:

```
** END OF FILE ENCOUNTERED **
```

However, if the file contains more than 20 records, the following line should be displayed after displaying the 20th record from the file:

```
** FILE CONTAINS MORE THAN 20 RECORDS **
```

Chapter 6
SOME USEFUL CLISTs
ESPECIALLY FOR SYSTEMS
PROGRAMMERS

In this chapter we will discuss some more CLISTs which will be of special interest to the systems programmers. This does not mean that other professionals cannot make good use of these CLISTs. In fact, the CLIST described below that is used to submit a job after changing one line in it can be used by application programmers as well. The CLISTs which follow are all examples of CLISTs that have proven to the author to be highly useful in his day-to-day work in systems programming. These CLISTs can be easily copied to your own CLIST library and executed. They can also be easily modified to suit your unique needs. In this regard, it must stressed that only a good understanding of these CLISTs will enable you to write similar CLISTs that will best meet your own unique requirements. This is why each CLIST will be explained in detail. However, if there is anything you do not understand in the CLISTs given below, you are advised to read the appendices in this book or refer to some other appropriate book or IBM manual.

A CLIST TO SUBMIT A JOB AFTER CHANGING ONE LINE IN IT

Here is an example of a CLIST that I use a lot at my work. As a CICS Systems Programmer responsible for eight CICS

```
//GEN09SCA JOB (789110,104W,99,99),'BARRY NIRMAL',MSGCLASS=Q,CLASS=K,
//      NOTIFY=GEN09,TYPRUN=SCAN
//*==========================================================================*
//* THIS JOB WILL SCAN A PROCEDURE STORED IN SYS1.PROCLIB FOR ANY SYNTAX
//* ERRORS. MAKE SURE THE JOB CARD HAS TYPRUN=SCAN OPERAND.
//*==========================================================================*
//STEP01   EXEC CICSXXXX
```

Figure 6.1.   The MVS job stored in GEN09.CICS.JOBS(PROCSCAN)
that will scan a procedure for starting up CICS for syntax
errors.

regions, I often had to modify the procedures for starting
the various CICS regions. Suppose I modified SYS1.PRO-
CLIB(CICSPRD1). I would edit the dataset that contains the
job shown in Figure 6.1 and change CICSXXXX on the last
line to CICSPRD1. Then I would submit this job. If TSO
notification indicated that the job ended without any JCL
error, I would know that the procedure CICSPRD1 that I
modified in SYS1.PROCLIB had no syntax errors.

Suppose that five minutes later I had to modify
SYS1.PROCLIB(CICSTST2). I would follow this same procedure to verify whether the procedure contained any syntax
errors. One day I got an idea: why not write a CLIST that I
could invoke passing it the name of the CICS region. This
CLIST would edit the dataset shown in Figure 6.1 and
would then submit the job. This would save me a lot of time
and effort in having to manually edit the dataset, having to
issue the SUBMIT command, and having to wait for system
response after each and every command. The CLIST I wrote
is shown in Figure 6.2. If this CLIST is present as member
PS1 in a partitioned dataset allocated under DDname
SYSPROC during my TSO session, and I want to check procedure CICSPRD3 in SYS1.PROCLIB for syntax errors, all I
would need to do is to issue the following TSO command:

```
%PS1 PRD3
```

```
Line      Statement
Number

1         PROC 1 SYSID
2         CONTROL NOMSG NOLIST
3         SET CICSNAME = CICS&SYSID
4         DATA
5         EDIT 'GEN09.CICS.JOBS(PROCSCAN)' NONUM OLD DATA
6         CHANGE * 100 'CICSXXXX' '&CICSNAME' ALL
7         SUBMIT
8         END NOSAVE
9         ENDDATA
10        EXIT
```

Figure 6.2. A CLIST that automates the function of submitting the job shown in Figure 6.1.

This CLIST would submit the job shown in Figure 6.1 after changing the last line in it from CICSXXXX to CICSPRD3. It would then end the EDIT command without saving the changes made to the job. This is necessary because the next time this CLIST is invoked, it would try to change the string CICSXXXX in this job.

This CLIST is quite straightforward. The CHANGE subcommand on line 6 indicates that 100 lines (from where the current line pointer is positioned) are to be scanned and all occurrences of the string CICSXXXX are to be changed to CICSnnnn where nnnn is the four character string passed to this CLIST by the user. (The asterisk following the word CHANGE indicates the line where the current line pointer is pointing.) So 100 lines (from the top of the dataset) are scanned for string CICSXXXX and all occurrences of this string are changed to CICSnnnn. Since this dataset contains far less than 100 lines, specifying 100 on line 6 ensures that all lines in the dataset are covered.

```
1        PROC 0
2        CONTROL MAIN NOMSG NOLIST END(ENDX)
3        /* THIS CLIST WILL EXECUTE THE IBM SUPERZAP PROGRAM INTERACTIVELY
4        FREE F(SYSIN SYSPRINT SYSLIB)
5        WRITE ENTER FULLY-QUALIFIED NAME OF LOAD LIBRARY WHICH MUST BE
6        WRITE CATALOGUED (NO QUOTES PLEASE) ===>>>
7        READ &DSN
8        WRITE ============================================================
9        WRITE CLIST ZAPBKN WILL ZAP DSN=&DSN
10       WRITE ENTER SYSIN STATEMENTS ONE LINE AT A TIME WHEN PROMPTED
11       WRITE ============================================================
12       CONTROL MSG
13       ALLOC F(SYSLIB) DA('&DSN.') SHR
14       ALLOC F(SYSIN) DA(*)
15       ALLOC F(SYSPRINT) DA(*)
16       CALL 'SYS1.LINKLIB(AMASPZAP)'
17       CONTROL NOMSG
18       FREE F(SYSIN SYSPRINT SYSLIB)
```

Figure 6.3.   A CLIST to execute the superzap program interactively rather than in batch.

A CLIST TO EXECUTE THE SUPERZAP PROGRAM INTERACTIVELY

Figure 6.3 shows a CLIST that can be used to execute the superzap program of IBM, interactively. For example, suppose that you wish to obtain a dump on your screen of load module BNMSGPGM in load library CICS.TEST.LOADLIB. The commands you enter and the messages displayed by the CLIST and program AMASPZAP are shown in Figure 6.4, where OPR stands for operator action and SYS stands for system response. It is assumed that this CLIST is stored in member ZAPBKN in a PDS allocated under DDname SYSPROC during the user's TSO session. Note: When the user types /* as the command for program AMASPZAP, this signals the end of SYSIN file and program AMASPZAP terminates. The program displays message number AMA100I before terminating. Control then flows to line 17 in the CLIST. On line 18 the DDnames which were previously allocated for use by program AMASPZAP are freed. The

```
OPR : %ZAPBKN
SYS : ENTER FULLY-QUALIFIED NAME OF LOAD LIBRARY WHICH MUST BE
      CATALOGUED (NO QUOTES PLEASE) ===>>>
OPR: cics.test.loadlib
SYS:  ==============================================================
      CLIST ZAPBKN WILL ZAP DSN=CICS.TEST.LOADLIB
      ENTER SYSIN STATEMENTS ONE LINE AT A TIME WHEN PROMPTED
      ==============================================================
      AMASPZAP  INSPECTS, MODIFIES, AND DUMPS CSECTS OR SPECIFIC DATA RECORDS
      ON DIRECT ACCESS STORAGE
OPR: absdumpt bnmsgpgm
SYS:  ABSDUMPT BNMSGPGM

      **CCHHR- 01FD000D0C   RECORD LENGTH- 000028     MEMBER NAME  BNMSGPGM
      - - - - - -
      - - - - - -
      AMA113I COMPLETED DUMP REQUIREMENTS
OPR: /*
SYS: AMA100I AMASPZAP PROCESSING COMPLETED
      ***
```

Figure 6.4.   The commands entered by the user and messages displayed by the system when the user executes the CLIST of Figure 6.3.

CLIST then ends and control is given to TSO which displays the familiar three asterisks or the READY message depending on whether the CLIST was executed from ISPF or native TSO. At this point, if the screen has three asterisks, the user presses the Enter key to return to TSO or to the ISPF panel from where the CLIST was invoked.

Now let us suppose that you have analyzed the dump produced by this CLIST and you find that at offset Hex '860' in CCHHR = Hex '01FD000D11' there is the string with the value of Hex 'C3C1F2F0' or Character 'CA20'. Suppose you wish to change this string to Character 'D915'. You can use the CLIST of Figure 6.3 to do this modification. The commands that you would enter and the system responses are shown in Figure 6.5. In executing this CLIST, it is assumed that the user made a mistake in entering the REPLACE statement the first time around, which he corrects after receiving system message informing him of the error.

```
OPR : %ZAPBKN
SYS : ENTER FULLY-QUALIFIED NAME OF LOAD LIBRARY WHICH MUST BE
      CATALOGUED (NO QUOTES PLEASE) ===>>>
OPR: cics.test.loadlib
SYS:  ===========================================================
      CLIST ZAPBKN WILL ZAP DSN=CICS.TEST.LOADLIB
      ENTER SYSIN STATEMENTS ONE LINE AT A TIME WHEN PROMPTED
      ===========================================================
      AMASPZAP  INSPECTS, MODIFIES, AND DUMPS CSECTS OR SPECIFIC DATA RECORDS
      ON DIRECT ACCESS STORAGE
OPR: cchhr 01fd000d11
SYS:  CCHHR 01FD000D11
OPR: ver 0860 c3c1f2f0
SYS:  VER 0860 C3C1F2F0
OPR: rep 080 c4f9f1f5
SYS:  REP 080 C4F9F1F5
      AMA109I ERROR - ODD NO. DIGITS - IGNORED
OPR: rep 0860 c4f9f1f5
SYS:  REP 0860 C4F9F1F5
      AMA122I OLD DATA WAS C3C1F2F0
OPR: /*
SYS:  AMA100I AMASPZAP PROCESSING COMPLETED
      ***
```

Figure 6.5.   The commands entered by the user and messages displayed by the system when the user executes the CLIST of Figure 6.3 to zap a load module.

VERY IMPORTANT WARNING REGARDING THE USE OF SUPERZAP PROGRAM

Program AMASPZAP, described above, is commonly called the superzap program. This is an authorized program which is made available only to the systems programmers at an installation. Under no circumstances should any application programmer be allowed to use this program. If your installation has security software such as RACF, ACF2 or TOP-SECRET, the security software can be used to properly control the use of AMASPZAP or any other such sensitive programs. In case your installation has not yet acquired the security software, this may be yet another justification for acquiring it. However, if you are a systems programmer responsible for MVS at such an installation, you can easily take some other measure to control access to this program. For example you can move this program from SYS1.LINKLIB where it usually resides, to some other load library, whose name is known only to you and other people authorized to use this program.

The reason for controlling access to AMASPZAP is obvious. This program can be used by an application programmer knowledgeable about his company's payroll compute program to change it so that it may double the salary payable to him. It can also be used to change a load module so that it becomes unusable and abends whenever it is executed. This way various nasty problems can be easily created in the data center. People who create such problems will, most probably, be caught and punished at the end, but why not make it impossible for them to create problems by denying them access to sensitive programs?

A CLIST TO DEFINE AN ALIAS IN THE MASTER CATALOG

Let us suppose that an applications programmer wants to allocate a dataset with prefix TRPPY. Of course before he can do so, this prefix must be defined as an alias in the master catalog. This means that an ALIAS type entry must be created in the master catalog specifying the name of the user catalog which is to contain all datasets with that prefix. In our example, let us suppose that user catalog ICAT.CICS20 is to contain all datasets with prefix TRPPY. So, an ALIAS type entry must be defined for alias TRPPY in the master catalog that specifies that user catalog ICAT.CICS20 is to contain all datasets with prefix TRPPY. A CLIST that can be used to define this alias is shown in Figure 6.6. This CLIST will prompt the user for the name of the alias to be defined as well as the name of the user catalog to which this alias is related. When program IDCAMS is called that program will prompt the user for the password of the master catalog, because the master catalog, being a very important resource, is usually password protected so that only those who know its password can update it.

In this CLIST, the following points are worth noting. The CALL command is used to invoke program IDCAMS on line 23. It should be noted that when this program is called from TSO (e.g., using command CALL 'SYS1.LINKLIB(IDCAMS)'), file SYSIN is normally allocated to the terminal, because IDCAMS expects all commands to be entered through file SYSIN. When IDCAMS is called from TSO, it waits for the user to type one line of command and press the Enter key. The user must enter at least one space before entering the command itself. The program then processes that command, displays any output on file SYSPRINT which is also normally allocated to the terminal, and then waits for the user to enter another command and press the Enter key. The user can enter /* in positions 1 and 2 on the terminal and then press the Enter key to indicate that there are no more commands in which case IDCAMS would terminate.

When IDCAMS is called from within a CLIST, as shown in Figure 6.6, IDCAMS opens the disk file allocated to SYSIN for input. It then reads the first record from this file which has the DEFINE ALIAS command and processes it, displaying any messages on the terminal because DDname SYSPRINT is assigned to the terminal. IDCAMS then reads the second record from the SYSIN file. This record has /* in positions 1 and 2, which signals to IDCAMS that the end of file has been reached. IDCAMS then terminates and control flows to line 24 in the CLIST of Figure 6.6.

This CLIST illustrates the very important technique of storing SYSIN records in a dataset and then calling a utility program such as IDCAMS which would process all the record stored in the SYSIN file.

```
Line      Statement
Number

1         WRITE PLEASE ENTER THE NAME OF THE PREFIX TO BE DEFINED:
2         WRITENR (NO QUOTES) ==>>>
3         READ &PREFIX
4         WRITE PLEASE ENTER THE NAME OF THE USER CATALOG (NO QUOTES PLEASE):
5         READ &USERCAT
6         /*================================================================
7         /* HERE YOU CAN PUT CODE TO VALIDATE &PREFIX SO THAT IT IS NOT MORE
8         /* THAN 8 CHARACTERS LONG. YOU CAN ALSO VALIDATE &USERCAT SO THAT
9         /* IT IS ONE OF THE VALID USER CATALOG NAMES. HOWEVER, NOTE THAT
10        /* EVEN WITHOUT THIS VALIDATION, THIS CLIST WILL FUNCTION PROPERLY.
11        /*================================================================
12        CONTROL NOMSG
13        FREE F(SYSIN SYSPRINT)
14        CONTROL MSG
15        ALLOC F(SYSIN) NEW BLOCK(80) SPACE(200,20)
16        ALLOC F(SYSPRINT) DA(*)
17        OPENFILE SYSIN OUTPUT
18        SET SYSIN = &STR( DEFINE ALIAS(NAME(&PREFIX) RELATE('&USERCAT')))
19        PUTFILE SYSIN
20        SET SYSIN = /*
21        PUTFILE SYSIN
22        CLOSFILE SYSIN
23        CALL 'SYS1.LINKLIB(IDCAMS)'
24        FREE F(SYSIN)
25        ALLOC F(SYSIN) DA(*)
26        WRITE CLIST DEFALIAS NOW TERMINATES
```

Figure 6.6.   A CLIST to define an alias in the master catalog.

A CLIST TO DELETE AN ALIAS FROM THE MASTER CATALOG

Now let us suppose that alias TRPAY is to be deleted from the master catalog. What are the steps involved in doing this? Of course, the first thing to do is to issue the following command to check whether there are any datasets with this prefix:

```
LISTC L(TRPAY)
```

If there are any datasets with this prefix, they would be listed and the return code from this command would be zero. But if there are no datasets, a message to this effect would be displayed and the return code would be non-zero. If

```
Line        CLIST
Number      Statement

1           PROC 0
2           CONTROL MSG NOLIST
3           CLEAR
4           WRITE PLEASE ENTER THE PREFIX TO BE DELETED FROM MASTER CATALOG
5           WRITENR (WITHOUT QUOTES) ===>>>
6           READ &PREFIX
7           WRITE PLEASE ENTER THE UPDATE PASSWORD OF THE MASTER CATALOG
8           READ &MASTPASS
9           /*================================================================
10          /* LIST CATALOG ENTRIES WITH PREFIX = &PREFIX TO ENSURE THERE ARE NO
11          /* ENTRIES WITH THIS PREFIX.
12          /*================================================================
13          LISTC L(&PREFIX)
14          IF &LASTCC = 0 THEN DO
15             WRITE THERE ARE STILL DATA SETS WITH PREFIX = &PREFIX AS LISTED
16             WRITE ABOVE. PLEASE DELETE THESE DATA SETS BEFORE TRYING TO
17             WRITE DELETE THE PREFIX ITSELF.
18             GOTO GETOUT
19          END
20          DELETE '&PREFIX' ALIAS CATALOG('ICAT.MASTER'/&MASTPASS)
21          WRITE PREFIX &PREFIX HAS BEEN DELETED UNLESS MESSAGES DISPLAYED.
22          GETOUT: EXIT
```

Figure 6.7.   A CLIST to delete an alias from the master catalog.

there are any datasets with prefix TRPAY, they must be first deleted before deleting alias TRPAY itself. To delete alias TRPAY from the master catalog, the following command can be used:

```
DELETE 'TRPAY' ALIAS CATALOG('ICAT.MASTER'/ORANGE01)
```

where ICAT.MASTER is the name of the master catalog and the update password of the master catalog is ORANGE01.

A CLIST that automates the task of deleting an alias from the master catalog is shown in Figure 6.7. In this CLIST, the CLEAR command clears the screen. Note: CLEAR is not an IBM command, but a command developed in-house. If your installation does not have such a command, you can delete the line with the CLEAR command from this CLIST without affecting the function of the CLIST significantly.

Chapter 7
SOME MORE USEFUL CLISTs FOR SYSTEM AND APPLICATION PROGRAMMERS

A CLIST TO MIGRATE SOURCE MEMBERS FROM A TEST PANVALET LIBRARY TO A PRODUCTION PAN-VALET LIBRARY

In this section we will discuss a CLIST, a complete COBOL program, and an MVS job that can be used to automate the task of promoting source modules containing programs, JCL, data, etc. from any Panvalet test library to any Panvalet production library. After you have understood the material that follows, you can easily modify the CLIST, the COBOL program and the job that are presented here to suit your particular needs.

Figure 7.1 shows a CLIST that can be used to promote source programs from Panvalet test source library to Panvalet production source library. Let us consider an example. Suppose that Mary, application programmer on the Payroll/ Personnel System has modified program PPPY001 in SYS3.PANTEST.SOURCE and she asks Joe to promote this source program from SYS3.-PANTEST.SOURCE to the production library SYS3.PAN-PROD.SOURCE. Bill, the Project Leader on the Billing System, has modified AR01 in SYS3.PANTEST.SOURCE, and he requests that Joe migrate this program from the panvalet test library to the Panvalet production library. We

```
LINE       STATEMENT
NUMBER
1          PROC 0
2          CONTROL MSG NOLIST
3          CLEAR
4          WRITE *******************************************************************
5          WRITE *                                                                 *
6          WRITE *                 SOFTWARE PROMOTION FACILITY                     *
7          WRITE *                    &SYSDATE    &SYSTIME                          *
8          WRITE *                                                                 *
9          WRITE *******************************************************************
10         WRITE
11         FREE F(PANPARM1 PANPARM2)
12         ALLOCATE F(PANPARM1) DA('SYS3.PAN.PARM1') SHR
13         ALLOCATE F(PANPARM2) DA('SYS3.PAN.PARM2') SHR
14         OPENFILE PANPARM1 OUTPUT
15         OPENFILE PANPARM2 OUTPUT
16         ASKUSER: +
17           WRITENR TYPE THE NAME OF SOURCE MODULE ($$ TO QUIT) ===>>>>
18           READ SMOD
19           IF &SMOD = $$ THEN GOTO THATSIT
20           SET &PANPARM1 = &STR(++TRANSFER &SMOD)
21           SET &PANPARM2 = &STR(++DELETE NAME=&SMOD)
22           PUTFILE PANPARM1
23           PUTFILE PANPARM2
24           GOTO ASKUSER
25         THATSIT: +
26           CLOSFILE PANPARM1
27           CLOSFILE PANPARM2
28           FREE F(PANPARM1 PANPARM2)
29           SUBMIT 'SYS3.PAN.JCL(PANMIG1)'
30           WRITE ===========================================================
31           WRITE JOB PANMIGR HAS BEEN SUBMITTED FOR EXECUTION. PLEASE CHECK
32           WRITE CAREFULLY JOB OUTPUT AFTER IT HAS FINISHED. IF THIS JOB
33           WRITE DOES NOT ABEND, THEN YOU CAN REST ASSURED THAT EVERYTHING
34           WRITE WENT OK, ELSE CONTACT YOUR GOOD OLD FRIEND, BARRY NIRMAL
35           WRITE IN COMPUTER SCIENCE DIVISION FOR ASSISTANCE.
36           WRITE *** PLEASE PRESS ENTER KEY TO PROCEED. THANKS A LOT. ****
37         EXIT
```

Figure 7.1.   A CLIST to promote Panvalet source members from test
to production.

also have Anand, the CICS Systems Programmer. He has
modified CICS table source named CICS001 in SYS3.PAN-
TEST.SOURCE, and he requests that Joe migrate it from
the test source library to the production source library.

   After having received these requests, Joe executes the
CLIST in Figure 7.1 to perform this migration. Let us see
how this CLIST works. If this CLIST is stored as member

PANPROM in a CLIST library allocated under DDname SYSPROC during Joe's TSO session, he can execute it by typing %PANPROM on option 6 of ISPF or by typing TSO %PANPROM on the command line of any of the ISPF panels. The CLEAR command on line 3 executes a TSO command that clears the screen. (If your installation does not have CLEAR or an equivalent TSO command that clears the screen, you can simply delete line 3 from this CLIST without affecting its function in any way.) On line 11, two DDnames are freed. On lines 12 and 13, two existing datasets are allocated with the disposition of SHR, meaning that these allocations will not fail even if any other user in the MVS system is allocating any of these datasets with disposition of SHR. Let us suppose that these two datasets have been preallocated with the following parameters:

Logical Record Length:	80
Block Size:	3120
Primary Space Quantity:	1 track
Secondary Space Quantity:	1 track

On line 14 the dataset with the DDname of PANPARM1 is opened for output operation. This is followed by one more open operation on line 15. On lines 17 and 18, the user is prompted to enter the name of the first source module being promoted. Supposing that the name entered by the user is PPPY001, the statement on line 22 will write the following line to file PANPARM1:

```
++TRANSFER PPPY001
```

and the statement on line 23 will write the following line to file PANPARM2:

```
++DELETE NAME=PPPY001
```

Control then flows to line 16, where the user is prompted to enter the name of the next source module being promoted. If the user wants to indicate that there are no more source modules to promote, he can just enter $$, which will cause the control to flow to line 25.

Let us suppose for the sake of understanding this CLIST that the user is promoting the three source programs mentioned above, i.e. PPPY001, AR01 and CICS001, and he or she enters the program names in the same sequence. Then he can verify that when control comes to line 25, the following is the content of file PANPARM1:

```
++TRANSFER PPPY001
++TRANSFER AR01
++TRANSFER CICS001
```

And the content of file PANPARM2 is the following:

```
++DELETE PPPY001
++DELETE AR01
++DELETE CICS001
```

On line 29 the content of member PANMIG1 in the partitioned dataset SYS3.PAN.JCL is submitted as a job to the MVS. The content of this member is shown in Figure 7.2. This is followed by a number of message lines being written to the terminal. The EXIT statement on line 37 ends the execution of this CLIST. The user is then taken to the panel from where he invoked this CLIST. It is the job in Figure 7.2 that carries out the actual migration of source modules.

How Does the Job in Figure 7.2 Work?

Let us discuss how the job in Figure 7.2 performs the migration of source modules from the test Panvalet library to the production Panvalet library. In Figure 7.2, each

```
//PANMIGR JOB (PANV,202E,1,99),'JOE -X6345',CLASS=N,
//     NOTIFY=A7JKY,MSGLEVEL=(1,1)
//*=========================================================================*
//* WRITE RECORDS IN FILES UNDER DDNAMES TESTFILE, PRODFILE AND BOTHFILE
//*=========================================================================*
//STEP01    EXEC PGM=UTIL01,PARM='TSTPRD'
//STEPLIB   DD DISP=SHR,DSN=SYS3.PAN.LOAD
//TESTFILE  DD DISP=SHR,DSN=SYS3.PAN.TESTFILE
//PRODFILE  DD DISP=SHR,DSN=SYS3.PAN.PRODFILE
//BOTHFILE  DD DISP=SHR,DSN=SYS3.PAN.BOTHFILE
//SYSOUT    DD SYSOUT=*
//SYSDBOUT  DD SYSOUT=*
//SYSUDUMP  DD SYSOUT=*
//*=========================================================================*
//* ABEND IF STEP01 ENDED IN NON-ZERO CONDITION CODE.
//*=========================================================================*
//STEP02    EXEC PGM=UTIL01,COND=(0,EQ,STEP01),PARM='ABEND$'
//STEPLIB   DD DISP=SHR,DSN=SYS3.PAN.LOAD
//SYSOUT    DD SYSOUT=*
//SYSDBOUT  DD SYSOUT=*
//SYSDUMP   DD SYSOUT=*
//*=========================================================================*
//* SORT RECORDS IN SYS3.PAN.PARM1
//*=========================================================================*
//STEP03    EXEC PGM=SORT,REGION=2048K
//SORTLIB   DD  DISP=SHR,DSN=SYS1.SORTLIB
//SORTWK01 DD   UNIT=SYSDA,SPACE=(CYL,(1))
//SORTWK02 DD   UNIT=SYSDA,SPACE=(CYL,(1))
//SORTWK03 DD   UNIT=SYSDA,SPACE=(CYL,(1))
//SYSOUT    DD  SYSOUT=*
//SORTIN    DD  DISP=SHR,DSN=SYS3.PAN.PARM1
//SORTOUT   DD  DISP=SHR,DSN=SYS3.PAN.PARM1
//SYSIN     DD  *
  SORT FIELDS(12,10,CH,A)
  RECORD TYPE=F
//*=========================================================================*
//* ABEND IF STEP03 ENDED IN NON-ZERO CONDITION CODE.
//*=========================================================================*
//STEP04    EXEC PGM=UTIL01,COND=(0,EQ,STEP03),PARM='ABEND$'
//STEPLIB   DD DISP=SHR,DSN=SYS3.PAN.LOAD
//SYSOUT    DD SYSOUT=*
//SYSDBOUT  DD SYSOUT=*
//SYSDUMP   DD SYSOUT=*
//*=========================================================================*
//* SORT RECORDS IN SYS3.PAN.PARM2
//*=========================================================================*
//STEP05    EXEC PGM=SORT,REGION=2048K
//SORTLIB   DD  DISP=SHR,DSN=SYS1.SORTLIB
//SORTWK01 DD   UNIT=SYSDA,SPACE=(CYL,(1))
//SORTWK02 DD   UNIT=SYSDA,SPACE=(CYL,(1))
//SORTWK03 DD   UNIT=SYSDA,SPACE=(CYL,(1))
//SYSOUT    DD  SYSOUT=*
```

Figure 7.2. Listing of the job that is submitted by the CLIST of Figure 7.1.

```
//SORTIN    DD  DISP=SHR,DSN=SYS3.PAN.PARM2
//SORTOUT   DD  DISP=SHR,DSN=SYS3.PAN.PARM2
//SYSIN     DD  *
  SORT FIELDS(15,10,CH,A)
  RECORD TYPE=F
//*============================================================================*
//* ABEND IF STEP05 ENDED IN NON-ZERO CONDITION CODE.
//*============================================================================*
//STEP06    EXEC PGM=UTIL01,COND=(0,EQ,STEP05),PARM='ABEND$'
//STEPLIB   DD DISP=SHR,DSN=SYS3.PAN.LOAD
//SYSOUT    DD SYSOUT=*
//SYSDBOUT  DD SYSOUT=*
//SYSDUMP   DD SYSOUT=*
//*============================================================================*
//* PRINT LIST OF ALL MEMBERS PRESENT IN TEST PAN LIBRARY ALONG WITH THEIR
//* USER CODES AND WRITE THE PRINTOUT IN DATA SET &&REFTEST
//*============================================================================*
//STEP07    EXEC PGM=PAN#2
//SYSPRINT  DD  DSN=&&REFTEST,
//             DISP=(NEW,PASS),
//             UNIT=SYSDA,SPACE=(TRK,(1,1),RLSE),
//             DCB=(RECFM=FBA,LRECL=133,BLKSIZE=9044)
//PANDD2    DD  DUMMY
//PANDD3    DD  DUMMY
//PANDD1    DD  DISP=SHR,DSN=SYS3.PANTEST.SOURCE
//SYSIN     DD  DISP=SHR,DSN=SYS3.PAN.TESTFILE
//          DD  *
++PRINT 2-UP
//*============================================================================*
//* ABEND IF STEP07 ENDED IN NON-ZERO CONDITION CODE.
//*============================================================================*
//STEP08    EXEC PGM=UTIL01,COND=(0,EQ,STEP08),PARM='ABEND$'
//STEPLIB   DD DISP=SHR,DSN=SYS3.PAN.LOAD
//SYSOUT    DD SYSOUT=*
//SYSDBOUT  DD SYSOUT=*
//SYSDUMP   DD SYSOUT=*
//*============================================================================*
//* WRITE RECORDS IN FILE UNDER DDNAME OUTFILE
//*============================================================================*
//STEP09    EXEC PGM=UTIL01,PARM='ACCESS,PANTEST,PROD,++WRITE$'
//STEPLIB   DD DISP=SHR,DSN=SYS3.PAN.LOAD
//TRANSIN   DD DISP=SHR,DSN=SYS3.PAN.PARM2
//REFERIN   DD DISP=(OLD,PASS),DSN=&&REFTEST
//OUTFILE   DD DSN=&&TESTWORK,
//             DISP=(NEW,PASS),
//             UNIT=SYSDA,
//             SPACE=(TRK,(1,1),RLSE),
//             DCB=(RECFM=FB,LRECL=80,BLKSIZE=9040)
//SYSOUT    DD SYSOUT=*
//SYSDBOUT  DD SYSOUT=*
//SYSUDUMP  DD SYSOUT=*
```

Figure 7.2.   Listing of the job that is submitted by the CLIST of Figure 7.1 (continued).

```
//*====================================================================*
//* ABEND IF STEP09 ENDED IN NON-ZERO CONDITION CODE.
//*====================================================================*
//STEP10    EXEC PGM=UTIL01,COND=(0,EQ,STEP09),PARM='ABEND$'
//STEPLIB  DD DISP=SHR,DSN=SYS3.PAN.LOAD
//SYSOUT    DD SYSOUT=*
//SYSDBOUT DD SYSOUT=*
//SYSDUMP   DD SYSOUT=*
//*====================================================================*
//* NOW DELETE MEMBERS BEING MIGRATED FROM PRODUCTION PANVALET LIBRARY.
//*====================================================================*
//STEP11    EXEC PGM=PAN#2
//SYSPRINT DD  SYSOUT=*
//PANDD3    DD  DUMMY
//PANDD1    DD  DISP=SHR,DSN=SYS3.PANPROD.SOURCE
//PANDD2    DD  DUMMY
//SYSIN     DD  DISP=SHR,DSN=SYS3.PAN.PRODFILE
//          DD  DISP=SHR,DSN=SYS3.PAN.PARM2
//*====================================================================*
//* ABEND IF STEP11 ENDED IN CONDITION CODE GREATER THAN 8
//*====================================================================*
//STEP12    EXEC PGM=UTIL01,COND=(8,GE,STEP01),PARM='ABEND$'
//STEPLIB  DD DISP=SHR,DSN=SYS3.PAN.LOAD
//SYSOUT    DD SYSOUT=*
//SYSDBOUT DD SYSOUT=*
//SYSDUMP   DD SYSOUT=*
//*====================================================================*
//* NOW COPY MEMBERS BEING MIGRATED FROM TEST PANVALET LIBRARY TO PROD PAN LIB
//*====================================================================*
//STEP13    EXEC PGM=PAN#2
//SYSPRINT DD  SYSOUT=*
//PANDD3    DD  DUMMY
//PANDD1    DD  DISP=SHR,DSN=SYS3.PANTEST.SOURCE
//PANDD2    DD  DISP=SHR,DSN=SYS3.PANPROD.SOURCE
//SYSIN     DD  DISP=SHR,DSN=SYS3.PAN.BOTHFILE
//          DD  DISP=SHR,DSN=SYS3.PAN.PARM1
//*====================================================================*
//* ABEND IF STEP13 ENDED IN NON-ZERO CONDITION CODE.
//*====================================================================*
//STEP14    EXEC PGM=UTIL01,COND=(0,EQ,STEP13),PARM='ABEND$'
//STEPLIB  DD DISP=SHR,DSN=SYS3.PAN.LOAD
//SYSOUT    DD SYSOUT=*
//SYSDBOUT DD SYSOUT=*
//SYSDUMP   DD SYSOUT=*
//*====================================================================*
//* DELETE FROM TEST PANVALET LIBRARY MEMBERS THAT HAVE BEEN MIGRATED
//*====================================================================*
//STEP15    EXEC PGM=PAN#2
//SYSPRINT DD  SYSOUT=*
//PANDD3    DD  DUMMY
//PANDD1    DD  DISP=SHR,DSN=SYS3.PANTEST.SOURCE
//PANDD2    DD  DUMMY
```

Figure 7.2.   Listing of the job that is submitted by the CLIST of Figure 7.1 (continued).

```
//SYSIN    DD  DISP=SHR,DSN=SYS3.PAN.TESTFILE
//         DD  DISP=SHR,DSN=SYS3.PAN.PARM2
//*=============================================================================*
//* ABEND IF STEP15 ENDED IN NON-ZERO CONDITION CODE.
//*=============================================================================*
//STEP16   EXEC PGM=UTIL01,COND=(0,EQ,STEP15),PARM='ABEND$'
//STEPLIB  DD DISP=SHR,DSN=SYS3.PAN.LOAD
//SYSOUT   DD SYSOUT=*
//SYSDBOUT DD SYSOUT=*
//SYSDUMP  DD SYSOUT=*
//*=============================================================================*
//* PRINT LIST OF MEMBERS IN PRODUCTION LIBRARY ALONG WITH THEIR USER CODES
//* AND WRITE THE PRINTOUT IN DATA SET &&REFER
//*=============================================================================*
//STEP17   EXEC PGM=PAN#2
//SYSPRINT DD  DSN=&&REFER,
//             DISP=(NEW,PASS),
//             UNIT=SYSDA,SPACE=(TRK,(1,1),RLSE),
//             DCB=(RECFM=FBA,LRECL=133,BLKSIZE=9044)
//PANDD2   DD  DUMMY
//PANDD3   DD  DUMMY
//PANDD1   DD  DISP=SHR,DSN=SYS3.PANPROD.SOURCE
//SYSIN    DD  DISP=SHR,DSN=SYS3.PAN.PRODFILE
//         DD  *
++PRINT 2-UP
//*=============================================================================*
//* ABEND IF STEP17 ENDED IN NON-ZERO CONDITION CODE.
//*=============================================================================*
//STEP18   EXEC PGM=UTIL01,COND=(0,EQ,STEP17),PARM='ABEND$'
//STEPLIB  DD DISP=SHR,DSN=SYS3.PAN.LOAD
//SYSOUT   DD SYSOUT=*
//SYSDBOUT DD SYSOUT=*
//SYSDUMP  DD SYSOUT=*
//*=============================================================================*
//* WRITE RECORDS IN FILE UNDER DDNAME OUTFILE
//*=============================================================================*
//STEP19   EXEC PGM=UTIL01,PARM='ACCESS,PANPROD,PROD,++STATUS'
//STEPLIB  DD DISP=SHR,DSN=SYS3.PAN.LOAD
//TRANSIN  DD DISP=SHR,DSN=SYS3.PAN.PARM2
//REFERIN  DD DISP=(OLD,PASS),DSN=&&REFER
//OUTFILE  DD DSN=&&ACTION,
//            DISP=(NEW,PASS),
//            UNIT=SYSDA,
//            SPACE=(TRK,(1,1),RLSE),
//            DCB=(RECFM=FB,LRECL=80,BLKSIZE=9040)
//SYSOUT   DD SYSOUT=*
//SYSDBOUT DD SYSOUT=*
//SYSUDUMP DD SYSOUT=*
```

Figure 7.2.   Listing of the job that is submitted by the CLIST of Figure 7.1 (continued).

```
//*==========================================================================*
//* ABEND IF STEP19 ENDED IN NON-ZERO CONDITION CODE.
//*==========================================================================*
//STEP20    EXEC PGM=UTIL01,COND=(0,EQ,STEP19),PARM='ABEND$'
//STEPLIB   DD DISP=SHR,DSN=SYS3.PAN.LOAD
//SYSOUT    DD SYSOUT=*
//SYSDBOUT  DD SYSOUT=*
//SYSDUMP   DD SYSOUT=*
//*==========================================================================*
//* CHANGE STATUS OF MIGRATED PROGRAMS FROM TEST TO PRODUCTION IN THE PRDO LIB
//*==========================================================================*
//STEP21    EXEC PGM=PAN#1
//SYSPRINT  DD  SYSOUT=*
//PANDD1    DD  DISP=SHR,DSN=SYS3.PANPROD.SOURCE
//PANDD2    DD  DUMMY
//PANDD3    DD  DUMMY
//SYSIN     DD  DISP=(OLD,PASS),DSN=&&ACTION
//*==========================================================================*
//* ABEND IF STEP21 ENDED IN NON-ZERO CONDITION CODE.
//*==========================================================================*
//STEP22    EXEC PGM=UTIL01,COND=(0,EQ,STEP21),PARM='ABEND$'
//STEPLIB   DD DISP=SHR,DSN=SYS3.PAN.LOAD
//SYSOUT    DD SYSOUT=*
//SYSDBOUT  DD SYSOUT=*
//SYSDUMO   DD SYSOUT=*
//*==========================================================================*
//* CLEAR THE CONTENTS OF FILES UNDER DDNAMES TESTFILE, PRODFILE AND BOTHFILE
//*==========================================================================*
//STEP99    EXEC PGM=UTIL01,PARM='CLEAR$'
//STEPLIB   DD DISP=SHR,DSN=SYS3.PAN.LOAD
//TESTFILE  DD DISP=SHR,DSN=CICS.PAN.TESTFILE
//PRODFILE  DD DISP=SHR,DSN=SYS3.PAN.PRODFILE
//BOTHFILE  DD DISP=SHR,DSN=SYS3.PAN.BOTHFILE
//SYSDBOUT  DD SYSOUT=*
//SYSDUMP   DD SYSOUT=*
```

Figure 7.2.   Listing of the job that is submitted by the CLIST of Figure 7.1 (continued).

step's function has been documented briefly. To understand this job, you need to have some understanding of how Panvalet library management programs PAN#1 and PAN#2 work. This job also executes the SORT program with which you should be familiar if you have worked in application or system programming. It also executes program UTIL01, which is shown in Figure 7.3. Let us assume that at the time the programmers requested migration of source modules, their status in the test Panvalet library are

```
      IDENTIFICATION DIVISION.
      PROGRAM-ID.          UTIL01
      AUTHOR.              B. K. NIRMAL
      DATE-WRITTEN.        89-04-15.
      DATE-COMPILED.
     *=================================================================*
     * THIS PROGRAM IS USED IN :
     *
     *
     *
     *=================================================================*
     *USER CODE IS A 4-DIGIT NUMBER, FROM 0 TO 9999                    *
     *ACCESS CODE CAN HAVE A VALUE FROM 1 TO 75533.                    *
     *LIB   CODE CAN HAVE A VALUE FROM 0 TO 32767                      *
     *INSTALL CODE CAN HAVE  VALUE FROM 0 TO 32767                     *
     *CNTL    CODE CAN HAVE  A VALUE OF 0 IF BOTH INSTALL AND LIB CODES
     *        ARE ZERO.
     *CNTL    CODE CAN HAVE  A MAX VALUE OF 65534 IF BOTH INSTALL AND
     *        LIB CODES HAVE A MAX VALUE OF 32767.
     *=================================================================*
     *  +++++++++++++++ A T T E N T I O N +++++++++++++++++++++++++++++*
     *=================================================================*
     * CHANGE VALUES OF WS-TEST-LIB-CODE, WS-PROD-LIB-CODE AND         *
     * WS-INSTALL-CODE IN W-S TO HAVE CORRECT VALUES AT ALL TIMES.     *
     *=================================================================*
     *                      CHANGE CONTROL                            *
     *                                                                *
     *  PLEASE UPDATE THIS BOX WHENEVER MAKING CHANGES TO THIS        *
     *  PROGRAM.  ADD 1 TO VERSION NUMBER AND FLAG ALL OF YOUR        *
     *  CHANGES WITH VERSION NUMBER IN THE FORMAT V#NNNN WHERE        *
     *  NNNN = PREVIOUS VERSION + 1.                                  *
     *                                                                *
     *  VERSION   DATE     PGMR     DESCRIPTION/EAR REFERENCE         *
     *  ===#=== ========   ======  ================================== *
     *  001  89/04/15  Z2BKN    NEW PROGRAM                           *
     *                                                                *
     *=================================================================*
      ENVIRONMENT DIVISION.
      INPUT-OUTPUT SECTION.
      FILE-CONTROL.
          SELECT REFER-FILE        ASSIGN TO REFERIN.
          SELECT TRANS-FILE        ASSIGN TO TRANSIN.
          SELECT OUT-FILE          ASSIGN TO OUTFILE.
          SELECT TEST-FILE         ASSIGN TO TESTFILE.
          SELECT PROD-FILE         ASSIGN TO PRODFILE.
          SELECT BOTH-FILE         ASSIGN TO BOTHFILE.

      DATA DIVISION.
      FILE SECTION.
      FD  REFER-FILE
          LABEL RECORD STANDARD
          BLOCK CONTAINS 0 RECORDS.
```

Figure 7.3.   Source code of program UTIL01 executed in CLIST of Figure 7.4 and job of Figure 7.2.

```
01  REFER-REC               PIC X(133).

FD  TRANS-FILE
    LABEL RECORD STANDARD
    BLOCK CONTAINS 0 RECORDS.

01  TRANS-REC               PIC X(80).

FD  OUT-FILE
    LABEL RECORD STANDARD
    BLOCK CONTAINS 0 RECORDS.

01  OUT-REC                 PIC X(80).

FD  TEST-FILE
    LABEL RECORD STANDARD
    BLOCK CONTAINS 0 RECORDS.

01  TEST-REC                PIC X(80).

FD  PROD-FILE
    LABEL RECORD STANDARD
    BLOCK CONTAINS 0 RECORDS.

01  PROD-REC                PIC X(80).

FD  BOTH-FILE
    LABEL RECORD STANDARD
    BLOCK CONTAINS 0 RECORDS.

01  BOTH-REC                PIC X(80).

WORKING-STORAGE SECTION.
*=================================================================*
01  WS-INSTALL-CODE         PIC 9(05) VALUE 1234.
*=================================================================*
01  WS-CT-LIB-CODE          PIC 9(05) VALUE 23145.
01  WS-CP-LIB-CODE          PIC 9(05) VALUE 23145.
*=================================================================*
01  WS-TEST-LIB-CODE        PIC 9(05) VALUE 90.
01  WS-PROD-LIB-CODE        PIC 9(05) VALUE 500.
*=================================================================*
01  WS-LIB-CODE             PIC 9(05).
01  WS-TEXT-CNTL            PIC 9(05).
01  WS-PROD-CNTL            PIC 9(05).

01  DASHES                  PIC X(120) VALUE ALL '='.
01  WS-HIT-USER             PIC X(04).
01  WS-HIT-USER-N   REDERINES WS-HIT-USER
                            PIC 9(04).
01  WS-HIT-ACCESS           PIC 9(05).
01  WS-HIT-SEC              PIC X(01).
```

Figure 7.3.   Source code of program UTIL01 executed in CLIST of Figure 7.4 and job of Figure 7.2 (continued).

```
01  WS-TRANS-REC.
    05 FILLER                     PIC X(14).
    05 TR-PROG                    PIC X(10).

01  WS-OUT-REC0                   PIC X(14)    VALUE
    '++OPTION OUTPUT,NEWPDS'.

01  WS-OUT-REC1
    05 FILLER                     PIC X(09) VALUE '++ACCESS '.
    05 OR1-ACCESS                 PIC 9(5).

01  WS-OUT-REC2.
    05 FILLER                     PIC X(09) VALUE '++STATUS '.
    05 OR2-F1.
       10  OR2-PROG                  PIC X(10).
       10  OR2-FIXED                 PIC X(05).

01  WS-OUT-REC3.
    05 FILLER                     PIC X(13) VALUE '++WRITE WORK,'.
    05 OR3-PROG                   PIC X(10).

01  WS-OUT-REC4.
    05 FILLER                     PIC X(10) VALUE '++CONTROL '.
    05 OR4-CNTL                   PIC 9(5).
    05 FILLER                     PIC X(56) VALUE SPACES.
    05 OR4-CODE                   PIC X(01) VALUE SPACE.

01  WORK-AREA-1.
    05 W1-CHAR        OCCURS 15 TIMES PIC X.

01  WORK-AREA-2.
    05 W2-CHAR        OCCURS 15 TIMES PIC X.

01  WS-REFER-REC              PIC X(133).
01  WS-REFER-REC1    REDEFINES WS-REFER-REC.
    05 RR1-TEXT              PIC X(05).

01  WS-REFER-REC2    REDEFINES WS-REFER-REC.
    05 RR2-TEXT              PIC X(10).

01  WS-REFER-REC3    REDEFINES WS-REFER-REC.
    05 FILLER               PIC X(01).
    05 RR-PROG1             PIC X(10).
    05 FILLER               PIC X(07).
    05 RR-USER1             PIC X(04).
    05 FILLER               PIC X(01).
    05 RR-SEC1              PIC X(01).
    05 FILLER               PIC X(39).
    05 RR-PROG2             PIC X(10).
    05 FILLER               PIC X(07).
    05 RR-USER2             PIC X(04).
    05 FILLER               PIC X(01).
    05 RR-SEC2              PIC X(01).
```

Figure 7.3. Source code of program UTIL01 executed in CLIST of Figure 7.4 and job of Figure 7.2 (continued).

```
01  JOB-DONE-SW                     PIC 9  VALUE ZERO.
01  EOF-TRANS-SW                    PIC 9  VALUE ZERO.
    88 EOF-TRANS                    VALUE 1.

01  EOF-REFER-SW                    PIC 9  VALUE ZERO.
    88 EOF-REFER                    VALUE 1.

01  VALID-REC-SW                    PIC 9  VALUE ZERO.
01  WS-NAME-FOUND-SW                PIC 9  VALUE ZERO.

01  ABORT-CODE                      PIC S9(8) COMP.
01  IX1                             PIC S9(8) COMP.
01  IX2                             PIC S9(8) COMP.
01  TABLE-SIZE                      PIC S9(4) COMP VALUE ZERO.
01  HIT-FOUND-SW                    PIC 9.
    88 HIT-FOUND                    VALUE 1.

01  WS-USER-TBL.
    05 WS-USER-TABLE                OCCURS 2000 TIMES.
       10 UT-PROG                         PIC X(10).
       10 UT-USER                         PIC X(4).
       10 UT-SEC                          PIC X(1).

01  WS-MSG-1.
    05 FILLER                            PIC X(57) VALUE
    'UTIL01 - NO. OF PROGRAMS READ FROM REFERENCE FILE = '.
    05 MSG1-TABLE-SIZE              PIC ZZZ9.

LINKAGE SECTION.
01  LINKAGE-PARM.
    04  FILLER              PIC X(02).
    04  RUN-TYPE            PIC X(06).

        88 ABEND-PGM            VALUE 'ABEND$'.
        88 TRANSFER-CT-TO-CP     VALUE 'CTTOCP'.
        88 TRANSFER-CP-TO-CT     VALUE 'CPTOCT'.
        88 TRANSFER-TEST-TO-PROD  VALUE 'TSTPRD'.
        88 TRANSFER-PROD-TO-TEST  VALUE 'PRDTST'.
        88 DECIDE-ACCESS        VALUE 'ACCESS'.
        88 CLEAR-FILES          VALUE 'CLEAR$'.
    04  FILLER              PIC X(01).
    04  PAN-LIB             PIC X(07).
        88 PANTEST      VALUE 'PANTEST'.
        88 PANPROD      VALUE 'PANPROD'.
        88 KIKTEST      VALUE 'KIKTEST'.

        88 KIKPROD      VALUE 'KIKPROD'.
    04  FILLER              PIC X(01).
    04  RUN-MODE            PIC X(04).
        88 TEST MODE    VALUE 'TEST'.
        88 PROD-MODE    VALUE 'PROD'.
    04  FILLER              PIC X(01).
```

Figure 7.3.   Source code of program UTIL01 executed in CLIST of Figure 7.4 and job of Figure 7.2 (continued).

```
     04  OUTFILE-TYPE        PIC X(08).
         88 GIVE-STATUS      VALUE '++STATUS'.
         88 GIVE-WORK        VALUE '++WRITES'.
*==================================================================*
PROCEDURE DIVISION USING LINKAGE-PARM.
    IF ABEND-PGM
       DISPLAY DASHES
       DISPLAY 'UTIL01 HAS EXECUTED WITH RUN-TYPE = ' RUN-TYPE
       DISPLAY 'UTIL01 IS TERMINATING BY CAUSING USER ABEND 100'
       DISPLAY DASHES
       MOVE -100 TO ABORT-CODE
       CALL 'ABORT' USING ABORT-CODE.

    IF TRANSFER-TEST-TO-PROD OR
       TRANSFER-CT-TO-CP      OR
       TRANSFER-PROD-TO-TEST OR
       TRANSFER-CP-TO-CT
       PERFORM WRITE-PARM-RTN THRU WRITE-PARM-EXIT
       GOBACK.

    IF CLEAR-FILES
       PERFORM CLEAR-FILES-RTN THRU CLEAR-FILES-EXIT
       GOBACK.

    IF DECIDE-ACCESS
       PERFORM ACCESS-RTN THRU ACCESS-EXIT
       GOBACK.

    DISPLAY DASHES
    DISPLAY 'RUN-TYPE PASSED TO UTIL01 IS = ' RUN-TYPE
    DISPLAY 'THIS VALUE IS NOT CURRENTLY SUPPORTED BY UTIL01'
    DISPLAY 'UTIL01 IS BEING ABORTED ON USER ABEND CODE = 999'
    DISPLAY DASHES
    MOVE -999 TO ABORT-CODE
    CALL 'ABORT'USING ABORT-CODE.

ACCESS-RTN.
       OPEN INPUT  REFER-FILE
                   TRANS-FILE
             OUTPUT OUT-FILE.
       IF PANTEST
         MOVE WS-TEST-LIB-CODE TO WS-LIB-CODE
       ELSE
         IF PANPROD
           MOVE WS-PROD-LIB-CODE TO WS-LIB-CODE
       ELSE
       IF KIKTEST
         MOVE WS-CT-LIB-CODE TO WS-LIB-CODE
       ELSE
         IF KIKPROD
           MOVE WS-CP-LIB-CODE TO WS-LIB-CODE
```

Figure 7.3.   Source code of program UTIL01 executed in CLIST of Figure 7.4 and job of Figure 7.2 (continued).

```
        ELSE
         DISPLAY DASHES
         DISPLAY 'VALUE OF PAN-LIB PASSED THRU PARM = ' PAN-LIB
         DISPLAY 'INVALID VALUE FOR PANVALET LIBRARY PASSED THRU'
         DISPLAY 'LINKAGE PARM TO PROGRAM UTIL01'
         DISPLAY 'UTIL01 IS TERMINATING BY CAUSING USER ABEND 200'
         DISPLAY DASHES
         MOVE -200 TO ABORT-CODE
         CALL 'ABORT' USING ABORT-CODE.

        IF GIVE-STATUS
          NEXT SENTENCE
        ELSE
          IS GIVE-WORK
             WRITE OUT-REC FROM WS-OUT-REC0
        ELSE
         DISPLAY DASHES
         DISPLAY 'VALUE OF OUTFILE-TYPE PASSED THRU PARM = '
           OUTFILE-TYPE
         DISPLAY 'INVALID VALUE FOR OUT FILE TYPE PASSED THRU '
         DISPLAY 'LINKAGE PARM TO PROGRAM UTIL01'
         DISPLAY 'UTIL01 IS TERMINATING BY CAUSING USER ABEND 300'
         DISPLAY DASHES
         MOVE -300 TO ABORT-CODE
         CALL 'ABORT' USING ABORT-CODE.

        IF TEST-MODE OR PROD-MODE
          NEXT SENTENCE
        ELSE
         DISPLAY DASHES
         DISPLAY 'VALUE OF RUN-MODE PASSED THRU PARM = '
           RUN-MODE
         DISPLAY 'THIS VALUE IS INVALID'
         DISPLAY 'UTIL01 IS TERMINATING BY CAUSING USER ABEND 400'
         DISPLAY DAHES
         MOVE -400 TO ABORT-CODE
         CALL 'ABORT' USING ABORT-CODE.

        MOVE LOW-VALUES TO WS-USER-TBL.
        PERFORM LOAD-USER-TABLE THRU LOAD-USER-EXIT
          UTIL EOF-REFER.
        MOVE TABLE-SIZE TO MSG1-TABLE-SIZE.
        DISPLAY DASHES.
        DISPLAY WS-MSG-1.
        DISPLAY DASHES.
        CLOSE REFER-FILE.
        IF TABLE-SIZE LESS THAN 1 OR GREATER THAN 2000
          DISPLAY '==============================================='
          DISPLAY 'IN UTIL01 OCCURRED THE ERROR DESCRIBED BELOW:'
          DISPLAY 'NUMBER OF RECORDS READ FROM REFER-FILE HAS '
          DISPLAY 'LESS THAN 1 OR MORE THAN 2000 RECORDS. THIS '
```

Figure 7.3.   Source code of program UTIL01 executed in CLIST of Figure 7.4 and job of Figure 7.2 (continued).

```
            DISPLAY 'IS A SYMPTOM OF A SERIOUS ERROR AND NEEDS TO BE'
            DISPLAY 'INVESTIGATED BY BARRY NIRMAL IN EDP DEPT'
            DISPLAY '*** ERROR *** ERROR *** ERROR *** ERROR ******'
            PERFORM Z100-DISPLAY-STD-MSGS
            MOVE -300 TO ABORT-CODE
            CALL 'ABORT' USING ABORT-CODE.

        PERFORM PROCESS-TRANS THRU PROCESS-EXIT UNTIL
          EOF-TRANS.
        CLOSE TRANS-FILE OUT-FILE.
        GO TO ACCESS-EXIT.

    ACCESS-EXIT.   EXIT.

    WRITE-PARM-RTN.
        OPEN OUTPUT TEST-FILE   PROD-FILE   BOTH-FILE.
        IF TRANSFER-TEST-TO-PROD OR
           TRANSFER-PROD-TO-TEST
          COMPUTE WS-TEST-CNTL = WS-TEST-LIB-CODE + WS-INSTALL-CODE
          COMPUTE WS-PROD-CNTL = WS-PROD-LIB-CODE + WS-INSTALL-CODE
        ELSE
          COMPUTE WS-TEST-CNTL = WS-CT-LIB-CODE + WS-INSTALL-CODE
          COMPUTE WS-PROD-CNTL = WS-CP-LIB-CODE + WS-INSTALL-CODE.

        MOVE WS-PROD-CNTL TO OR4-CNTL.
        WRITE PROD-REC FROM WS-OUT-REC4.

        MOVE WS-TEST-CNTL TO OR4-CNTL.
        WRITE TEST-REC FROM WS-OUT-REC4.

        IF TRANSFER-TEST-TO-PROD OR
           TRANSFER-CT-TO-CP
          MOVE WS-TEST-CNTL TO OR4-CNTL
          WRITE BOTH-REC FROM WS-OUT-REC4
          MOVE '++OPTION OUTPUT' TO BOTH-REC
          WRITE BOTH-REC
          MOVE WS-PROD-CNTL TO OR4-CNTL
          MOVE 'A' TO OR4-CODE
          WRITE BOTH-REC FROM WS-OUT-REC4

        ELSE
          MOVE WS-PROD-CNTL TO OR4-CNTL
          WRITE BOTH-REC FROM WS-OUT-REC4
          MOVE '++OPTION OUTPUT' TO BOTH-REC
          WRITE BOTH-REC
          MOVE WS-TEST-CNTL TO OR4-CNTL
          MOVE 'A' TO OR4-CODE
          WRITE BOTH-REC FROM WS-OUT-REC4.

        CLOSE TEST-FILE   PROD-FILE   BOTH-FILE.
    WRITE-PARM-EXIT.   EXIT.
```

Figure 7.3.   Source code of program UTIL01 executed in CLIST of
Figure 7.4 and job of Figure 7.2 (continued).

```
CLEAR-FILES-RTN.
        OPEN OUTPUT TEST-FILE    PROD-FILE    BOTH-FILE.
        WRITE TEST-REC FROM DASHES.
        WRITE PROD-REC FROM DASHES.
        WRITE BOTH-REC FROM DASHES.
        CLOSE TEST-FILE    PROD-FILE    BOTH-FILE.
CLEAR-FILES-EXIT.  EXIT.

PROCESS-TRANS.
     READ TRANS-FILE INTO WS-TRANS-REC AT END
        MOVE 1 TO EOF-TRANS-SW
        GO TO PROCESS-EXIT.

     MOVE ZERO TO HIT-FOUND-SW.
     PERFORM SEARCH-USER-TABLE THRU SEARCH-USER-EXIT
        VARYING IX1 FROM 1 BY 1 UNTIL IX1 GREATER THAN TABLE-SIZE
        OR HIT-FOUND-SW = 1 OR HIT-FOUND-SW = 9.

     IF HIT-FOUND
        PERFORM HIT-FOUND-RTN THRU HIT-FOUND-EXIT
     ELSE
        DISPLAY DASHES
        DISPLAY '*** ERROR *** ERROR *** ERROR *** ERROR ******'
        DISPLAY 'PROGRAM: ' TR-PROG ' NOT FOUND IN USER TABLE'
        DISPLAY 'THIS IS SYMPTOM OF A SERIOUS ERROR AND NEEDS TO '
        DISPLAY 'BE INVESTIGATED BY BARRY NIRMAL IN EDP DEPT'
        DISPLAY '*** ERROR *** ERROR *** ERROR *** ERROR ******'
        DISPLAY DASHES
        PERFORM Z100-DISPLAY-STD-MSGS
        MOVE -400 TO ABORT-CODE
        CALL 'ABORT' USING ABORT-CODE.

PROCESS-EXIT.
     EXIT.

HIT-FOUND-RTN.
     MOVE WS-HIT-ACCESS       TO OR1-ACCESS.
     IF GIVE-STATUS
        MOVE TR-PROG TO OR2-PROG
        MOVE ',PROD' TO OR2-FIXED
        MOVE OR2-F1 TO WORK-AREA-1
        MOVE SPACES TO WORK-AREA-2
        MOVE ZERO TO IX2   JOB-DONE-SW
        PERFORM EXAMINE-RTN THRU EXAMINE-EXIT VARYING IX1 FROM 1
          BY 1 UNTIL JOB-DONE-SW = 1 OR IX1 > 15
        MOVE   WORK-AREA-2 TO OR2-F1
        WRITE OUT-REC FROM WS-OUT-REC1
        WRITE OUT-REC FROM WS-OUT-REC2
     ELSE
        IF GIVE-WORK
           WRITE OUT-REC FORM WS-OUT-REC1
           MOVE TR-PROG TO OR3-PROG
```

Figure 7.3. Source code of program UTIL01 executed in CLIST of Figure 7.4 and job of Figure 7.2 (continued).

```
                WRITE OUT-REC FROM WS-OUT-REC3.

        HIT-FOUND-EXIT.  EXIT.

        EXAMINE-RTN.

            IF W1-CHAR (IX1) = SPACE
              GO TO EXAMINE-EXIT.

            IF W1-CHAR (IX1) NOT = ','
              ADD 1 TO IX2
              MOVE W1-CHAR (IX1) TO W2-CHAR (IX2)
              GO TO EXAMINE-EXIT
            ELSE
              ADD 1 TO IX2
              MOVE ',' TO WS-CHAR (IX2)
              ADD 1 TO IX2
              MOVE 'P' TO W2-CHAR (IX2)
              ADD 1 TO IX2
              MOVE 'R' TO W2-CHAR (IX2)
              ADD 1 TO IX2
              MOVE 'O' TO W2-CHAR (IX2)
              ADD 1 TO IX2
              MOVE 'D' TO W2-CHAR (IX2)
              MOVE 1 TO JOB-DONE-SW.
        EXAMINE-EXIT.  EXIT.

        LOAD-USER-TABLE.
            MOVE ZERO TO VALID-REC-SW
                         WS-NAME-FOUND-SW.
            PERFORM GET-FIRST-VALID-REC THRU GET-FIRST-EXIT    UNTIL
              VALID-REC-SW = 1 OR EOF-REFER.
            IF EOF-REFER
              GO TO LOAD-USER-EXIT.
            PERFORM GENERAL-RTN THRU GENERAL-EXIT UNTIL EOF-REFER.
        LOAD-USER-EXIT.  EXIT.

        GENERAL-RTN.
            PERFORM HANDLE-THIS-RECORD THRU HANDLE-EXIT.
            MOVE ZERO TO VALID-REC-SW.
            PERFORM GET-NEXT-VALID-REC THRU GET-NEXT-EXIT UNTIL
              VALID-REC-SW = 1 OR EOF-REFER.

        GENERAL-EXIT.
            EXIT.

        HANDLE-THIS-RECORD.
            ADD 1 TO TABLE-SIZE.
            IF TABLE-SIZE > 2000 OR RR-PROG1 = SPACE
              GO TO HANDLE-EXIT.
            IF TEST-MODE
              DISPLAY 'STORING PGM= ' RR-PROG1 ' USER CODE= ' RR-USER1
```

Figure 7.3. Source code of program UTIL01 executed in CLIST of Figure 7.4 and job of Figure 7.2 (continued).

```
                    ' SEC = ' RR-SEC1.
          MOVE RR-PROG1 TO UT-PROG (TABLE-SIZE).
          MOVE RR-USER1 TO UT-USER (TABLE-SIZE).
          MOVE RR-SEC1  TO UT-SEC  (TABLE-SIZE).

          ADD 1 TO TABLE-SIZE.
          IF TABLE-SIZE > 2000 OR RR-PROG2 = SPACES
            GO TO HANDLE-EXIT.

          IF TEST-MODE
            DISPLAY 'STORING PGM= ' RR-PROG1 ' USER CODE= ' RR-USER1
                   ' SEC = ' RR-SEC1.
          MOVE RR-PROG1 TO UT-PROG (TABLE-SIZE).
          MOVE RR-USER1 TO UT-USER (TABLE-SIZE).
          MOVE RR-SEC1  TO UT-SEC  (TABLE-SIZE).

          ADD 1 TO TABLE-SIZE.
          IF TABLE-SIZE > 2000 OR RR-PROG2 = SPACES
            GO TO HANDLE-EXIT.
          IF TEST-MODE
            DISPLAY 'STORING PGM= ' RR-PROG2 ' USER CODE= ' RR-USER2
                    ' SEC = ' RR=SEC2.
          MOVE RR-PROG2 TO UT-PROG (TABLE-SIZE).
          MOVE RR-USER2 TO UT-USER (TABLE-SIZE).
          MOVE RR-SEC2  TO UT-SEC  (TABLE-SIZE).

      HANDLE-EXIT.    EXIT.

      SEARCH-USER-TABLE.
          IF UT-PROG (IX1) = LOW-VALUE
            MOVE 9 TO HIT-FOUND-SW
            GO TO SEARCH-USER-EXIT.

          IF UT-PROG (IX1)  = TR-PROG
             MOVE 1 TO HIT-FOUND-SW
             MOVE UT-USER (IX1) TO WS-HIT-USER
             MOVE UT-SEC  (IX1) TO WS-HIT-SEC
             PERFORM DETERMINE-ACCESS THRU DETERMINE-EXIT
             GO TO SEARCH-USER-EXIT.

      SEARCH-USER-EXIT.          EXIT.

      DETERMINE-ACCESS.
          EXAMINE WS-HIT-USER REPLACING ALL SPACES BY ZEROES.
          IF WS-HIT-SEC = ZERO OR SPACES
            MOVE ZERO TO WS-HIT-ACCESS
          ELSE
            IF WS-HIT-SEC = '1'
              COMPUTE WS-HIT-ACCESS = WS-HIT-USER-N
            ELSE
              IF WS-HIT-SEC = '2'
                COMPUTE WS-HIT-ACCESS = WS-HIT-USER-N + WS-LIB-CODE
```

Figure 7.3. Source code of program UTIL01 executed in CLIST of Figure 7.4 and job of Figure 7.2 (continued).

```
            ELSE
             IF WS-HIT-SEC = '3'
                COMPUTE WS-HIT-ACCESS = WS-HIT-USER-N + WS-LIB-CODE
                       + WS-INSTALL-CODE
               ELSE
            DISPLAY DASHES
            DISPLAY 'PROCESSING PROGRAM: ' TR-PROG
            DISPLAY 'SEC OF THIS PROGRAM = ' WS-HIT-SEC
            DISPLAY 'THIS IS INVALID SEC. '
            DISPLAY CASHES
            PERFORM Z100-DISPLAY-STD-MSGS
            MOVE -888 TO ABORT-CODE
            CALL 'ABORT' USING ABORT-CODE.

DETERMINE-EXIT.  EXIT.

GET-FIRST-VALID-REC.

    READ REFER-FILE INTO WS-REFER-REC AT END
      MOVE 1 TO EOF-REFER-SW
      GO TO GET-FIRST-EXIT.
    IF RR1-TEXT  = 'ONAME'

      MOVE 1 TO WS-NAME-FOUND-SW
      GO TO GET-FIRST-EXIT.
    IF WS-NAME-FOUND-SW = ZERO
      GO TO GET-FIRST-EXIT.
    MOVE 1 TO VALID-REC-SW.

GET-FIRST-EXIT.   EXIT.

GET-NEXT-VALID-REC.
    READ REFER-FILE INTO WS-REFER-RECT AT END
      MOVE 1 TO EOF-REFER-SW
      GO TO GET-NEXT-EXIT.
    IF RR2-TEXT  = '1PANSOPHIC'
      MOVE 0 TO WS-NAME-FOUND-SW
              VALID-REC-SW
      PERFORM GET-FIRST-VALID-REC THRU GET-FIRST-EXIT UNTIL
        VALID-REC-SW = 1 OR EOF-REFER
      GO TO GET-NEXT-EXIT.
    MOVE 1 TO VALID-REC-SW.

GET-NEXT-EXIT.   EXIT.

Z100-DISPLAY-STD-MSGS.
    DISPLAY '===================================================='
    DISPLAY 'THIS PROGRAM HAS BEEN TERMINATED BY CAUSING AN'
    DISPLAY 'USER ABEND. PLEASE TAKE THIS OUTPUT AND ANY OTHER '
    DISPLAY 'DOCUMENTS TO MR. BARRY NIRMAL IN EDP DEPT. FOR '
    DISPLAY 'PROBLEM RESOLUTION. THANK YOU VERY MUCH'
    DISPLAY '===================================================='.
```

Figure 7.3. Source code of program UTIL01 executed in CLIST of Figure 7.4 and job of Figure 7.2 (concluded).

TEST and ENABLED. After the job in Figure 7.2 has ended, the source modules will have been transferred from the test Panvalet library to the production Panvalet library; their status in the Panvalet production library will have become PRODUCTION and ENABLED; and the modules that were migrated will have been deleted from the test Panvalet library. The migrated modules in the production library will carry the same user code and security level which they had prior to the migration process. Of course, if the library codes of the test and production libraries are different, the access codes of the migrated modules will be different on production library from those on the test library prior to the migration process.

The job in Figure 7.2 has been set up in such a manner that if no step abends, the job was completely successful. This is accomplished by executing program UTIL01 with a parameter of 'ABEND$' after STEP01, STEP03, and so on until STEP21. If you study the COBOL program in Figure 7.3, you will conclude that when this program is executed with parameter 'ABEND$', it calls program ABORT after moving -100 in field ABORT-CODE. The sole purpose of ABORT is to cause an user abend. Now if STEP01 in Figure 7.2 ended successfully, i.e., it executed with condition code of zero, then STEP02 would be bypassed; otherwise, STEP02 would execute which would mean that UTIL01 would abend with user abend code of 100. This will mean that all succeeding steps of the job would be bypassed. This is a very useful technique of ensuring that if a job did not abend, the job was completely successful. This way the user needs only to check whether the job abended or not; he need not check each and every step in the job output, find out the condition code of each step, and try to make sense whether or not that condition code is indicative of an error condition. Once in a long time, if this job abends in a particular step, the systems analyst can fix the cause of the problem and rerun the job from the step that failed by specifying RESTART=STEPxx on the job card where STEPxx is the step that failed. Alternatively, he can fix the files updated by the failing job and reexecute the CLIST in Figure 7.1, causing the job to be submitted again.

In this context, note that the Panvalet production library has been allocated by using Panvalet program PAN#4 with the following parameters under DDname SYSIN:

```
++CLEAR RECORDS=16
++SUPPRESS ++RENAME
++SUPPRESS ++USER
++SUPPRESS DISABLE
++SUPPRESS INACTIVE
```

and the Panvalet test library has been allocated by using Panvalet program PAN#4 with the following parameters under DDname SYSIN:

```
++CLEAR RECORDS=16
```

You must understand how program UTIL01 given in Figure 7.3 works in order to understand how the job in Figure 7.2 works. You must also refer to Panvalet manuals that describe the philosophy of Panvalet security and the working of programs PAN#1 and PAN#2 while trying to understand the program in Figure 7.3 and the job in Figure 7.2. You also must have a good knowledge of the COBOL language in order to understand the program in Figure 7.3.

There is no need to completely explain the working of the program in Figure 7.3, because it is self-documenting. Note: The program has been written assuming that the Panvalet installation code is 1234, the library code of SYS3.PANTEST.SOURCE is 90, and the library code of SYS3.PANPROD.SOURCE is 500. You can easily change this program if your installation code or the library codes of your test and production Panvalet libraries are different from these values. Another point is that, when executing the migration CLIST, if a source module name is entered that is not present in the test library, STEP09 of the job would abend with user abend code of 400. This way the person performing the migration would be informed that he entered a wrong source module name. He can then re-execute the CLIST and again enter all the module names because no source module would have been migrated yet. However, if a source module entered is present in the test Panvalet library but not in the production library, this would not cause any error. In this case, STEP11 would end with non-zero condition code because Panvalet would try to delete a module from the production library that is not present there. However, STEP12 would still be bypassed because the condition code of STEP11 would still be less than or equal to 8. In fact, this is the only situation in which any step of this job would end in a non-zero condition code.

The program in Figure 7.3 has been tested to work with the listing of members in a Panvalet library created by running PAN#2 of Panvalet Release 12.0B. If a future release of this software creates the printout in a slightly different format, slight modification of the program in Figure 7.3 will be necessary to make it work.

A CLIST TO COPY ONE OR MORE MEMBERS FROM A PRODUCTION PANVALET LIBRARY TO A TEST PANVALET LIBRARY

Figure 7.4 is a CLIST that can be used to copy one or more members from a production Panvalet library to a test Panvalet library. This CLIST can be used by all members of a team, be it CICS support team or an application development and support team, for copying members into the test library. The production library has its members in PROD status which cannot be modified. This is correct for soft-

```
Line   CLIST Statement
Number
1      PROC 0
2      CONTROL NOMSG NOLIST
3      CLEAR
4      ***********************************************************************
5      *            THE GREAT LAKES ELECTRONICS COMPANY - EDP DEPT
6      *            FACILITY TO COPY ONE OR MORE MEMBERS FROM
7      *                        CICSPROD.PANLIB
8      *                            TO
9      *                        CICSTEST.PANLIB
10     *
11     *     CURRENT DATE: &SYSDATE        CURRENT TIME:  &SYSTIME
12     ***********************************************************************
13     WRITE
14     WRITE WOULD YOU PLEASE WAIT WHILE I DO SOME PRELIMINARY WORK......
15     FREE F(TESTFILE PRODFILE BOTHFILE SYSOUT SYSPRINT SYSDBOUT SYSUDUMP)
16     FREE F(INPUT1)
17     DELETE '&SYSUID..PANTEST.TEMPFILE'
18     DELETE '&SYSUID..PANPROD.TEMPFILE'
19     DELETE '&SYSUID..PANBOTH.TEMPFILE'
20     ALLOC F(TESTFILE) DA('&SYSUID..PANTEST.TEMPFILE') NEW TRACKS +
21       SPACE(1 1) LRECL(80) BLKSIZE(3120) RECFM(F B)
22     ALLOC F(PRODFILE) DA('&SYSUID..PANPROD.TEMPFILE') NEW TRACKS +
23       SPACE(1 1) LRECL(80) BLKSIZE(3120) RECFM(F B)
24     ALLOC F(BOTHFILE) DA('&SYSUID..PANBOTH.TEMPFILE') NEW TRACKS +
25       SPACE(1 1) LRECL(80) BLKSIZE(3120) RECFM(F B)
26     ALLOC F(SYSPRINT) SYSOUT(Q)
27     ALLOC F(SYSOUT)    SYSOUT(Q)
28     ALLOC F(SYSDBOUT) SYSOUT(Q)
29     ALLOC F(SYSUDUMP) SYSOUT(Q)
30     CALL 'SYS3.PAN.LOAD(UTIL01)' 'CPTOCT'
31     DELETE '&SYSUID..PAN.PARMA'
32     ALLOC F(INPUT1) DA('&SYSUID..PAN.PARMA') NEW TRACKS SPACE(1 1) +
33       LRECL(80) BLKSIZE(3120) RECFM(F B)
34     OPENFILE INPUT1 OUTPUT
35     WRITE =================================================================
36     WRITE PLEASE ENTER NAMES OF MODULES YOU WANT COPIED FROM CICS PRODUCTION
37     WRITE LIBRARY TO CICS TEST LIBRARY. THE NAMES ENTERED MUST BE IN
38     WRITE ASCENDING SEQUENCE. NOT DOING SO WILL MEAN THAT ALL MEMBERS
39     WRITE STARTING WITH THE MEMBER WHICH IS OUT OF SEQUENCE WILL NOT
40     WRITE GET COPIED. ALSO NOTE THAT IF A MEMBER IS ALREADY PRESENT IN
41     WRITE TEST LIBRARY, IT WILL NOT GET COPIED.
42     WRITE =================================================================
43     ASKUSER: +
44       WRITENR ENTER NAME OF MEMBER ($$ TO INDICATE NO MORE) ====>>>
45       READ &MODULE
46       IF &MODULE = $$ THEN GOTO SUBJOB
47       SET &INPUT1 = &STR(++TRANSFER &MODULE)
48       PUTFILE INPUT1
49       GOTO ASKUSER
```

Figure 7.4.   A CLIST to copy members from a production Panvalet library to a test Panvalet library.

```
50      SUBJOB: +
51        WRITE NOW COPYING SOURCE MODULE....
52        CLOSFILE INPUT1
53        FREE F(SYSIN INPUT1 PANDD1 PANDD2 PANDD3)
54        ALLOC F(PANDD1) DA('CICSPROD.PANLIB') SHR
55        ALLOC F(PANDD2) DA('CICSTEST.PANLIB') SHR
56        ALLOC F(PANDD3) DUMMY
57        ALLOC F(SYSIN) DA('&SYSUID..PANBOTH.TEMPFILE' +
58                          '&SYSUID..PAN.PARMA') SHR
59        CALL 'SYS3.PAN.LOAD(PAN#2)'
60        IF &LASTCC > 0 THEN DO
61          WRITE
62          WRITE THERE HAS BEEN A PROBLEM WHILE COPYING MEMBERS.
63          WRITE ONE OR MORE MEMBERS MAY NOT HAVE BEEN COPIED.
64          WRITE PLS CHECK JOB OUTPUT UNDER USERID: &SYSUID (SYSOUT CLASS=Q)
65          WRITE IF YOU NEED ASSISTANCE, CONTACT YOUR GOOD OLD FRIEND
66          WRITE MR. BARRY K. NIRMAL IN THE EDP DEPARTMENT
67        END
68        ELSE DO
69          WRITE REQUESTED PANVALET MEMBERS HAVE BEEN SUCCESSFULLY COPIED
70          WRITE PLEASE WAIT A FEW SECONDS .....
71        END
72        DELETE '&SYSUID..PANTEST.TEMPFILE'
73        DELETE '&SYSUID..PANPROD.TEMPFILE'
74        DELETE '&SYSUID..PANBOTH.TEMPFILE'
75        DELETE '&SYSUID..PAN.PARMA'
76        FREE F(SYSOUT SYSPRINT PANDD1 PANDD2 PANDD3 SYSIN)
77        FREE F(SYSDBOUT SYSUDUMP)
78        EXIT
```

Figure 7.4.   A CLIST to copy members from a production Panvalet library to a test Panvalet library (continued).

ware security and management. So, if a team member wants to modify a source, he can use this CLIST to copy it from the production library into the test library. When he has modified the source and tested it, he then asks the Project Leader of the team to have it migrated from the test library to the production library. The person performing the migration uses the CLIST shown in Figure 7.1 for carrying out the migration process.

This CLIST also uses the program in Figure 7.3. However, this CLIST has been set up to copy members from CICSPROD.PANLIB to CICSTEST.PANLIB which, according to the program in Figure 7.3, are assumed to have identical library codes of 23145. This has been done to demonstrate that the same COBOL program shown in Figure 7.3 can be used to support two sets of Panvalet libraries, which are:

```
- CICSTEST.PANLIB  AND  CICSPROD.PANLIB
- SYS3.PANTEST.SOURCE  AND  SYS3.PANPROD.SOURCE
```

Now let us see how this CLIST works. On lines 17 thru 19, three datasets under the user's TSO ID are deleted. Normally these datasets would not exist and these deletions would fail. But, just in case the last execution of this CLIST ended abnormally and these datasets did not get deleted, it is a good idea to delete them so that the allocations on lines 20 thru 25 do not fail. Next, on lines 20 thru 25, these three datasets are allocated. On line 30 program UTIL01 is called. This program, because of the parameter (CPTOCT) passed to it, writes records into files allocated under DDnames TESTFILE, PRODFILE and BOTHFILE. On line 31 one dataset under user's TSO ID is deleted for the same reason described above. This is followed by its allocation on line 32. On lines 44 and 45, the user is prompted to enter the name of the source module he wants to copy. If he enters $$ as the name, control flows to line 50, otherwise, on line 48, one record (containing ++TRANSFER module-name) is written to the file under DDname INPUT1. So, if the user entered five names, five records would be written to the file with DDname INPUT1. On line 52, this file is closed. This is followed by some more dataset allocations required by Panvalet program PAN#2. Finally, on line 59, program PAN#2 is called. This program does the copying of members from the dataset allocated under DDname PANDD1 to the dataset allocated under DDname PANDD2. If there was some problem in copying, PAN#2 would return a non-zero condition code. This is why on line 60 we check the condition code returned by program PAN#2 and, if it is not zero, we write a number of lines of messages on lines 62 thru 66, otherwise we write successful completion message on lines 69 and 70. Finally the datasets allocated under user's TSO ID are deleted on lines 72 thru 75. Next a number of DDnames are freed and the CLIST is terminated by executing the EXIT statement on line 78.

A CLIST TO CHANGE ALL OCCURRENCES OF ONE STRING TO ANOTHER STRING IN A DATASET (SEQUENTIAL OR PARTITIONED)

Figure 7.5 is a CLIST that can be used to change all occurrences of one string to another in a sequential or partitioned dataset. Take a few minutes to study this CLIST. You will notice that the old string cannot have a null value whereas the new string can have a null value. When the new string has a null value, this amounts to deleting all occurrences of the old string from the dataset. The following points are worth noting about this CLIST:

1. When the dataset being edited does not have proper sequence numbers (e.g., the dataset is not of TEXT type, has record format of fixed blocked with logical record length of 80, and positions 73-80 in each record do not have proper sequence number.), when the EDIT command on line 96 or 139 is executed, the system would inform the user that the dataset is not line-numbered. In this case, positions 73-80 of each record would participate in the change process. This is to say that suppose that an old string of 4 bytes is replaced by a new string of 5 bytes, and position 72 of a record contains X, then X would be moved to position 73. However, if the dataset has proper sequence number in positions 73-80 of each record, then letter X in position 72 of that record would be truncated, and the system would display the following message to the user:

   ```
   LINE TRUNCATED+
   ```

```
Line   Statement
Number
1      PROC 0
2      CONTROL LIST MSG END(ENDX) NOFLUSH
3      /*-----------------------------------------------------------------*/
4      /* THIS CLIST WILL CHANGE ALL OCCURRENCES OF ONE STRING TO ANOTHER IN */
5      /* A SEQUENTIAL OR PARTITIONED DATA SET.                           */
6      /* THE OLD STRING, NEW STRING AS WELL AS DATA SET NAME AND PDS MEMBER */
7      /* NAMES ARE OBTAINED BY PROMPTING THE USER.                       */
8      /* DATA SET MAY OR MAY NOT HAVE PROPER SEQUENCE NUMBER IN RECORDS.  */
9      /*-----------------------------------------------------------------*/
10     SET &BLANKS = &STR(                                           )
11     SET &S5     = &SUBSTR(1:5,&BLANKS)
12     SET &S10    = &SUBSTR(1:10,&BLANKS)
13
14     CLEAR
15     PROMPT1: WRITENR ENTER OLD STRING (NULL NOT ALLOWED) ===>>
16     READ &OLDSTR
17     IF &STR(&OLDSTR)  =  &STR() THEN GOTO PROMPT1
18     PROMPT2: WRITENR ENTER NEW STRING (NULL ALLOWED) ===>>
19     READ &NEWSTR
20     IF &LENGTH(&STR(&NEWSTR))  GT &LENGTH(&STR(OLDSTR))  THEN +
21       DO
22         WRITE NEW STRING IS LONGER THAN OLD STRING.
23         WRITE THIS MAY CAUSE TRUNCATION ON SOME LINES IN DATA SET.
24         WRITE HAVING WARNED YOU, THIS CLIST IS PROCEEDING WITH ITS JOB.
25       ENDX
26     WRITE NOTE, ALL OCCURRENCES OF '&OLDSTR' WILL BE CHANGED TO '&NEWSTR'
27
28     /*-----------------------------------------------------------------*/
29     /* THIS ERROR ROUTINE IS INVOKED WHEN A CLIST ERROR OCCURS. THE    */
30     /* ERROR CAN BE CAUSED WHILE EXECUTING THE CHANGE SUBCOMMAND WHEN  */
31     /* THE OLD STRING IS NOT PRESENT IN THE DATA SET. IT CAN ALSO OCCUR */
32     /* WHEN ATTEMPTING TO ALLOCATE A DATA SET THAT DOES NOT EXIST.     */
33     /*-----------------------------------------------------------------*/
34     ERROR DO
35       SET &RETCODE = &LASTCC
36       IF &SYSPCMD = EDIT AND +
37          &SYSSCMD = CHANGE THEN DO        /* OLD STRING NOT FOUND */
38            SET &ERRPCMD = &SYSPCMD
39            SET &ERRSCMD = &SYSSCMD
40            WRITE
41            WRITE STRING '&OLDSTR' NOT FOUND IN '&BKNDSN' OR
42            WRITE AN ERROR OCCURRED WHEN EXECUTING CHANGE SUBCOMMAND
43            WRITE NOTE, THIS DATA SET OR PDS MEMBER WILL NOT BE CHANGED.
44            RETURN
45          ENDX
46       /*-----------------------------------------
47       /* AN ERROR HAS OCCURRED IN A SITUATION OTHER THAN EXECUTING CHANGE
48       /* SUBCOMMAND OF EDIT COMMAND. TERMINATE CLIST EXECUTION.
49       /*-----------------------------------------
50       WRITE
51       WRITE ERROR ROUTINE HAS BEEN INVOKED.
52       WRITE PRIMARY COMMAND =   &SYSPCMD
53       WRITE SECONDARY COMMAND = &SYSSCMD
54       WRITE RETURN CODE       = &RETCODE
```

Figure 7.5. A CLIST to change all occurences of one string to another in a sequential or partitioned dataset.

```
55       WRITE
56       WRITE CLIST PROCESSING IS BEING ABNORMALLY TERMINATED.
57       EXIT
58     ENDX
59     /*------- END OF ERROR ROUTINE -----------------*/
60     /*---------------------------------------------*/
61     /*    GET DATA SET NAME NOW               */
62     /*---------------------------------------------*/
63
64     GETDSN: +
65     WRITE &S05 ENTER A FULLY-QUALIFIED DATA SET NAME (NO QUOTES PLS. )
66     WRITE &S05                     OR
67     WRITE &S05 ENTER A QUESTION MARK (?) TO LIST ALL YOUR DATA SET NAMES
68     WRITE &S05                     OR
69     WRITE &S05 SIMPLY PRESS THE ENTER KEY TO TERMINATE PROCESSING.
70     WRITE
71     WRITENR DSN ===>>
72     READ &DSN
73     WRITE
74
75     IF &DSN = THEN GOTO GETOUT
76     IF &DSN = ? THEN DO
77       LISTCAT
78       WRITE ***
79       READ
80       GOTO GETDSN
81     ENDX
82     LISTDS '&DSN'
83     GETTYPE: +
84       WRITENR IS THIS DATA SET SEQUENTIAL (PS) OR PARTITIONED (PO) ??
85       READ &DSTYPE
86       IF &DSTYPE = PS THEN GOTO SEQDS
87       IF &DSTYPE = PO THEN GOTO PDS
88       WRITE INVALID DATA SET TYPE ENTERED
89       GOTO GETTYPE
90
91     /*----DATA SET IS SEQUENTIAL ------------------*/
92     SEQDS: +
93       SET &ERRPCMD =
94       SET &ERRSCMD =
95       SET &BKNDSN = &DSN
96       EDIT '&DSN' DATA
97       CHANGE * 999999 /&OLDSTR/&NEWSTR/ ALL
98       IF &ERRPCMD = EDIT AND +
99         &ERRSCMD = CHANGE THEN DO
100           END NOSAVE
101           GOTO GETDSN
102       ENDX
103       END SAVE
104       WRITE
105       WRITE DATA SET '&DSN' HAS BEEN SUCCESSFULLY CHANGED
106       WRITE ***
107       READ
108       GOTO GETDSN
109
```

Figure 7.5.   A CLIST to change all occurences of one string to another in a sequential or partitioned dataset (continued).

```
110       /*————-DATA SET IS PARTITIONED ——————————*/
111       PDS: +
112         WRITE WARNING: LOAD MODULE SHOULD NOT BE CHANGED USING THIS CLIST
113         WRITE
114         WRITE IS '&DSN' A LOAD LIBRARY (Y OR NULL) ??
115         READ &ANS
116         IF &SUBSTR(1:1,&ANS) = Y THEN GOTO GETDSN
117       GETMEM: +
118         WRITE
119         WRITE &S10 ENTER A MEMBER NAME
120         WRITE &S10        OR
121         WRITE &S10 ENTER A QUESTION MARK (?) TO LIST ALL MEMBERS
122         WRITE &S10        OR
123         WRITE &S10 JUST PRESS ENTER KEY TO END PROCESSING OF THIS PDS
124         WRITE
125         WRITENR MEMBER NAME PLEASE ===>>
126         READ &MEM
127
128         IF &MEM =  THEN GOTO ENDPDS
129         SET &BKNDSN = &DSN(&MEM)
130         IF &MEM = ? THEN DO
131           LISTDS '&DSN' MEM
132           WRITE ***
133           READ
134           GOTO PDS
135         ENDX
136
137         SET &ERRPCMD =
138         SET &ERRSCMD =
139         EDIT '&DSN(&MEM)' DATA
140         CHANGE * 999999 /&OLDSTR/&NEWSTR/ ALL
141         IF &ERRPCMD = EDIT AND +
142            &ERRSCMD = CHANGE THEN DO      /* STRING NOT FOUND */
143              END NOSAVE
144              GOTO GETMEM
145         ENDX
146         END SAVE
147         WRITE MEMBER '&MEM' OF PDS '&DSN' HAS BEEN SUCCESSFULLY CHANGED.
148         GOTO GETMEM
149
150       /*————-END OF PDS ————————————-*/
151       ENDPDS: +
152         WRITE PROCESSING COMPLETE FOR LIBRARY '&DSN'
153         WRITENR DO YOU WISH TO COMPRESS THIS PDS (Y OR NULL) ??
154         READ &ANS
155         IF &SUBSTR(1:1,&ANS) = Y THEN DO
156           COMPRESS '&DSN'
157           WRITE ***
158           READ
159         ENDX
160         GOTO GETDSN
161       /*————-END OF CLIST PROCESSING ——————————-*/
162       GETOUT: EXIT
```

Figure 7.5.   A CLIST to change all occurences of one string to another in a sequential or partitioned dataset (continued).

This message would be displayed for each line where truncation has occurred.

2. As stated in Appendix A, the CHANGE subcommand does not work across line boundary, except when the dataset being edited is of TEXT type and the EDIT command executes with the NONUM option in effect.

3. Suppose you have a dataset with record length of 80 bytes and it contains Assembler macros. Let us suppose that this dataset has the following record:

```
DISP=SHR,                                             X
```

Note that this record has X in position 72 which is a continuation character in the Assembly language. When you edit this dataset through ISPF and issue the following command:

```
C SHR SHARE
```

the changed line looks like this:

```
DISP=SHARE,                                           X
```

Note that the X in position 72 was not affected by the change because there were enough spaces before the X to make room for the expansion of SHR into SHARE. However, instead of making this change through ISPF, if you made this change using the CLIST of Figure 7.5 (i.e., with old string of SHR and new string of SHARE), the changed line would appear like this:

```
DISP=SHARE,
```

Note that the X in position 72 would be truncated if the dataset had proper sequence number on each record, and it would be moved to position 74 in the other case.

A CLIST TO DEFINE THE BASE OF A GENERATION DATA GROUP (GDG)

Application programmers as well as systems programmers frequently must define the bases of generation data groups (GDGs). Figure 7.6 shows a CLIST that can be used for this purpose. Suppose you want to define GDG base named SYS4.PAN.BKUP, and you want to keep 4 generations of datasets under this GDG. This means that at any time you would be able to access only the following four datasets:

```
Line      CLIST
Number    Statement

1         PROC 2 DSN GENER
2         CONTROL MSG LIST
3         /*==================================================================
4         /* THIS CLIST WILL BUILD AND SUBMIT A JOB TO DEFINE THE BASE OF A
5         /* GENERATION DATA GROUP (GDG). THE PARAMETERS REQUIRED ARE FULLY
6         /* QUALIFIED DATA SET NAME AND NUMBER OF GENERATIONS REQUIRED.
7         WRITE ==============================================================
8         WRITE A BATCH JOB WILL BE SUBMITTED THAT WILL DEFINE THE GDG WITH
9         WRITE GDG BASE NAME= &DSN
10        WRITE NUMBER OF GENERATIONS = &GENER
11        WRITE PLEASE CHECK JOB OUTPUT AND MAKE SURE IT ENDED IN CONDITION
12        WRITE CODE OF ZERO. IF JOB WAS UNSUCCESSFUL, CONTACT YOUR SYSTEMS
13        WRITE SUPPORT SPECIALIST.
14        WRITE ==============================================================
15        SET &BLANKS = &STR(  )
16        SET &CONT = &STR(-)
17        SUBMIT * END(@@)
18        //&SYSUID.G JOB (645110,107W,99,99),'ANY PROGRAMMER',
19        //       CLASS=K,MSGCLASS=X,NOTIFY=&SYSUID
20        //STEP01   EXEC PGM=IDCAMS
21        //SYSPRINT DD SYSOUT=*
22        //SYSIN    DD *
23        &BLANKS   DEFINE GDG   &CONT
24        &BLANKS   (NAME(&DSN)  &CONT
25        &BLANKS   LIMIT(&GENER) &CONT
26        &BLANKS   NOEMPTY &CONT
27        &BLANKS   SCRATCH)
28        @@
```

Figure 7.6.   A CLIST to define the base of a generation data group (GDG).

```
SYS4.PAN.BKUP(0)
SYS4.PAN.BKUP(-1)
SYS4.PAN.BKUP(-2)
SYS4.PAN.BKUP(-3)
```

To define this GDG base you can issue the following command, provided the CLIST in Figure 7.6 is stored as member DEFGDG in a PDS allocated under DDname SYSPROC during your TSO session:

```
TSO %DEFGDG  SYS4.PAN.BKUP   4
```

This CLIST will submit a job whose name will be your TSO user ID followed by letter G. It is this job that will define the GDG base for you. This CLIST issues the SUBMIT command on line 17 which specifies that the job to be submitted is right in the CLIST and follows the SUBMIT command. When a line with string @@ is found, it indicates the end of the job. The line with @@ in positions 1 and 2 is itself not considered part of the job. In this CLIST you will notice that the variable &CONT has been used and it contains a hyphen. This is important because for example if we had used a hyphen at the end of line 23, it would have been considered a continuation character for the CLIST line and not for the command line for program IDCAMS. This is why we have used variable &CONT. For similar reason the use of variable &BLANKS has been made.

A CLIST TO DEFINE A KEY-SEQUENCED VSAM DATASET

Figure 7.7 shows a CLIST which can be of immense help to applications programmers in defining VSAM key-sequenced clusters. Defining VSAM clusters is an intimidating task, especially to new programmers because the DEFINE CLUSTER command has many parameters with many

```
Line       CLIST
Number     Statement

1          PROC 0
2          CONTROL MSG NOLIST NOFLUSH
3          SET &RET = 0
4          WRITE KINDLY ENTER FULLY-QUALIFIED VSAM CLUSTER NAME (NO QUOTES) ===>
5          READ &FILENAME
6          WRITE ENTER ESTIMATED NUMBER OF RECORDS THIS FILE IS TO CONTAIN ====>
7          READ &NUMREC
8          WRITE ENTER SIZE IN BYTES OF RECORDS THIS FILE IS TO CONTAIN =====>
9          READ &RECSIZE
10         WRITE ENTER KEY LENGTH OF PRIMARY KEY ========>>
11         READ &KEYLEN
12         GETKEY: WRITE VSAM KEY STARTS AT WHAT POSITION IN THE RECORD ??
13         READ &STARTPOS
14         IF &STARTPOS = 0 THEN DO
15           WRITE KEY START POSITION CAN NOT BE ZERO, DID YOU MEAN 1 ??
16           GOTO GETKEY
17           END
18         SET &STARTPOS = &STARTPOS - 1
19         WRITE ENTER THE DASD VOLUME WHERE THIS FILE SHOULD BE DEFINED ===>>
20         READ &VOLSER
21         ERROR OFF
22         DELETE '&FILENAME'
23         ERROR DO
24           SET &RET = &LASTCC
25           WRITE NOW IN ERROR ROUTINE
26           WRITE LAST CONDITION CODE WAS &RET
27           WRITE LAST PRIMARY COMMAND WAS &SYSPCMD
28           WRITE LAST SECONDARY COMMAND WAS &SYSSCMD
29           WRITE THIS CLIST ABNORMALLY TERMINATES
30           EXIT
31         END
32         DEFINE CLUSTER +
33           (NAME('&FILENAME')   +
34                 RECORDS(&NUMREC)      +
35                 SHAREOPTIONS(2 3)     +
36                 VOLUME(&VOLSER)       +
37                 RECSZ(&RECSIZE &RECSIZE)  +
38                 CISZ(2048)   +
39                 FREESPACE(10 10)   +
40                 KEYS(&KEYLEN &STARTPOS))   +
41           DATA(NAME('&FILENAME..DATA'))    +
42           INDEX (NAME('&FILENAME..INDEX'))
43         WRITE SIR/MADAM, THE VSAM FILE HAS BEEN SUCCESSFULLY DEFINED.
44         WRITE DO YOU WANT THIS FILE LOADED WITH A RECORD WHOSE KEY
45         WRITE CONSISTS OF ALL 9'S (THIS IS RECOMMENDED) ======>>
46         WRITENR PLEASE REPLY Y/N ===>>>
47         READ &ANS
48         IF &ANS = N THEN GOTO GETOUT
49         ALLOC F(INPUT) DA('SYS3.PARMLIB(VSAM9999)') SHR
50         ALLOC F(OUTPUT) DA('&FILENAME') SHR
51         REPRO INFILE(INPUT) OUTFILE(OUTPUT)
52         WRITE SIR/MADAM, THIS FILE HAS BEEN LOADED WITH ONE RECORD
53         GETOUT:  EXIT
```

Figure 7.7.   A CLIST to define a key-sequenced VSAM cluster and load it with a record containing all 9's.

```
1    PROC 1 DSN CLASS(A) DEST(R00) CC()
2    /* THIS CLIST PRINTS A SEQUENTIAL OR A MEMBER OF A PARTITIONED DATA
3    /* SET AFTER TRANSLATING ALL CHARACTERS OF EACH RECORD FROM
4    /* LOWERCASE TO UPPERCASE. NOTE EVEN CHARACTER IN POSITION 1 IS
5    /* CONVERTED IF IT CONTAINS A LOWERCASE CHARACTER.
6    /*==================================================================
7    CONTROL NOMSG
8    FREE F(INPUT OUTPUT)
9    CONTROL MSG
10   ALLOC F(OUTPUT) SYSOUT(&CLASS) DEST(&DEST) RECFM(F B &CC)
11   ALLOC F(INPUT) DA(&DSN) SHR
12   CALL 'SYS3.LINKLIB(PRINTUP)'
13   WRITE DATA SET &DSN HAS BEEN PRINTED OFF AFTER CONVERTING ALL
14   WRITE LOWERCASE CHARACTERS TO UPPERCASE.
15   FREE F(INPUT OUTPUT)
16   FREE DA('SYS3.LINKLIB')
17   END
```

Figure 7.8.   A CLIST to print a data set after converting lowercase characters to uppercase.

interdependencies and technical considerations to keep in mind. So if an installation sets up a CLIST that can be used by the new programmers to define VSAM clusters, it would help them a great deal. They can use this CLIST to define VSAM files and get down to the task of writing applications programs, whether on-line or batch, that access these files. Once they have gained sufficient experience, they can take a course on VSAM that explains how to choose the parameters on DEFINE CLUSTER for optimum performance.

In this CLIST, the user is prompted to enter values for parameters such as the VSAM file name, record length, etc. If the record key starts at first position in the record, the user must enter 1 and not zero, even though the LISTCAT command displays zero as RKP (Relative Key Position). When RKP displayed is zero, the key is at offset zero from the beginning of the record; that is, it starts at position 1 in the record. If the user entered 1 as the value of STARTPOS, the CLIST subtracts 1 from this value on line 18, resulting in STARTPOS assuming a value of zero. So, on KEYS parameter of the DEFINE CLUSTER, the value used for STARTPOS would be zero, which would be correct.

After obtaining all the necessary parameters from the user, the ERROR option is turned off on line 21 so that if the DELETE command on line 22 ended in error (caused by the dataset being deleted not existing), control would flow to the next sequential statement rather than executing any error routine that might be active. The statements on lines 23 thru 31 set up an ERROR routine which would be invoked if an error occurred in DEFINE CLUSTER, ALLOC or REPRO commands. Next, the DEFINE CLUSTER command is issued. This is an Access Method Services (AMS) command which is executed by the Access Method Services program (IDCAMS) that is used to define and maintain VSAM datasets. The AMS commands are described in full detail in the following IBM publications:

MVS/Extended Architecture Access Method Services Reference
OS/VS2 Access Method Services Reference

If an error occurred in executing the DEFINE CLUSTER command, control would go to line 24 where, after displaying some message lines, the CLIST would be terminated. If the DEFINE CLUSTER ended successfully, the user would be informed of this. (See line 43.) Next, the user is prompted to indicate whether he wants a record with all 9's in the key loaded to this file. This is recommended if the file is to be subsequently opened by a batch program or CICS. The user may not want to load a record with all 9's if he wants to load this file from a sequential file containing one or more records. If the user enters Y in response to the query on lines 44 thru 46, the CLIST attempts to allocate under DDname INPUT the dataset 'SYS3.PARMLIB(VSAM9999)' whose record length must be less than or equal to the record length of the VSAM file and which contains 9's in the key positions of the record. On line 50 the VSAM file is allocated under DDname OUTPUT, which is followed by executing the REPRO command of Access Method Services. This command copies all records (actually only one record in this case) from the file allocated under DDname INPUT to the file allocated under DDname OUTPUT. The CLIST then terminates.

A CLIST TO PRINT A DATASET AFTER CONVERTING LOWERCASE CHARACTERS TO UPPERCASE CHARACTERS ON A PRINTER

Figure 7.8 shows a CLIST that can be used to print a dataset, whether sequential, a member of a PDS on the main printer, or on a remote printer. The dataset can have logical record length of 80 or 133. Each record in the dataset is scanned, including position 1, and all lowercase characters are converted to uppercase characters. The program then writes the converted record to the SYSOUT file with DDname OUTPUT. This CLIST can be very useful in a situation where a dataset contains lowercase characters and the user wants to print it on the main printer, because a remote printer is not available or is available but its ribbon is not very dark. As you know, main printers usually print garbage for lowercase characters.

Now suppose you, with TSO prefix Z2SSA have a dataset called Z2SSA.SDSF.PRINT and its record format is FBA, i.e. the first position of each record contains ANSI carriage control character, and its logical record length is 133. You want the first position to be interpreted as a carriage control character while printing. If you want to print this dataset on the main printer, you can issue the following command, provided the CLIST of Figure 7.8 is stored as member PRINTUP in a PDS allocated under DDname SYSPROC during your TSO session:

```
PRINTUP SDSF.PRINT CC(A)
```

And, if you want to print this dataset on remote printer R20, you may issue the following command assuming that SYSOUT datasets to be printed on remote printers at your installation must have SYSOUT class of Y:

```
PRINTUP SDSF.PRINT CLASS(Y) DEST(R20) CC(A)
```

Now, suppose you have a dataset named Z2SSA.PRINT1 which has record length of 80 and record format of FB (Fixed Blocked). You want to print this dataset on the main printer, but you want that the character in position of each record be treated as data and not as carriage control character. You can then issue the following command:

```
PRINTUP PRINT1
```

And, if you want that the character in position 1 of each record be interpreted as ANSI carriage control character and not as data, you can issue the following command:

```
PRINTUP PRINT1 CC(A)
```

The program used by this CLIST resides in SYS3.LINKLIB as member PRINTUP. Its source code is not shown. The reader is urged to code this program in COBOL or Assembler, preferably in Assembler with the help of a colleague who is good at writing Assembler programs. The program should work as described above. The program should read each record from the input file, convert all characters from lowercase to uppercase characters and then write out the converted record to the output file. Unlike IBM's utility program IEBGENER, this program should not copy record format from the input file to the output file.

Chapter 8
ADVANCED CLIST FACILITIES

HANDLING ONE-DIMENSIONAL ARRAYS

An array is basically an organized collection of data. An array can be one-dimensional, two-dimensional, and so on up to n-dimensional, where n can be an infinite number. For most commercial and business applications though, a three-dimensional array is the most one deals with. Let us suppose that we have 40 employees in our EDP department and we want to store the basic salary of each employee in the form of an array. Then the collection of 40 basic salaries can be considered a one-dimensional array or a vector. Thus vector A is represented by its n components a_1, a_2, . . . a_n. Figure 8.1 shows the values of each elements of the vector consisting of 40 elements, where the value of each element represents an employee's monthly basic salary amount.

Let us suppose that we are to write a CLIST that will store these 40 elements and then display on the terminal the entire array. The CLIST shown in Figure 8.2 does this job. In this CLIST you will notice that on line 12 we are creating by means of concatenation of symbolic variables, &SALARY and &ELEMENT, a third variable name. Since &ELEMENT takes values from 1 thru 40, we are creating 40 new symbolic variables with names &SALARY1, &SALARY2, and so on up to &SALARY40. The value of each

```
Array          Value of Array Element
Element        (Monthly Basic Salary
Number          in U.S. Dollars)

  1                  2500
  2                  3000
 - - - - - - - - - - -
 - - - - - - - - - - -
 40                  1980
```

Figure 8.1.   A one-dimensional array with 40 elements.

of these 40 variables represents the basic salary amount of
that particular employee.

It is very important to note that the statement on line
12 creates 40 new variables which are &SALARY1,
&SALARY2,...&SALARY40. In this statement, the fact that
&SALARY was assigned the value of BERRIE on line 2 is

```
1     CONTROL MAIN LIST MSG END(ENDX)
2     SET &SALARY = BERRIE
3     SET &ELEMENT = 1
4     SET &MAXELE = 40
5     WRITE DEAR USER, YOU WILL NOW BE PROMPTED TO ENTER THE
6     WRITE BASIC SALARY OF &MAXELE EMPLOYEES OF THE EDP DEPT.
7     WRITE =====================================================
8     DO WHILE &ELEMENT LE &MAXELE
9        WRITE ENTER BASIC SALARY FOR EMPLOYEE
10       WRITENR NUMBER  &ELEMENT   (ONLY WHOLE NUMBER PLEASE) ===>
11       READ &DATAIN
12       SET &SALARY&ELEMENT = &DATAIN
13       SET &ELEMENT = &ELEMENT + 1
14    ENDX
15    /* NOW PRINT EACH ELEMENT OF THE ARRAY ON THE TERMINAL */
16    SET &ELEMENT = 1
17    DO WHILE &ELEMENT LE &MAXELE
18       SET &DATAOUT = &EVAL(&&SALARY&ELEMENT)
19       WRITE BASIC SALARY FOR EMPLOYEE # &ELEMENT = &DATAOUT
20       SET &ELEMENT = &ELEMENT + 1
21    ENDX
22    WRITE THIRD ELEMENT OF THE ARRAY HAS THE VALUE:   &SALARY3
23    EXIT
```

Figure 8.2.   A CLIST to read values of an array's elements and then
display them on the terminal.

immaterial, but the value of &ELEMENT is very important in creating new variable names &SALARY1, &SALARY2 and so on.

In this CLIST you will also notice on line 18 the use of the built-in function &EVAL and the use of two ampersands in &&SALARY&ELEMENT. If we had simply used the statement SET &DATAOUT = &SALARY&ELE-MENT, the value of &SALARY would be concatenated with the value of &ELEMENT. Since &SALARY was assigned a value of BERRIE on line 2, this variable when concatenated with the value of &ELEMENT (say 20), would result in &DATAOUT assuming the value of BERRIE20. But this is not what we want. We want &DATAOUT to have the value of &SALARY20, i.e., the value of the 20th element in our array. This necessitates the use of &EVAL(&&SALARY&ELEMENT). According to the rule of symbolic substitution, two ampersands are replaced by a single ampersand. Hence assuming that &ELEMENT has a value of 20, &&SALARY&ELEMENT after symbolic substi-tution becomes &SALARY20. And &EVAL is used to cause evaluation of this variable and the result to be moved to variable &DATAOUT.

It is very important to understand this concept. Supposing that we want to assign to &ITEM5 the value of the fifth element of this array, one of the following state-ments can be used:

```
SET &ITEM5 = &SALARY5
SET &ITEM5 = &EVAL(&SALARY5)
```

The following statements will not work:

```
SET &ITEM = 5
SET &ITEM5 = &SALARY&ITEM
```

Another point to note in the CLIST of Figure 8.2 is that by simply changing one statement located right in the beginning where the value of &MAXELE is set to 40, this CLIST will store all the elements of an array of a larger or smaller size than 40, and it will then print all the elements of that array. This makes the CLIST flexible. In fact, if this CLIST was to be used for handling arrays of varying sizes, it might be even better to prompt the user for the value of the array's size at the beginning, rather than setting it to a fixed value in the CLIST. This would make the CLIST even more flexible by sparing the CLIST user from having to modify it prior to executing it for handling an array of a different size.

HANDLING TWO-DIMENSIONAL ARRAYS

A two-dimensional array is basically a table of information. In mathematical language, it is also called a matrix. The elements of a k by l matrix are represented by the subscript notation:

$$b_{11} \cdots b_{1j} \cdots b_{11}$$

$$b_{21} \cdots b_{2j} \cdots b_{21}$$

$$\cdots \cdots \cdots \cdots$$

$$b_{k1} \cdots b_{kj} \cdots b_{kl}$$

For example, Figure 8.3 shows a 5 by 8 matrix. There are eight columns in this matrix. The first column represents the number of courses taught in the year 1982. The second columns represents the number of courses taught in the year 1983, and so on. Finally, the eighth column represents the total number of courses taught over the years 1982 thru 1988. The first row represents the first teacher named Wilson. The second row stands for the second teacher named Smith, and so on. Finally, the fifth row rep-

```
TEACHER NAME       - - - NUMBER OF COURSES TAUGHT IN THE YEAR - -
                   1982   1983   1984   1985   1986   1987   1988   TOTAL
WILSON              4      3      4      6      8      7      6      38
SMITH               5      5      5      5      5      5      5      35
HATTER              2      3      3      6      2      3      5      24
TIWARY              2      4      3      5      4      5      7      30
MANDELA             4      5      6      6      6      5      6      38
```

Figure 8.3.   A two-dimensional array with 5 rows and 8 columns (5 by 8 matrix).

resents data for the fifth teacher, named Mandela. Normally all elements of a matrix are of the same data type. This makes it easier to load the entire matrix into storage by a high-level language such as COBOL or CLIST. For example, all elements of the matrix in Figure 8.3 are whole numbers.

Suppose we are to write a CLIST that will store the names of the five teachers into an one-dimensional array after reading them from the terminal. It will also store into storage the 5 by 8 matrix. The data for columns 1 thru 7 will be read from the terminal, while the data in the eighth column will be calculated by the CLIST. Such a CLIST is shown in Figure 8.4. In this CLIST the statement on line 12 is not really necessary. It has been written merely to demonstrate that the value of &COUNT is not used on line 20, where new variables &COUNT11982, &COUNT11983, . . . &COUNT51988 are created. You will notice that on line 32, we have again used the built-in function &EVAL just as we used it in Figure 8.2. It should be also noted that the following statement could not be used to replace lines 32 and 33:

```
SET &TOT = &TOT + &EVAL(&&COUNT&TEACHER&YEAR)
```

This is due to the fact that &EVAL must not be written as a part of another expression. The CLIST in Figure 8.4 also illustrates the use of nested DO loops which are essential

```
1        PROC 0
2        CONTROL MAIN MSG LIST END(ENDX)
3        SET &TEACHER = 1
4        /* THE FOLLOWING LOOP WILL READ IN THE NAMES OF FIVE TEACHERS */
5        DO WHILE &TEACHER LE 5
6          WRITE ENTER LAST NAME OF TEACHER # &TEACHER
7          READ &DATAIN
8          SET &NAME&TEACHER = &DATAIN
9          SET &TEACHER = &TEACHER + 1
10       ENDX
11       SET &TEACHER = 1
12       SET &COUNT = XYZ    /* THIS STATEMENT IS NOT REALLY NECESSARY */
13       DO WHILE &TEACHER LE 5
14         SET &YEAR = 1982
15         SET &X = &EVAL(&&NAME&TEACHER)
16         WRITE PLEASE ENTER NUMBER OF COURSES TAUGHT BY TEACHER = &X
17         DO WHILE &YEAR LE 1988
18           WRITENR                    FOR YEAR &YEAR
19           READ &DATAIN
20           SET &COUNT&TEACHER&YEAR = &DATAIN
21           SET &YEAR = &YEAR + 1
22         ENDX
23         SET &TEACHER = &TEACHER + 1
24       ENDX
25       /* NOW CALCULATE TOTAL COURSES TAUGHT FOR 7 YEARS AND STORE THEM  */
26       /* IN THE EIGHTH COLUMN NAMED TOT                                 */
27       SET &TEACHER = 1
28       DO WHILE &TEACHER LE 5
29         SET &TOT = 0
30         SET &YEAR = 1982
31         DO WHILE &YEAR LE 1988
32           SET &COUNT = &EVAL(&&COUNT&TEACHER&YEAR)
33           SET &TOT = &TOT + &COUNT
34           SET &YEAR = &YEAR + 1
35         ENDX
36         SET &COUNT&TEACHER.TOT = &TOT     /* THIS IS THE 8TH COLUMN */
37         SET &X = &EVAL(&&NAME&TEACHER)
38         WRITE TOTAL COURSES TAUGHT BY TEACHER = &X  IS &TOT
39         SET &TEACHER = &TEACHER + 1
40       ENDX
41       EXIT
```

Figure 8.4.   A CLIST to handle the two-dimensional array shown in Figure 8.3.

for handling two-dimensional arrays. Similarly, to handle three-dimensional arrays, we would have to use three nested DO-loops. Three-dimensional arrays can be understood in the following manner. In Figure 8.3 is given a table of 5 rows and 8 columns, where each row represents a teacher and each of the columns 1 thru 7 represents one year and the eighth column represents all the years. If it was decided to keep the following counts of the students for each teacher, for each of the years 1982 thru 1988 as well as for all the years for each teacher:

Number of students enrolled in all the courses taught by the teacher

Number of students who failed any of the courses taught by the teacher

The resulting array would be a three-dimensional array or a 5 x 8 x 2 array. But since three-dimensional arrays are rarely used in non-scientific applications, we will not discuss them here. Having understood the technique of handling two-dimensional arrays, it should not be too difficult to write CLISTs for handling three-dimensional or even ten-dimensional arrays.

PROVIDING MULTIPLE CLIST ENTRY POINTS

How multiple CLIST entry points are provided is best explained by example. Let us suppose we have a CLIST called ALLOCALL which is stored in SYS3.CLIST. This CLIST frees a number of DDnames and then reallocates them. This CLIST is automatically executed when any programmer/analyst belonging to the Applications Division of the EDP Department logs on to TSO. The Applications Division consists of the Engineering Group and the Commercial Group. The requirement is that when users belonging to the Engineering Group execute this CLIST, execution should start with label ENG01 and when users belonging to the Commercial Group execute this CLIST, execution should start with the label COMM01. This is a situation where the CLIST has two entry points and execution starts with the one or the other. This problem can be solved in one of two ways.

Providing Multiple CLIST Entry Points Through Alias Assignment

In this method, the CLIST ALLOCALL has to be rewritten as shown in Figure 8.5. In this figure, we are using control variable &SYSICMD. This control variable provides the name by which the CLIST was implicitly executed. Let us now assign two alias names, ALLOCENG and ALLOCOMM, to member ALLOCALL in SYS3.CLIST. This can be done by executing the following TSO commands:

```
RENAME 'SYS3.CLIST(ALLOCALL)' (ALLOCENG) ALIAS
RENAME 'SYS3.CLIST(ALLOCALL)' (ALLOCOMM) ALIAS
```

These commands create two new alias entries in the directory of the PDS (partitioned dataset) 'SYS3.CLIST'. After these commands have been executed, if you browse this dataset and display the panel with member list, you will find members ALLOCENG and ALLOCOMM with the word ALIAS on the right of members' names. Having assigned two alias names, this CLIST can now be invoked by issuing any one of the following commands at the terminal or in the calling CLIST:

```
CONTROL MSG LIST END(ENDX)
- - - - - -
- - - - - -
IF &SYSICMD = ALLOCENG THEN GOTO ENG01
IF &SYSICMD = ALLOCOMM THEN GOTO COMM01
WRITE CLIST ALLOCALL IS DESIGNED TO BE IMPLICITLY EXECUTED
WRITE USING NAME ALLOCENG OR ALLOCOMM. THIS RULE HAS BEEN
WRITE FOUND TO BE BROKEN. THIS CLIST PREMATURELY ENDS.
EXIT
ENG01: +
- - -
- - -
COMM01: +
- - -
- - -
```

Figure 8.5.   One version of the CLIST ALLOCALL in SYS3.CLIST with two entry points.

```
ALLOCENG or %ALLOCENG
        or
ALLOCOMM or %ALLOCOMM
        or
ALLOCALL or %ALLOCALL
```

When control reaches the CLIST, the value of &SYSICMD is the name by which it was implicitly invoked. As shown in Figure 8.5, if ALLOCENG was used to invoke this CLIST, control would flow to label ENG01, and, if ALLOCOMM was used, control would flow to label COMM01. If ALLOCALL was used to invoke this CLIST, it would display a number of messages on the terminal before abnormally terminating.

   This method of supporting multiple entry points requires that the CLIST be implicitly invoked, and, as was discussed in Chapter 1, to implicitly invoke a CLIST, it must reside in a PDS that is allocated under DDname SYSPROC. If this CLIST was invoked explicitly, for example thru the following command:

```
EXEC 'SYS3.CLIST(ALLOCALL)'
```

the following messages would be displayed at the terminal:

```
CLIST ALLOCALL IS DESIGNED TO BE IMPLICITLY EXECUTED
USING NAME ALLOCENG OR ALLOCOMM. THIS RULE HAS BEEN
FOUND TO BE BROKEN. THIS CLIST PREMATURELY ENDS.
```

Providing Multiple CLIST Entry Points Through CLIST Parameters

Another way of providing multiple entry points is by using positional or keyword parameters which are specified on the PROC statement. Let us consider the CLIST in Figure 8.5. It has been rewritten in Figure 8.6 where one position-

```
PROC 1 ENTRYPT
CONTROL MSG LIST END(ENDX)
- - - - - -
- - - - - -
IF &ENTRYPT = ENG THEN GOTO ENG01
IF &ENTRYPT = COM THEN GOTO COMM01
WRITE THE VALUE OF ENTRYPT PASSED BY CALLER IS &ENTRYPT
WRITE THE VALUE SUPPLIED MUST BE ENG OR COM.
WRITE CLIST ALLOCALL ABNORMALLY TERMINATES.
EXIT
ENG01: +
- - -
- - -
COMM01: +
- - -
- - -
```

Figure 8.6.   Another version of the CLIST ALLOCALL in SYS3.CLIST with two entry points.

al parameter has been specified. This means that the caller must supply one parameter when executing this CLIST. This CLIST has been designed so that the caller will supply either ENG or COM as the value of positional parameter &ENTRYPT. Any other value would result in an abnormal termination of this CLIST.

The following are examples of valid commands for executing this CLIST, either from TSO, ISPF or from within another CLIST, assuming that SYS3.CLIST is allocated under DDname SYSPROC during the user's session:

```
EXEC 'SYS3.CLIST(ALLOCALL)' 'ENG'
ALLOCALL COM
%ALLOCALL ENG
```

When ENG is supplied as the value of &ENTRYPT, CLIST execution would start from label ENG01, and when COM is supplied as the value of &ENTRYPT, execution would start with label COMM01.

A number of statements belonging to attention and/or error routine may be present in the CLIST of Figure 8.5 and

Figure 8.6 after the CONTROL statement. Care must be taken so that the conditional statements that test for &SYSICMD in Figure 8.5 and &ENTRYPT in Figure 8.6 do not cause bypassing of the error and/or attention routine. Attention and error routines are usually placed at the beginning of a CLIST because they must be passed through in order to be activated. If they are branched around in the course of CLIST execution, they are not activated and, therefore, will not be used in case of an attention interrupt or an error condition arising.

NESTED CLISTs

The concept of nested CLISTs is a very basic and important concept. According to this concept, a CLIST can execute another CLIST in the same manner as a human operator can, i.e., explicitly, implicitly, or in an extended implicit manner, as discussed in Chapter 1. The CLIST that executes another CLIST is termed the calling CLIST, and the executed CLIST is termed a called CLIST. A called CLIST can, in turn, execute another CLIST and so on. The called CLIST should use the EXIT statement to return control to the caller. The CLIST that is at the top of the hierarchy can also use EXIT statement to return to TSO which is supposed to be its caller.

The CLIST which is at the top of the hierarchy, i.e., the one that is executed by the user (i.e., "called" by TSO) is supposed to be the outer-level CLIST and is supposed to be at level 1. The CLIST that it executes is supposed to be nested within it. For example, in Figure 8.7, CLISTA is the outer-level CLIST. It executes CLISTB and CLISTC which are, therefore, nested within it. CLISTB in turn invokes CLISTD and CLISTD invokes CLISTE. CLISTE is, therefore, nested within CLISTD; and CLISTD, within CLISTB. This figure shows three levels of nesting. The following points are worth-noting:

1. Nesting must be orderly. For example, in Figure 8.7, CLISTA invokes CLISTB prior to invoking CLISTC. Then CLISTD and CLISTE must execute before CLISTA can invoke CLISTC. It is also possible for CLISTC to invoke CLISTE, in which case CLISTE would exist both at levels 4 and 3 of the nested hierarchy. This is to say that the same CLIST can be at two or more levels of a nested hierarchy. This is made possible due to the rule that each time a CLIST is executed, a fresh copy of the CLIST is brought into virtual storage.
2. Nested CLISTs in the subcommand environment may contain only subcommands and CLIST statements. They must not contain TSO commands.
3. CONTROL statement options and ATTN exits established within a CLIST are in effect only as long as that CLIST is executing. These options are no longer in effect when that CLIST returns to its caller, or when it calls another CLIST.

You have probably realized that just as you can structure a complex program written in COBOL or PL/I with the main routine and subroutines arranged in a logically functional framework, you can also arrange a number of nested CLISTs to achieve programming objectives. However, it must be remembered that even though a programming problem can be solved thru nested CLISTs, it might be sometimes more appropriate to write a COBOL or a PL/I program instead.

THE GLOBAL STATEMENT

This statement is used to establish variables whose contents are modified and referenced by both a calling CLIST and one or more CLISTs nested within it. The nested CLISTs can be at the same or different levels. Let us illustrate this concept by means of a couple of examples:

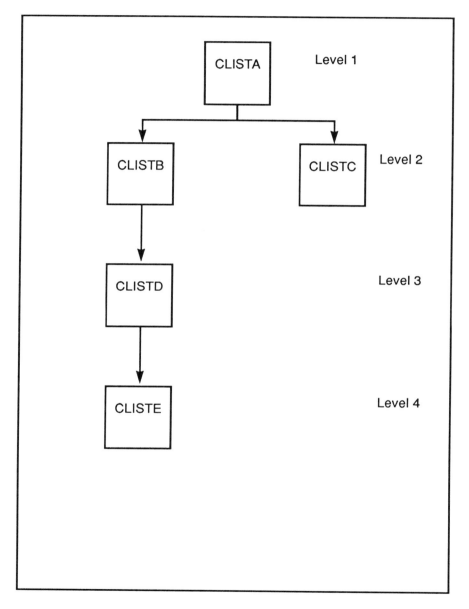

Figure 8.7.   A representation of nested CLISTS.

Example 1. Suppose there is CLIST C1 that invokes CLIST C2 and C3. Let us further suppose that C2 references two variables, V1 and V2 that are also referenced in C1. CLIST C3 references those two variables plus two additional variables, V3 and V4 that are also referenced in C1. In this situation, C1 must have a GLOBAL statement specifying four symbolic variables:

```
GLOBAL V1 V2 V3 V4
```

Since C3 references all the four variables referenced by C1, it must have a GLOBAL statement specifying four variables. For example:

```
GLOBAL V1 V2 V3 V4
```

Since V1 and V2 are the symbolic variables that are referenced both in C2 and C1, CLIST C2 must have a GLOBAL statement as follows:

```
GLOBAL V1 V2
```

The variable names used in the called CLIST may or may not be the same as those in the calling CLIST. However, for the sake of CLIST maintainability and understandability, it is recommended that the names of variables whose contents are modified or referenced by more than one CLIST be the same in all the CLISTs.

Example 2. Suppose that CLIST C1 invokes C2 and C2 in turn invokes C3. C2 uses four variables also referenced in C1. So, both C1 and C2 should have the following GLOBAL statement:

```
GLOBAL V1 V2 V3 V4
```

Now suppose that C3 references only V1 and V3. Then CLIST C3 should have the following statement:

```
GLOBAL V1 V2 V3
```

Note: Even though C3 does not use V2, it still supplies a name for it on the GLOBAL statement because the variables are position dependent. However, the name for the second variable on the GLOBAL statement in C3 can be a "dummy" name because it is merely a place holder. For example:

```
GLOBAL V1 DUMMY V3
```

THE EXIT STATEMENT

There are three ways for a CLIST to terminate and return to the caller, which can be another CLIST or TSO:

- Use the EXIT statement.
- Do not have EXIT statement or END command. The last line in the CLIST can be an executable statement, such as WRITE or SET. After this line is executed control is automatically transferred to TSO or to the calling CLIST.
- Use the END command of TSO

Of these three options, the use of EXIT statement is the most desirable method of terminating a CLIST and returning control to the caller.

```
[label:]     EXIT        [CODE(expression)]
                              [QUIT]
```

When no operands are present on the EXIT statement, control returns to the caller with &LASTCC containing the return code of the last command, subcommand or CLIST statement executed prior to the EXIT. On the EXIT statement one can indicate that a specific return code be sent to the caller. This is done by coding:

```
EXIT CODE(expression)
```

where 'expression' can be any simple expression whose result is numeric. TSO evaluates the expression and puts the result into system control variable &LASTCC. The calling CLIST can then interrogate &LASTCC. In this way, lower-level CLISTs can send back indications of errors or certain conditions encountered during execution. The following are valid examples of EXIT statements:

```
1.    EXIT CODE(10)
2.    SET &LASTCC = 2
      EXIT
3.    SET &RETCODE = 13
      EXIT CODE(&RETCODE)
4.    SET &RET = 14
      EXIT CODE(&RET-7)
```

Additionally, one can also include the QUIT operand on the EXIT statement. When QUIT is present, rather than returning to the caller, control goes up the hierarchy of nested CLISTs until a CLIST is found that has CONTROL statement with the MAIN or NOFLUSH option in effect, which means that it is protected from stack flushing. If no CLIST in the hierarchy has either MAIN or NOFLUSH option in effect, control flows to TSO which would flush all current CLISTs from the stack. TSO would then display the READY message in the native TSO mode or the three asterisks, if the CLIST was executed from within ISPF. The following are valid examples of specifying the QUIT operand:

```
1.    EXIT QUIT
2.    EXIT CODE(expression) QUIT
```

EXERCISES

1. Write a CLIST that will read a sequential file containing n records where n is 1 or greater. Each record has the following layout:

Positions	Data Type	Data Description
1 - 6	Integer Numeric	Employee Number
7 - 7	Alphanumeric	Not Used
8 - 9	Numeric	Grade Code
10 - 39	Aphanumeric	Employee Name

The CLIST will store the data in an array. When all records from the file have been stored, it will process the array and will display on the terminal a line containing employee number, employee name and grade code for each record where the grade code is greater than 20. At the end it will display a line with the text *** END OF FILE REACHED **. Use the file I/O statements taught in Chapter 5 and the array concepts taught in this chapter to write this CLIST.

2. Write a CLIST called KOMPRESS that will compress-in-place a partitioned dataset. Supposing that this CLIST is stored as member KOMPRESS in a PDS allocated under DDname SYSPROC, the user can issue the following command to compress dataset 'CICS.PDS.CNTL':

```
%KOMPRESS CICS.PDS.CNTL
```

This CLIST is to be a driver of three other CLISTs, as shown in Figure 8.8. The CLIST ALLOCF will allocate the PDS to DDname INFILE. It will also allocate file SYSIN and will write the following single record into this file:

```
COPY INDD=INFILE,OUTDD=INFILE
```

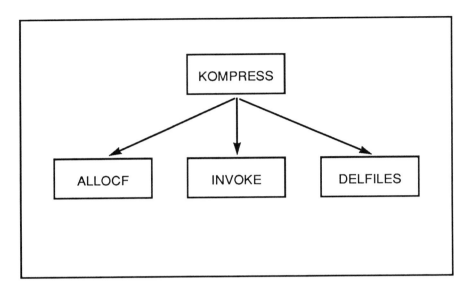

Figure 8.8.   KOMPRESS CLIST to compress-in-place any specified partitioned dataset.

This CLIST will also allocate files SYSPRINT, SYSUT3, and SYSUT4. SYSPRINT should be allocated to the terminal, whereas SYSUT3 and SYSUT4 are work files of about 15 tracks each.

The CLIST INVOKE will assume that all files allocations have been done, and it will CALL program IEBCOPY which is usually stored in SYS1.LINKLIB. The last CLIST called by KOMPRESS is DELFILES which deletes the work files allocated previously and frees up files, reallocating SYSIN to the terminal.

Before terminating, KOMPRESS should write the following message to the terminal:

```
PDS pds-name SUCCESSFULLY COMPRESSED
```

where pds-name is to be replaced by the name of the PDS supplied by the user.

Appendix A
COMMONLY USED TSO
COMMANDS

In this appendix, we will discuss those TSO commands which are most commonly used in command procedures (CLISTs). It has been mentioned that a command procedure (CLIST) consists of TSO commands, subcommands, and CLIST statements which have been arranged in an executable sequence. When CLISTs were first developed by IBM, they consisted entirely of TSO commands and subcommands; that is why the name is Command Procedure or Command List (CLIST). As time passed, a number of statements were made available for use while writing command procedures. These statements such as GOTO, IF-THEN-ELSE sequence, etc. allow command procedures to serve as a program written in a high level language. So, the CLIST language today is a highly evolved language, allowing us to write simple as well as highly complex and powerful CLISTs.

TSO COMMANDS COMMONLY USED IN CLISTs

Since TSO commands are frequently used in command procedures, let us now discuss the most commonly-used commands one by one. In the command descriptions that follow, an attempt will be made to keep the discussions at a general level, discussing only those aspects of the commands that are most frequently encountered in day-to-day work. It should be remembered that TSO commands can be issued from within a CLIST, from native mode of TSO, from TSO within ISPF, or from any of the ISPF panels. Of course, if you want to issue a TSO command from an ISPF panel, you have to precede the actual command with the word TSO and type the entire command on the command line which is at the top of the panel.

The ALLOCATE Command

The ALLOCATE command or the ALLOCATE subcommand of EDIT is used for the following purposes:

* To allocate an existing dataset before invoking a program written by you, or a program supplied by IBM such as a compiler, the linkage editor or the loader, etc.
* To create a new dataset that has unique characteristics. While creating a new dataset, you can allocate it under a specific DDname so that a program which will be called can access it or you can omit the DDname.
* Rather than allocating a dataset using ISPF option 3.2 or thru a batch job using program IEFBR14, you can use the ALLOC command to allocate it. Suppose you want to allocate 30 datasets. Rather than allocating them one by one, you can create a CLIST with 30 allocate commands and then execute that CLIST, or you can set up a batch job and use IEFBR14 with 30 DD statements and then submit that job for execution.

Note: The ALLOCATE command has many parameters and there are many interdependencies of the various parameters. Below we will use the simplified formats of this command which have only the commonly used parameters. This will be done for the sake of simplicity and practicality and to avoid this topic from getting overly complex. For a detailed discussion of this and other commands, refer to the following manual or an equivalent one applicable to your MVS environment:

MVS/Extended Architecture TSO Extensions TSO Command Language Reference

ALLOCATING AN EXISTING DATASET UNDER A SPECIFIC DDNAME

Before invoking a program written by you or an operating system program such as a compiler or the linkage editor, you must allocate certain datasets under specific DDnames. The DDnames are dependent on the program that is to be called, but the dataset name is not dictated by the program. When invoking such a program through MVS JCL, these datasets are allocated using DD (data definition) statements of JCL. The ALLOCATE command used for allocating an existing dataset has the following simplified format:

```
{ ALLOC    } [ FILE(ddname)    ] {{ DATASET(dsname-list or *) }}
{ ALLOCATE }  [ DDNAME(ddname) ] {{ DSNAME(dsname-list or *)  }}
                                  {{ DUMMY                     }}
              [ OLD            ]
              | SHR            |
              | MOD            |
              [ SYSOUT(class)  ]
```

Note: The FILE (or DDNAME) parameter can precede the DATASET (or DSNAME or DUMMY) parameter or follow it. FILE can be abbreviated as F or FI and DATASET can be abbreviated as DA.

DATASET(dsname-list or *) or DSNAME(dsname-list or*). This specifies the name(s) of the dataset(s) to be allocated. Multiple non-VSAM dataset can be concatenated by specifying a list of datasets. It is recommended that you use the fully-qualified dataset names enclosed within quotes, even though the system only requires that the right-most qualifier must be present. Also a member of a partitioned dataset may be specified by enclosing the member name within parentheses.

If you specify an asterisk (*) in the place of dataset name, this indicates that you want this DDname to be assigned to your terminal so that any input or output data will come from or go to your terminal. In case you use an asterisk, only the FILE (or DDNAME) parameter should be used along with the DSNAME parameter.

When a SYSOUT dataset is allocated, the dataset name parameter should not be used. This is because the system generates names for SYSOUT datasets. Any dataset name you supply for SYSOUT datasets will be ignored. To allocate a member of a generation data group, specify the fully qualified dataset name, including the generation number. You cannot concurrently allocate datasets that reside on the same physical tape.

The following should be noted when concatenating multiple datasets:

- The datasets specified in the list must be all cataloged. To catalog a dataset, you should use the dataset utility option of ISPF (normally option 3.2) or you can use the CATALOG option of ALLOCATE command at the time of creating the dataset.
- The datasets to be concatenated must be either all sequential or all partitioned. The maximum number of datasets that can be concatenated is 255, which is more than sufficient for normal requirements.

The DUMMY option. This specifies that no physical datasets or devices are to be allocated to this DDname. This option is helpful when, for example, a program writes records to the file allocated under DDname BILLOUT, and, for testing purposes, you do not want to write records to this file. In this case the following ALLOCATE statement can be used:

```
ALLOC F(BILLOUT) DUMMY
```

When DUMMY is specified only the FILE (Or DDNAME) operand should be used. However, when DDname SYSIN or SYSOUT is being dummied out, the system may require that DCB information also be supplied, in which case the USING operand may be used to supply following information: logical record length, blocksize, record format and dataset organization.

FILE(DDname) or DDNAME(DDname). This specifies the DDname to be associated with the dataset. The DDname supplied can not exceed eight characters. This DDname corresponds to the DDname specified on the DD (data definition) statement in the JCL and must match the DDname specified in the data control block (DCB) built in the program to be invoked. For a COBOL program, this name is the external-name used in the ASSIGN TO clause in the INPUT-OUTPUT SECTION. For a PL/I program, this name is the file name in a declare statement which has the form "DCL file-name FILE".

OLD. This indicates that the dataset presently exists and you want exclusive use of it, meaning that while you are allocating it, no other TSO user, job or a started task such as CICS can use this dataset. The dataset must be already cataloged otherwise you must specify the VOLUME parameter. Datasets allocated with OLD are retained when they are freed.

SHR. This indicates that the dataset presently exists and you want shared use of it, meaning that while you are allocating it, other TSO users, jobs or started tasks such as CICS can use this dataset concurrently. The dataset must be already cataloged otherwise you must specify the VOLUME parameter. Datasets allocated with SHR are retained when they are freed.

MOD.   This indicates that you want to append records at the end of the dataset. This is the only option which allows you to retain the records (if any) already present in the file. With all other options records are written starting from the beginning of the dataset which means that records already existing are wiped out when the dataset is closed.

   If the dataset does not exist it will be created provided you specify extra parameters on the ALLOC command (not discussed in detail in this book).

NEW.   This specifies that the dataset (non-VSAM only) does not already exist and that it is to be created. This dataset will be kept and cataloged provided dataset name was specified; otherwise it will be deleted when you FREE it or log off. When you use this operand, you must also specify a number of other operands which are not given here because it is recommended that the NEW operand not be used. Instead, the dataset can be allocated using option 3.2 of ISPF and then you can use the OLD, MOD or SHR operand.

SYSOUT [(class)].   This specifies that this dataset is a system output dataset. The optional class parameter specifies a SYSOUT class. When you use the SYSOUT operand, you can also use the optional operands: DEST (station ID of the remote station receiving output), COPIES (number of copies to be printed) and FCB (form control buffer).

Example 1.

```
ALLOC FILE(TEMPIN) DA(*)
```

This allocates DDname TEMPIN as an input or output file

and associates it with the terminal. To check that this command has worked, issue this command:

```
LISTA STAT H
```

You will see in the system-displayed messages:

```
TERMFILE TEMPIN
```

This message means that DDname TEMPIN is currently allocated to terminal.

Example 2.

```
ALLOC F(OUTFILE1) DA('Z2BKN.OUTFILE1') OLD
```

This allocates the specified dataset to DDname OUTFILE1 for exclusive use. Because the dataset name is enclosed in quotes, the name is the fully-qualified name of the dataset. The dataset is assumed to be cataloged. After this command has executed, if you issue command: LISTA STAT H, you will see something like this:

```
Z2BKN.OUTFILE1
    PO    08/31/89  00/00/00 RPWD OUTFILE1 KEEP
```

Example 3.

```
ALLOC F(OUTFILE2) DA('22BKN.OUTFILE2') SHR VOLUME(ST0010) UNIT(SYSALLDA)
```

This allocates this dataset for shared use. The VOLUME and UNIT operands are specified because the dataset is not cataloged. It has been assumed that unit SYSALLDA as defined by the installation allows the user to access all DASD devices.

Example 4. You want to allocate a partitioned dataset with the first qualifier of dataset name being the same as your TSO prefix. The following are the requirements:

Dataset Name:	Z2BKN.PDS.COBOL
Block Size :	6320
Primary Space Required in Tracks:	10
Secondary Space Required in Tracks:	10
Maximum number of directory Blocks:	4
Record Format:	Fixed Blocked

```
ALLOC DA(PDS.COBOL) DSORG(PO) TRACKS SPACE(10 10) +
LRECL(80) BLKSIZE(6320) RECFM(F B) DIR(4) NEW
```

This command will allocate the dataset on a volume selected by the installation and the dataset will also be cataloged. LISTA STAT H will show the following:

```
Z2BKN.PDS.COBOL
    PO  09/11/89 - - - - - - SYS00083
```

Here SYS00083 means that the dataset is only temporarily allocated. You can delete it by issuing the following command:

```
DELETE 'Z2BKN.PDS.COBOL'
```

The deletion will work because the dataset is temporarily allocated. Note that if a dataset is permanently allocated to a TSO user, a batch job or a started task, it can not be deleted unless it is first freed.

Example 5. You want to allocate a sequential dataset with the attributes specified in an attribute list. You want to specify space requirements in terms of blocks rather than tracks or cylinders.

```
ATRIB ATTLIST1 DSORG(PS) LRECL(800) BLKSIZE(6320) RECFM(F B)
ALLOC DA('PRPAY.EPAY001A') USING(ATTLIST1) BLOCK(200) SPACE(30,20) NEW
```

Example 6. You want to allocate a SYSOUT dataset which will be printed using FCB and you want three copies to be printed:

```
ALLOC F(OUT1) SYSOUT(Z) DEST(R11) FCB(PCHK) COPIES(3)
```

LISTA STAT H will show DDname as OUT1 with dataset name being a temporary name with the first qualifier of JES2.

The FREE Command

This command is used to free or deallocate datasets that have been previously allocated. It can also be used to change the output class of SYSOUT datasets and to delete attribute lists. Following are the main uses of this command:

- to deallocate a DDname such as SYSPROC so that it can be allocated to another dataset or a different concatenation of datasets.
- to free datasets no longer needed so that you do not reach the maximum limit of allocated datasets. This is because there is a limit to the number of datasets that can be allocated to you during your TSO session. (Check with your TSO Systems Programmer to find the maximum number.) Since datasets allocated by the LOGON and ALLOCATE commands are not freed automatically, it is recommended that you free datasets no longer required so that you do not reach the limit. This will prevent you from being denied allocation of further datasets.

When a SYSOUT dataset is freed, it becomes available immediately for output processing (non-held datasets) by JES or by the OUTPUT command (held datasets).

When a SYSOUT dataset is freed, its destination can be changed by specifying DEST operand or its output class can be changed by specifying SYSOUT operand.

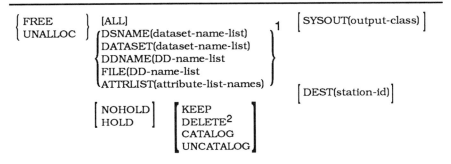

1. Choose one or more of the parameters within braces.
2. DELETE is the only disposition that is valid for SYSOUT datasets.

See the IBM manual mentioned above or an equivalent manual suitable for your MVS environment for a description of the various operands of this command.

Example 1.   Suppose you want to free datasets allocated under DDnames SYSUT1, SYSUT2, SYSIN, and SYSPROC.

```
Command: FREE F(SYSUT1,SYSUT2,SYSIN,SYSPROC)
```

Example 2.   Suppose you wish to free four datasets by specifying their dataset names only. Issue the following command:

```
FREE DA('PRPAY.CLIST', PDS.COBOL, OUTFIL1, 'PRPAY.PDS.COBOL')
```

Assuming your TSO ID is Z2BKN, the datasets freed will be:

```
PRPAY.CLIST
Z2BKN.PDS.COBOL
Z2BKN.OUTFILE1
PRPAY.PDS.COBOL
```

Note that a dataset which is a member of concatenation cannot be freed. A dataset that is open cannot be freed. A dataset that is being used by you or by another user, e.g., through option 3.2 (Dataset Utility) or option 1 (Browse) of ISPF, can not be freed.

Example 3. Suppose you wish to delete two attribute lists. Issue this command:

```
FREE ATTRLIST(ATTR01, ATTR02)
```

You might get this message, if attribute list ATTR01 is not currently allocated:

```
FILE ATTR01 NOT FREED, IS NOT ALLOCATED
```

Example 4. Suppose you wish to free all dynamically allocated datasets, DDnames, and attribute lists. Dynamically allocated datasets are those allocated through the ALLOC command, by a system command processor, or by a command processor written by you. The DDnames in your TSO log-on procedure are considered statically allocated as opposed to dynamically allocated datasets (allocated during the course of your TSO session).

```
Command: FREE All
```

This command will not free a dataset if it is currently being used by you or another user, e.g., through the Dataset Utility (3.2) or Browse (1) option of ISPF. Note that this command will free all dynamically allocated datasets and will also list on the terminal those datasets that have been freed up.

Example 5.   You wish to free four datasets by specifying dataset names for some and DD names for others. You also wish to change SYSOUT class of any SYSOUT datasets being freed. Issue this command:

```
FREE DA(PDS.DOC80) F(SYSUT1,PPSMAST,SYSPRINT) SYSOUT(Z)
```

The ATTRIB Command

This command is used to specify a list of attributes for non-VSAM datasets to be allocated dynamically thru the ALLOC command. Once an attribute list has been defined using ATTRIB command, you can use it during your TSO session in ALLOC commands which will convert the attributes into DCB parameters and LABEL parameters for datasets being allocated.

The ATTRIB command allocates a dataset with name being NULLFILE and DDname being the same as the attribute list name. The LISTALC STAT command can be used to list all active attribute lists.

You may choose not to use a attribute list on ALLOC command and specify the dataset attributes directly on the ALLOC command or use the LIKE operand on the ALLOC command.

Example 1.   Suppose you want to create an attribute list for use later in allocating new datasets. The following are the dataset attributes:

Record Format: Fixed-length Blocked Records
Block Size: 6000
Logical Record Length: 120
Dataset Organization: Physical Sequential

```
Command: ATTR ATTR01 RECFM(F B) LRECL(120) BLKSIZE(6000) DSORG(PS)
```

Example 2. This example shows how to define an attribute list, use it for allocating two datasets, and then delete the attribute list so that it cannot be used again.

> The name of the attribute list: ATTR02
> Block Size: 12000
> Buffering Technique: Simple Buffering

```
ATTRIB ATTR02 BLKSIZE(12000) BFTEK(S)
ALLOC DA('PRPAY.FILE1') NEW BLOCK(20) SPACE(2,1) VOLUME(ST0020) +
    USING(ATTR02)
ALLOC DA('PRPAY.FILE2') NEW BLOCK(80)    VOLUME(ST0010) USING(ATTR02)
FREE ATTRLIST(ATTR02)
```

The CALL Command

The CALL command is used to load into virtual storage and execute a program that is in the load-module (executable) format. You can specify an optional parameter to pass to the program.

```
CALL        { dataset-name                     }
            { load-library-name(member-name) }
            [ 'parameter-string']
```

The dataset you specify must be a partitioned dataset, and you must specify the name of the program to be executed. If you omit the member name, it defaults to 'TEMPNAME'.

Example 1. Suppose you wish to execute the load module PPPY200 resident in load library Z2BKN.PDS.LOAD, and you wish to pass a parameter string to it. If your dataset name prefix is Z2BKN, any of the following commands will work:

```
CALL PDS(PPPY200) 'CHECK-VACATION=N'
CALL 'Z2BKN.PDS.LOAD(PPPY200) 'CHECK-VACATION=N'
```

Example 2. Suppose you wish to execute program Z2BKN.LOAD(COMPUTE1). Any of the following commands will work, assuming that your TSO ID is Z2BKN:

```
CALL (COMPUTE1)
CALL 'Z2BKN.LOAD(COMPUTE1)'
```

Example 3. You wish to execute load module 'Z2BKN.PSNL.LOAD(TEMPNAME)', with parameters 'A,10,CHK'

```
CALL PSNL 'A,10,CHK'
```

The EXECUTE Command

The EXEC command is used to execute a command procedure (CLIST).

$$\left\{ \begin{array}{l} \left\{ \begin{array}{l} \text{EXEC} \\ \text{EX} \end{array} \right\} \quad \text{dataset-name} \\ \text{[\%]CLIST-name} \end{array} \right\} \quad \text{['value-list']} \quad \left[\begin{array}{l} \underline{\text{NOLIST}} \\ \text{LIST} \end{array} \right] \left[\begin{array}{l} \underline{\text{NOPROMPT}} \\ \text{PROMPT} \end{array} \right]$$

Dataset-name.   This specifies the dataset, either sequential or a member of a PDS that contains the CLIST to be executed. For details see Chapter 1.

%CLIST-name.   This specifies the member of a PDS containing CLISTs. If percent sign is entered, it causes TSO to search only the datasets allocated under DDname SYSPROC for the CLIST being executed.

Value-list. This specifies the values to be substituted for the symbolic variables specified on the PROC statement in the CLIST. The PROC statement was discussed in Chapter 2 and examples of EXEC command were given. It is important to note that the actual values to replace the positional parameters specified on the PROC statement must be in the same sequence as the positional operands. However, the actual values to replace the keyword parameters present on the PROC statement must follow the positional values and may be in any sequence.

When the explicit form of the EXEC command is used, the value-list must be enclosed within single quotes.

The PROMPT/NOPROMPT and LIST/NOLIST operands provide a means of specifying whether the user will be prompted for data during the course of CLIST execution and whether TSO commands and subcommands present within the CLIST will be listed at the terminal. It should be noted that these parameters can also be specified on the CONTROL statement within the CLIST. However, specifying them on the EXEC command provides flexibility and is useful for debugging purposes.

As discussed in Chapter 1, the EXEC command has three forms:

- The explicit form
  For example:

  ```
  EX 'SYS2.PROD.CLIST(CONVDATE)' 'CURR'
  ```

- The implicit form
  For example:

  ```
  GIVETIME
  ```

- The extended implicit form
  For example:

  ```
  %GIVETIME
  ```

The WHEN Command

The WHEN command is used to test return codes issued by a previously executed CALL command, and to take an appropriate action depending on the result of the test.

```
WHEN      SYSRC  (operator integer)
          ⎡ END                    ⎤
          ⎣ name-of-command        ⎦
```

You may or may not use the END command. If you do not specify any command after the SYSRC operand, the default command END is used, which ends the CLIST execution.

Operator. One of the following operators can be used:

Operator	Meaning
EQ or =	equal to
NE or ¬ =	not equal to
GT or >	greater than
LT or <	less than
GE or >=	greater than or equal to
LE or <=	less than or equal to
NL or ¬ <	not less than
NG or ¬ >	not greater than

It is important to remember that when the condition specified on the WHEN command is found to be true, the CLIST ends, and the command specified on the WHEN is executed. After the execution of that command, control does not come back to the CLIST. Another important point is that the WHEN command should be immediately preceded by the CALL command. This is best illustrated through the following code:

```
CALL 'SYS3.LINKLIB(PPPY001)'
WRITE THE RETURN CODE RETURNED BY PPPY001 = &LASTCC
WHEN SYSRC (EQ 751) %CLISTA
WHEN SYSRC (EQ 752) %CLISTB
WRITE THE RETURN CODE FROM PPPY001 WAS NEITHER 751 NOR 752
```

Here it is assumed that program PPPY001 returns a return code of 0, 751, or 752. If the return code is 751, we want to execute CLISTA, and if the return code is 752, we want to execute CLISTB. Now let us suppose that in one execution of PPPY001, this program returns a return code of 751. After control has come back to the CLIST, the WRITE statement displays the following message on the terminal:

```
THE RETURN CODE RETURNED BY PPPY001 = 751
```

The WRITE statement also sets &LASTCC to 0. So when the WHEN commands are executed, return code is zero and hence neither CLISTA nor CLISTB gets executed. and the following message is displayed on the terminal:

```
THE RETURN CODE FROM PPPY001 WAS NEITHER 751 NOR 752
```

Example 1. Suppose you write a COBOL program called TESTSTAT which reads the payroll/ personnel master file record for an employee, and, if his status on the master file indicates that the employee is inactive, the program issues a return code of 8, otherwise it issues a return code of zero. Suppose that if the employee is inactive you want to execute another CLIST which will write appropriate messages on the terminal and then end. The following commands can be used for this purpose:

```
CALL 'PRPAY.PDS.LOAD(TESTSTAT)' '090144'
WHEN SYSRC (= 8)  EXEC 'PRPAY.CLIST(MSGINACT)'
- - -
```

- - -

In this example, if the program TESTSTAT issues a return code of 8, the CLIST 'PRPAY.CLIST(MSGINACT)' is executed, otherwise control flows to the next consecutive statement in the CLIST, or you are returned to the TSO mode, if the above commands were executed one after another by you from TSO mode.

The method of receiving parameter in a COBOL program as passed through JCL or through the CALL command of TSO is shown in Figure A.1. This figure also shows the method of setting return code in a COBOL program. It should be noted that RETURN-CODE is a COBOL reserved word and is not defined anywhere in the COBOL program. If nothing is moved to RETURN-CODE in the program prior to executing STOP RUN or GOBACK, its value defaults to 0. The return code set by the COBOL program is also the same thing as the condition code that can be tested in the JCL. For example a JCL to execute this COBOL program might be set up as shown in Figure A.2. In this JCL, STEP02 will be bypassed if STEP01 ended in condition code of 8, that is if program TESTSTAT moved 8 to RETURN-CODE before terminating.

```
LINKAGE SECTION.
01  PARAM.
      05  FILLER             PIC X(02).
      05  LS-EMPLOYEE-NUM    PIC 9(6).

PROCEDURE DIVISION USING PARAM.
    - - - -
    - - - -
      IF EMPLOYEE-INACTIVE
         MOVE 8 TO RETURN-CODE
      ELSE
         MOVE ZERO TO RETURN-CODE.
```

Figure A.1.   Part of COBOL program TESTSTAT that checks the status of an employee and sets appropriate return code before terminating.

```
//STEP01    EXEC  PGM=TESTSTAT,PARM='090144'
//STEPLIB   DD  DSN=SYS3.LINKLIB,DISP=SHR
//EMPMAST   DD  DSN=SYS3.PAYROLL.MASTER.FILE,DISP=SHR
//SYSOUT    DD  SYSOUT=A
//SYSDBOUT  DD  SYSOUT=Q
//*
//STEP02    EXEC  PGM=PPPY002,COND=(8,EQ,STEP01)
 -  -  -
 -  -  -
```

Figure A.2.   A JCL to execute the COBOL program TESTSTAT part of which is shown in Figure A.1.

Example 2. This example illustrates how successive WHEN commands can be used to make multiple tests of the return codes issued by a previously executed program.

```
CALL LOAD(PROG01)
WHEN SYSRC ( = 0)   %SHOWVAC
WHEN SYSRC ( = 8)   %SHOWMENU
WHEN SYSRC ( > 8)   %ABORTJOB
```

THE DELETE COMMAND

The DELETE command is used to delete one or more datasets (both VSAM and non-VSAM) or one or more members of a partitioned dataset. After executing the DELETE command, the system lists the names of datasets and PDS members successfully deleted. DELETE can be abbreviated as DEL. The best way to understand how DELETE works is through some examples:

Example 1. To delete a dataset named 'TRAPY.ANY.NAME', you issue this command:

```
DEL 'TRPAY.ANY.NAME'
```

This dataset can be a non-VSAM sequential or direct access dataset, a partitioned dataset, or a VSAM cluster. When a VSAM KSDS is deleted, system automatically deletes three entries, the cluster, the data component and the index component and lists on the terminal the names of the cluster, the data component and the index component that were deleted. It should be noted that you only issue DELETE command for the cluster; you do not issue DELETE for the data component or the index component.

Example 2.   The following command deletes two members of a partitioned dataset:

```
DELETE  ('PRPAY.PDS.LIB(CPPAPPA1)'  'PRPAY.PDS.LIB(CPPAPPA2)')
```

This and the following example illustrate the rule that when more than one entry is to be deleted, the list of entry names must be enclosed within parentheses.

Example 3.   Suppose that your TSO dataset name prefix is Z2BKN and you wish to delete the following datasets:

```
Z2BKN.JUNK1
Z2BKN.JUNK2
PRPAY.TEMPFILE
TRPAY.DUMMY.CAS.RECORD
```

Issue the following command:

```
DELETE (JUNK1 JUNK2 'PRPAY.TEMPFILE'  'TRPAY.DUMMY.CAS.RECORD')
```

The datasets in this example can be a non-VSAM sequential or direct access dataset, a partitioned dataset, or a VSAM cluster. If one of these datasets is in use by you or another user, the system will delete the other datasets but not the one that is in use.

Example 4. Suppose there exists a generation data group with the GDG base name of 'TRPAY.GPAY302A'. If this GDG is empty, meaning that there are no datasets under this GDG, the following command will delete this GDG base entry from the catalog:

```
DELETE 'TRPAY.GPAY302A'
```

Example 5. Suppose that there exists dataset 'TRPPA.EPPA001A' and you wish to remove this dataset from the MVS catalog, but leave it on the disk volume where it resides. Then the following command can be used:

```
DELETE 'TRPPA.EPPA001A' NSCR
```

Here NSCR stands for Not Scratch, meaning do not scratch it from the DASD; simply delete it from the catalog. The default is scratch, that is delete it from the catalog as well as from the DASD.

The following are the considerations to keep in mind when using this command:

1. If you wish to delete only one or more members of a PDS, specify the member names explicitly as shown in Example 2, above. However, if you wish to delete an entire PDS, do not specify member name as shown in Example 1, above. A PDS is removed from the catalog only when the entire PDS is deleted. When you delete only one or more members of a PDS, the system deletes them by removing their names from the PDS directory. The name of the PDS in the catalog and on the DASD VTOC is left unaltered.

2. If a GDG base is to be deleted from the catalog, all datasets belonging to the GDG must have been previously deleted. For example suppose a GDG base 'TRPAY.GPAY001A' is defined in the catalog and there

are two datasets under this GDG. Then, if you wish to get rid of this GDG base and both of its datasets, then command DELETE 'TRPAY.GPAY001A' will not work, but the following sequence of commands will work:

```
DELETE 'TRPAY.GPAY001A.G0001V00'
DELETE 'TRPAY.GPAY001A.G0002V00'
DELETE 'TRPAY.GPAY001A'
```

3. If there are many datasets with similar names, an asterisk can be used on the DELETE command to delete multiple datasets. For example, suppose the following datasets exist:

```
TRPAY.PDS.SOURCE
TRPAY.PDS.COBOL
TRPAY.PDS.LOAD
TRPAY.PDS2.LIB
```

The following command will delete all datasets with three-qualifier names where the first qualifier is TRPAY and the second qualifier is PDS.

```
DELETE 'TRPAY.PDS.*'
```

Out of the four datasets mentioned above, only TRPAY.PDS2.LIB will remain after the execution of this command. However there are two restrictions:

- Only one asterisk can be used per dataset name
- The asterisk must not appear in the first position of the dataset name on the DELETE command.

You may ask this question. In the above example, will the command DELETE 'TRPAY.*' delete all datasets which have TRPAY as the first qualifier of their names?

The answer is NO. This command will delete only those datasets whose names consists of only two qualifiers; the first qualifier being TRPAY and the second qualifier being anything else. Similarly DEL TRPAY.*.FILE1 will delete all datasets with three-qualifier names, where the first qualifier is TRPAY and the third qualifier is FILE1.

4. DELETE 'CICS.SYSIN(CICSPRD1)' will delete this PDS member. However, if the dataset is being allocated by another user in the system, even with shared disposition (DISP=SHR), this delete will fail. To make this delete work, you must issue the following:

```
ALLOC F(DD1) DA('CICS.SYSIN') SHR
DEL 'CICS.SYSIN(CICSPRD1)' FILE(DD1)
```

These commands will delete the PDS member provided the ALLOC command does not fail due to the fact that another user is allocating this dataset for exclusive use (DISP=OLD).

The EDIT Command

The EDIT command is a very important command, without whose knowledge one's grasp of TSO/CLIST remains incomplete. This is because this command is the main means of entering and changing data in the datasets. You may remark that if you know how to edit datasets through the Edit option of ISPF, that should be sufficient for most purposes. It is true that this may be sufficient for most normal needs, but, if you know the EDIT command of TSO and all its subcommands thoroughly, you can put that knowledge to work in writing CLISTs that will save you time and effort. For example, suppose there is a PDS member containing MVS JCL, which you want to submit after changing the job name to a string consisting of your TSO ID and the

```
PROC 1 DSNAME
CONTROL NOMSG NOLIST
SET JOBNAME = &SYSUID.Y
DO
  DATA
     EDIT '&DSNAME.' OLD DATA
     CHANGE * 1 'JOBNAME' '&JOBNAME.'
     TOP
     SUBMIT
     END NOSAVE
  ENDDATA
END
EXIT
```

Figure A.3.   A CLIST that changes jobname on line 1 and submits the JCL in any specified dataset.

letter Y, but you do not want to save the changes made. One approach is to edit the dataset thru ISPF, change the job name, use the SUBMIT command to submit the job, and then cancel the changes. Another approach is to write a small CLIST as shown in Figure A.3, and, assuming that this CLIST is stored as member JOBSUB in a PDS allocated to DDname SYSPROC, to invoke it by issuing this command:

```
%JOBSUB data-set-name
```

This second option is definitely less time-consuming and less prone to error. This demonstrates the immense useful-ness of the EDIT command. This command also proves of great help, when ISPF can not be started for some reason, and the systems programmer has to edit some system datasets before it can be brought up. Also, if you as an applications programmer/analyst can not start up ISPF because of some error in a dataset such as a member of a CLIST library used at ISPF start-up time, you can use the EDIT command to change that dataset so that the ISPF command will work.

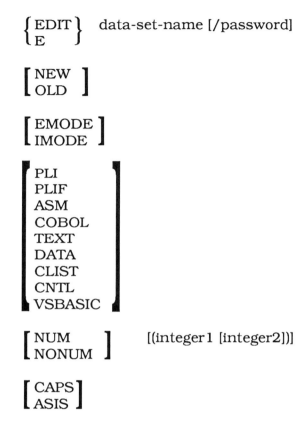

$\begin{Bmatrix} \text{EDIT} \\ \text{E} \end{Bmatrix}$ data-set-name [/password]

$\begin{bmatrix} \text{NEW} \\ \text{OLD} \end{bmatrix}$

$\begin{bmatrix} \text{EMODE} \\ \text{IMODE} \end{bmatrix}$

$\begin{bmatrix} \text{PLI} \\ \text{PLIF} \\ \text{ASM} \\ \text{COBOL} \\ \text{TEXT} \\ \text{DATA} \\ \text{CLIST} \\ \text{CNTL} \\ \text{VSBASIC} \end{bmatrix}$

$\begin{bmatrix} \text{NUM} \\ \text{NONUM} \end{bmatrix}$ [(integer1 [integer2])]

$\begin{bmatrix} \text{CAPS} \\ \text{ASIS} \end{bmatrix}$

Dataset-name. This specifies the name of the dataset to be created or edited. The dataset can be sequential or a member of a PDS, and may contain:

- Source program in COBOL, PL/I, FORTRAN, ASSEM-BLER, etc.
- Data used as input to a program
- Text
- A CLIST
- JCL statements for background jobs

The EDIT command will only work with datasets which have:

- Fixed blocked, unblocked, or standard block records with or without ASCII or machine carriage control characters.
- Variable blocked or unblocked, without ASCII or machine carriage control characters.

This means that the EDIT command can not be used to manipulate VSAM datasets or non-VSAM datasets with record formats other than F, FB, FBS, V, and VB. In this regard, note that a member of a partitioned dataset is treated as any other sequential dataset, for EDIT and many other purposes.

Password.   This specifies the password of the dataset, if it is password-protected for write, otherwise it is not necessary. If the dataset is password-protected for write and you omit this operand, system will prompt you for the password.

EMODE.   This specifies that the initial mode of operation is edit mode. This is the default for OLD datasets.

IMODE.   This specifies that the initial mode of operation is input mode. This is the default for NEW datasets.

NEW.   This specifies that the dataset does not exist. If an already cataloged dataset with the same name does not already exist, system will allocate this dataset (i.e., create it on a disk volume and place it in the MVS catalog), otherwise it will inform you when you try to save it. If NEW is specified without a member name, a sequential dataset is allocated, otherwise the system allocates a partitioned dataset and creates the specified member when you try to save it.

OLD. This specifies that the dataset named on the EDIT command already exists. If the system is unable to locate this dataset, you will be informed and you will have to reenter the EDIT command. When you specify OLD and do not specify a member name, the system will assume that the dataset is sequential. However if it is partitioned, the system will assume that the member name is TEMPNAME. When you specify OLD and do specify a member name, the system will inform you if dataset is not partitioned. If you specify neither OLD nor NEW, the system proceeds with the assumption that it is OLD. However, if the dataset can not be located, the system defaults to NEW.

As regards dataset type keywords, the following are some of the most commonly used dataset types:

COBOL. This specifies that the dataset is for COBOL statements.

CNTL. This specifies that the dataset contains JCL statements or SYSIN data.

TEXT. This specifies that the dataset may contain both lowercase and uppercase characters.

DATA. This specifies that the dataset is for data that is intended to be read as input by an application program.

NUM. This specifies that the lines in datasets are numbered. Only for assembler language programs, line numbers can be specified on the NUM operand.

NONUM. This specifies that the dataset records do not contain line numbers. NONUM must not be specified for VSBASIC and CLIST dataset types, since they must always contain line numbers.

CAPS.   This specifies that the input data keyed by the user and data on any modified lines are to be converted to uppercase. CAPS is the default when neither CAPS nor ASIS is specified, with the exception of dataset type being TEXT.

ASIS.   This specifies that no conversion of lowercase characters to uppercase be performed by the system. ASIS is the default only when dataset type is TEXT and you omit both CAPS and ASIS keywords.

Before discussing this command further, let us consider an example which will help you realize the technique of using this command for a practical problem, and will also help you understand the various concepts such as current line pointer, etc.

Example 1.   Let us suppose that we are to write a CLIST that can be used to define the base of a generation data group (GDG). Suppose that the user wants to define a GDG base named PRPAY.GPAY030A, and keep a maximum of 10 generations of this dataset. If this CLIST is stored as member DEFGDG in a CLIST library allocated under DDname SYSPROC during the user's TSO session, the following command can be used for this purpose:

```
%DEFGDG PRPAY.GPAY030A 10
```

This CLIST will submit a batch job with the jobname equal to TSO User ID followed by letter G.

Our Plan to Solve This Problem

Suppose there exists dataset 'Z2HSM.LIB.CNTL(DUMMY)' which contains two lines, whose content is unimportant. We will edit this dataset using the EDIT command. Next, we will delete the existing two lines from this dataset and then insert the following JCL lines into it:

```
//job-name JOB (645110,107E,99,99),'CLIST-STUDENT',
//       CLASS=K,MSGCLASS=Q,NOTIFY=user-id
//STEP01   EXEC PGM=IDCAMS
//SYSPRINT DD SYSOUT=*
//SYSIN    DD *
  DEFINE GDG  -
    (NAME(gdg-base-name) -
    LIMIT(max-generations) -
    NOEMPTY
    SCRATCH)
/*
```

where job-name will be replaced by a string consisting of the user's TSO ID and letter G. Other names written in lowercase characters in the JCL are to be replaced by user-supplied parameters.

After inserting these lines into the dataset, we will issue the SUBMIT subcommand of EDIT to submit this JCL as a job to MVS. We will then end the EDIT command without saving the changes into the dataset. One CLIST that implements this plan is given in Figure A.4.

Let us see how this CLIST works. On line 1, the digit 2 after PROC means that there are two required positional parameters to be passed to this CLIST via the EXEC command used to invoke this CLIST. These positional parameters are given the symbolic names of DSN and GENER. On line 2, we specify a number of processing options on the CONTROL statement. You can look up the meaning of these options in an IBM manual. Lines 3 thru 9 are comment lines. On line 10 we define the symbolic variable JOBNAME and equate it to the concatenation of the control variable &SYSUID and letter G. The DO statement on line 11 starts a DO group which has its END on line 34. Within this DO-group, we placed the DATA-ENDDATA group which is

```
Line      CLIST Statement
Number

1         PROC 2 DSN GENER
2         CONTROL MSG PROMPT NOLIST NOSYMLIST FLUSH NOCONLIST
3         /*=====================================================================*
4         /*    THIS CLIST WILL BUILD AND SUBMIT A JOB TO DEFINE              *
5         /*    THE BASE OF A GENERATION DATA GROUP (GDG).                    *
6         /*    PARAMETERS REQUIRED ARE FULLY-QUALIFIED NAME OF GDG BASE      *
7         /*    AND THE NUMBER OF GENERATIONS OF THE GDG TO BE DEFINED, IN    *
8         /*    THE SAME ORDER.                                               *
9         /*=====================================================================*
10        SET JOBNAME = &SYSUID.G
11        DO
12          DATA
13            EDIT 'Z2HSM.LIB.CNTL(DUMMY)' NONUM OLD DATA
14            DELETE
15            DELETE
16            INSERT //&JOBNAME JOB (645110,107E,99,99),'CLIST-STUDENT',
17            INSERT //        CLASS=K,MSGCLASS=Q,NOTIFY=&SYSUID
18            INSERT //STEP01   EXEC PGM=IDCAMS
19            INSERT //SYSPRINT DD SYSOUT=*
20            INSERT //SYSIN    DD *
21            INSERT    DEFINE GDG  @
22            INSERT      (NAME(&DSN)  @
23            INSERT      LIMIT(&GENER)  @
24            INSERT      NOEMPTY  @
25            INSERT      SCRATCH)
26            INSERT ***BARRY***
27            CHANGE '***BARRY***' '/*'
28            TOP
29            CHANGE * 100 '@' '-' ALL
30            TOP
31            SUBMIT
32            END NOSAVE
33          ENDDATA
34        END
35        /*=====================================================================*
36        /* NOW WE EXIT FROM THIS CLIST                                      *
37        /*=====================================================================*
38        END
```

Figure A.4. A CLIST to define the base of a generation data group (GDG).

used to designate a group of TSO commands and sub-commands. Note that there can be no command procedure statements within a DATA-ENDDATA group, because TSO will attempt to execute them as TSO commands or subcommands. In our example, the first thing we do within the DATA-ENDDATA group is edit the dataset

'Z2HSM.LIB.CNTL(DUMMY)' which, as we discussed before, contains just two lines. The current line pointer points to the first record. The DELETE subcommand on line 14 deletes the first line and that on line 15 deletes the second line from the dataset. Next we insert a number of lines in this dataset by using the INSERT subcommand of EDIT (lines 16 thru 26). On line 27, we change the string 'BARRY' to '/*' on the line where the current line pointer is positioned. This has been done merely to illustrate how we can change the contents of lines within a dataset being edited. Each INSERT subcommand causes the current line pointer (CLP) to point to the inserted line. (See Figure A.5.)

Next we go to the top of the dataset by issuing the TOP subcommand of EDIT on line 28. Then we issue the CHANGE subcommand which asks the system to change all occurrences of '@' to '-' for 100 lines on all lines starting from the current position of the line pointer. This covers all the lines in the dataset, from the first line to the last line. The reason why we used the @ characters instead of hyphens on INSERT subcommands is that the use of hyphens should be avoided due to possible confusion on the part of TSO. Since IDCAMS requires the use of hyphens at the end of each continued line, we change all @ to hyphens thru the CHANGE subcommand. Next we issue the SUBMIT subcommand on line 31 which submits the content of this dataset as a job to the MVS system. On line 32, we issue the END subcommand of EDIT to end the edit operation without saving the changes made to the dataset. (We must not save our changes because the next invocation of this CLIST will assume that member DUMMY of Z2HSM.LIB.CNTL contains just two lines.)

Line 33 marks the end of the DATA-ENDDATA group, and line 34 marks the end of the DO-group. On line 38 we have the END command of TSO which should be contrasted with the END subcommand of EDIT on line 32 and the END statement on line 34 which is used to end the DO-group started on line 11. The END command on line 38 ends the execution of this CLIST, and the system is ready to accept another command from the terminal.

Note: Lines numbered 11, 26, 27, 30 and 34 in this CLIST are not really necessary. They can be deleted without affecting the function of this CLIST in any manner.

Two modes of operation of the EDIT Command. The EDIT command has two modes of operation:

* The Input Mode
* The Edit Mode

In the input mode, the user enters data into the dataset, and, in the edit mode, the user enters the subcommands of EDIT and their operands for various purposes. When you issue the EDIT command you have the option of specifying NEW or OLD as the dataset disposition. If NEW is specified or the dataset already exists but is empty, the system puts you in input mode, otherwise it puts you in edit mode.

The input mode of the EDIT Command. In the input mode, you enter one line of data and press the Enter key, at which time the data goes into the dataset as one record. You can enter as many lines of data as you wish while you are in the input mode. Unless you specify otherwise, the system assigns a line number to each line of data you enter. The line numbers make it easy to identify each record of the dataset, because you can refer to each line by its line number. The default increment of consecutive line numbers is 10. Line numbers are placed at the beginning of variable length records and at the end of fixed-length records, with the exception of datasets with the COBOL attribute, when line numbers occupy the first six positions of each record.

Note: Unless you specify the TEXT or the ASIS operand on the EDIT command, all data entered will be converted to uppercase before being stored in the file.

Special considerations apply to the use of hyphens. In the input mode, when working with non-CLIST type datasets, the system removes the last hyphen from each line. In case of CLIST type datasets which are of variable-length formats (the recommended record format), the hyphens are not removed and become part of the stored data and will be interpreted as continuation characters by the EXEC command processor. This is to say that you should avoid ending a line with a hyphen in the input mode for non-CLIST type datasets.

The above rule for using hyphens applies only to the input mode. In the edit mode, when using the EDIT sub-commands such as CHANGE, REPLACE, INSERT, etc, a hyphen at the end of the line indicates continuation of the subcommand itself, and it causes the system to append the continued line to the subcommand itself. This is why in Figure A.4, we used character @ at the end of line numbers 21 thru 24, and on line 29 we changed them to hyphens.

This means that you should avoid ending a line with a hyphen in the edit mode as well as in the input mode. However, hyphens can be used when editing CLIST type datasets in input mode only.

The edit mode of the EDIT Command. In this mode, you can modify a dataset. If the dataset has line numbers, you can refer to the line you wish to edit by referring to its line number. This greatly simplifies the process of editing and is called line-number editing. Alternatively, you can edit the lines by referring to the specific items of text within them. This is called context editing. When a dataset has no line numbers, you can only use context editing to edit it. However, when a dataset has line numbers, you can either use line number editing or context editing, depending on which one is more convenient in a particular situation.

In context editing, the concept of current line pointer (CLP) is very important. The system maintains a pointer that marks a particular line within the dataset. Normally this pointer marks the last line that was referred to. However, you can issue subcommands of EDIT to change the value of the CLP so that it points to any line you choose. You can then refer to the line pointed to by the CLP by specifying an asterisk (*) instead of the line number. For example in Figure A.4, the TOP subcommand on line 28 makes the CLP assume a value of zero, which means that it points to the position before the first record. Then the CHANGE subcommand on line 29 is issued, which indicates that 100 lines are to be scanned, starting from the position of the CLP, and all occurrences of character @ are to be changed to hyphens.

Figure A.5 shows how the various subcommands of EDIT affect the value of the CLP. It should be noted that a dataset may or may not contain a record with line number zero. A CLP value of zero means that the CLP points to the position before the first line, if the first line has non-zero line number, and to the first line if its line number is zero. When a dataset is empty or it has no line numbers, a CLP value of zero means that it points to the top of the dataset.

Another point to keep in mind is that when you edit a dataset with line numbers, the line number field will not be affected by any modifications made to the lines due to commands such as the CHANGE subcommand. Also, only when NONUM and TEXT have been specified on the EDIT command, the CHANGE and FIND subcommands will work across record boundaries. In all other situations, an editing operation including FIND and CHANGE will be performed across only one record boundary at a time.

The subcommands of EDIT. The subcommands of EDIT are used to manipulate and edit data. These subcommands are summarized in Figure A.6. The ALLOCATE, EXEC, SUBMIT, HELP, PROFILE, and SEND commands have the same syntax and function as the TSO command with the same name. For a more detailed description of these sub-

Edit Subcommands	Value of the Pointer at Completion of Subcommand
ALLOCATE	No change
BOTTOM	Last line (or zero for empty datasets)
CHANGE	Last line changed
COPY	Last line copied
DELETE	Line preceding deleted line (or zero if the first line of the dataset has been deleted
DOWN	Line n relative lines below the last line referred to, where n is the value of the 'count' parameter, or bottom of the dataset (or line zero for empty datasets)
END	No change
EXEC	No change
FIND	Line containing specified string, if any; else, no change
FORMAT (a program product)	No change
HELP	No change
INPUT	Last line entered
INSERT	Last line entered
INSERT/REPLACE/DELETE	Inserted line or replaced line or line preceding the deleted line if any (or zero, if no preceding line exists)
LIST	Last line listed
MERGE (a program product)	Last line
MOVE	Last line moved
PROFILE	No change
RENUM	Same relative line
RUN	No change
SAVE	No change or same relative line
SCAN	Last line scanned, if any
SEND	No change
SUBMIT	No change
TABSET	No change
TOP	Zero value
UNNUM	Same relative line
UP	Line n relative lines above the last line referred to where n is the value of the 'count' parameter, (or line zero for empty datasets)
VERIFY	No change

Figure A.5.   How EDIT subcommands affect the line pointer value.

ALLOCATE	Allocates datasets and filenames
BOTTOM	Moves the pointer to the last record in the dataset
CHANGE	Alters the contents of a dataset
COPY	Copies records within the dataset
DELETE	Removes records
DOWN	Moves the pointer toward the end of the data
END	Terminates the EDIT command
EXEC	Executes a command procedure
FIND	Locates a character string
FORMAT (available as an optional program product)	Formats and lists data
HELP	Explains available subcommands
INPUT	Prepares the system for data input
INSERT	Inserts records
INSERT/REPLACE/DELETE	Inserts, replaces, or deletes a line
LIST	Prints out specific lines of data
MERGE (available as an optional program product)	Combines all or parts of datasets
MOVE	Moves records within a dataset
PROFILE	Specifies characteristics of your user profile
RENUM	Numbers or renumbers lines of data
RUN	Causes compilation and execution of dataset
SAVE	Retains the dataset
SCAN	Controls syntax checking
SEND	Allows you to communicate with the system operator and with other terminal users
SUBMIT	Submits a job for execution in the background
TABSET	Sets the tabs
TOP	Sets the pointer to zero value
UNNUM	Removes line numbers form records
UP	Moves the pointer toward the start of the dataset
VERIFY	Causes current line to be listed whenever the current line pointer changes or the text of the current line is modified

Figure A.6.   Subcommands of the EDIT command.

commands, refer to an appropriate IBM manual. Now let us consider some examples which will help clarify the syntax and functions of the EDIT command and its various subcommands.

Example 1. Suppose that your TSO userid is Z3HJK and dataset Z3HJK.NEWSYS.CNTL does not exist. You want the system to allocate this dataset and you want to insert the following lines into this dataset before saving it:

```
LINE ONE
LINE TWO
LINE THREE
```

You would type the following either from native TSO or from TSO within ISPF to achieve this objective:

```
EDIT NEWSYS NEW CNTL
line one
LINE two
Line three
(You press the ENTER key without typing anything)
END S
```

Note: Since you issued an EDIT command for a dataset that does not already exist, you are placed in the input mode. In input mode whatever you type on the screen, even commands or subcommands, are interpreted as data and become one logical record of the dataset. To switch from input mode to edit mode, you just press the ENTER key. Once in edit mode, you issue the END subcommand of EDIT to terminate the EDIT command. The three lines entered are saved in the dataset. The S after END stands for SAVE. You are basically 'telling' TSO to end the EDIT operation and 'requesting' that all changes made to the dataset be saved.

Once this dataset has been created, you can edit it again and change its content. The following describes the steps you might follow to replace the content of the existing three lines in the dataset:

```
OPR:  EDIT NEWSYS OLD CTNL
SYS:  EDIT
OPR:  10 BARRY
      (Press Enter key)
OPR:  20 HARRY
      (Press Enter key)
OPR:  30 JERRY
      (Press Enter key)
OPR:  END S
```

Now if you browse this dataset, you will find that its content is as follows:

Data in columns 1- 72	Line Number in columns 73-80
BARRY	10
HARRY	20
JERRY	30

If you want to add records with line numbers 15 and 40 in the same dataset, you might use the following steps:

```
OPR:  EDIT NEWSYS OLD CNTL
SYS:  EDIT
OPR:  15  NIRMAL
      (PRESS ENTER KEY)
OPR:  40  RICHARD
      (PRESS ENTER KEY)
OPR:  END SAVE
```

When you browse this dataset, you will find that it has five records with line numbers 10, 15, 20, 30 and 40.

To want to write a CLIST that will change line number 15 to MURPHY and line number 20 to MARY, you might use the following CLIST:

```
CONTROL MSG LIST
DATA
  EDIT NEWSYS OLD CNTL
  15  MURPHY
  20  MARY
  END SAVE
ENDDATA
EXIT
```

After executing this CLIST, if you browse this dataset, you would find that its content is as follows:

Data in columns 1- 72	Line Number In Columns 73- 80
BARRY	10
MURPHY	15
MARY	20
JERRY	30
RICHARD	40

Example 2. To add some records at the end of an existing sequential dataset 'PRPAY.EPAY062A', you might use the following steps:

```
OPR: EDIT 'PRPAY.EPAY062A'
SYS: DATASET 'PRPPY.EPPY062A' NOT LINE NUMBERED, USING NONUM
     EDIT
OPR: (Enters following lines one after another, pressing Enter key after
       each line)
     INSERT 90144
     INSERT 90146
     END SAVE
```

If you browse this dataset, you would find that the last two lines are:

```
90144
90146
```

Example 3. Suppose you are a systems programmer and you are starting up the MVS system. TSO can be started but due to some error ISPF cannot be started. You want to change the contents of SYS1.PROCLIB(JES2) and then restart the system. The first thing to do is to display the contents of the dataset so that you can decide what changes must be made. The following describes the commands you would enter to list the records in the dataset:

```
OPR: EDIT 'SYS1.PROCLIB(JES2)' OLD CNTL
SYS: EDIT
OPR: LIST
SYS: (lists the records in this dataset from the beginning to the end. The
     display might look as follows:)
  10000 //JES2    PROC MEMBER=JES2PARM,      * SYMBOLIC PARAMETERS
  20013 //        S1=SYS1,S2=SYS2,HLQ=SYS1, * HLQ FOR STEPLIB DD
  - - -
  - - -
  - - -
```

Now let us suppose that you want to change line number 200013 so that HLQ=SYS1 is changed to HLQ=SYS3. When the system displays END OF DATA after displaying the last line in the dataset, you type the following and then press the Enter key:

```
  200013 //        S1=SYS1,S2=SYS2,HLQ=SYS3,
```

Basically you would type the line number in the dataset to be replaced (or added) followed by one space followed by the new content of the line. When you press the Enter key, that line gets replaced by what you entered on the screen. You can confirm this by entering LIST and pressing the Enter key. TSO would display the entire content of the dataset starting from the first line. Finally you would enter END SAVE to end the EDIT command and specify that the changes made to the dataset be saved.

Example 4. In a CLIST you can issue the EDIT command and delete lines from the same CLIST. For example, suppose that a CLIST stored in member START of userid.CLIST is executed every time a TSO user logs on. Now this CLIST can be set up as shown below by the TSO systems programmer at the time of defining a new TSO user ID. This CLIST, on line numbers 40 thru 200, displays a number of message lines on the terminal when the user logs on to TSO the very first time. Then on lines 210 thru 250, EDIT operation is performed on this same CLIST and lines numbered 40 thru 250 are deleted from the dataset containing this CLIST. The idea behind this deletion is that the messages written on lines 40 thru 200 are intended to be displayed only the very first time and not every time that user logs on to TSO.

```
10     PROC 0
20      - - - -
30      - - - -
40     WRITE - - -
50     WRITE - - -
- - - - - - - -
200    WRITE - - -
210    DATA
220      EDIT '&SYSUID..CLIST(START)' CL
230      DELETE 40 250
240      END SAVE
250    ENDDATA
260     - - -
270     - - -
```

This example shows that every time you execute a CLIST, it gets loaded into virtual storage from the dataset where it is stored and then executed from virtual storage.

The RENAME Command

This command is used for the following purposes:

- to change the name of a non-VSAM dataset which is cataloged
- to create an alias for a partitioned dataset member
- to rename a member of a partitioned dataset

$\left\{ \begin{array}{l} \text{RENAME} \\ \text{REN} \end{array} \right\}$ present-name new-name

[ALIAS]

Example 1. Suppose there exists a PDS called 'Z2BKN.PDS.COBOL'. You wish to rename member PPPY200 to PPPY201. The following command can be used:

```
RENAME 'Z2BKN.PDS.COBOL(PPPY200)' (PPPY201)
```

And if your TSO prefix is Z2BKN, the following command will also work:

```
RENAME PDS.COBOL(PPPY200) (PPPY201)
```

Remember that you can use the PROFILE command of TSO to change your TSO prefix, set it to null, or add one if it is already null. We recommend that TSO prefix of every TSO user be the same as his TSO ID. This eliminates confusion and possibilities of error. For example, issue the following command to view all the options in your profile:

```
PROFILE
```

And, to set your dataset name prefix to null, issue the following command:

```
PROFILE NOPREFIX
```

And to change your prefix to say XYZ1, issue the following command:

```
PROFILE PREFIX(XYZ1)
```

Example 2. Suppose there exists a PDS called 'TRPAY.PDS.COBOL' and you wish to assign an alias of PPPY200 to member PPPY299. The following command will work:

```
REN 'TRPAY.PDS.COBOL(PPPY299)' (PPPY200) ALIAS
```

After this alias has been created, the name PPPY200 will appear in the directory of member names when you browse or edit this dataset thru ISPF, and, when you select member PPPY200, you will actually be selecting member PPPY299 because PPPY200 is an alias of PPPY299. If you edit member PPPY200 and modify it, it will cease being an alias of member PPPY299.

Example 3. Suppose the following datasets are cataloged:

```
TRPAY.ADHOC.COBOL
TRPAY.PDS.COBOL
TRPAY.PROD.COBOL
TRPAY.OLDSYS.COBOL
```

And suppose you wish to change their names to:

```
TRPAY.ADHOC.SRCEPGM
TRPAY.PDS.SRCEPGM
TRPAY.PROD.SRCEPGM
TRPAY.OLDSYS.SRCEPGM
```

The following command will work:

```
RENAME 'TRPAY.*.COBOL' 'TRPAY.*.SRCEPGM'
```

And, if TRPAY happens to be your TSO prefix, one of the following commands will work (requiring far less typing):

```
REN *.COBOL *.SRCEPGM
REN *COBOL,*.SRCEPGM
```

The following considerations apply to the RENAME command:

* RENAME 'data-set-name(A)' (B) will rename this PDS member. But this rename will fail if the PDS is allocated to another user such as CICS even in shared disposition (DISP=SHR).
* When a password protected dataset is renamed, the dataset ceases to have password protection. For example, suppose that a dataset was protected from update, and you rename it. After renaming, when you go to modify it, you are prompted for password, but any password you supply, including the password of the dataset prior to rename is considered invalid. To overcome this difficulty, you should use the PROTECT command to assign a password to the dataset after it has been renamed, or, preferably, you should remove the password before renaming it and then add the password after it has been renamed. In fact it is recommended that before deleting or renaming a password protected dataset, you should remove the password by issuing the following command:

```
PROTECT 'data-set-name' DEL(password)
```

Then, after renaming it, add the same password or a different password by issuing this command:

```
PROTECT 'data-set-name' ADD(password) PWREAD
                     or
PROTECT 'data-set-name' ADD(password) PWWRITE
```

- The RENAME command should not be used to assign an alias to a load module in a load library, which was created by linkage editor.
- An asterisk can be used in the place of dataset name qualifier in the present name and new name. When this is done to rename several datasets, the system changes all dataset names that match the present-name in the command, except for the qualifier that corresponds to the asterisk's position, as shown in Example 3 above.

Example 4. Suppose that your TSO userid is Z2BKN and, when you log on to TSO, member START of Z2BKN.CLIST is executed. This CLIST does some dataset allocations before executing command ISPF to start up ISPF. Because of an error in this CLIST, ISPF cannot be started. You know, however, that the older version of this CLIST is in member STARTO and this backup copy was working previously. You want to rename START to STARTX and then rename STARTO to START. The following commands issued from TSO mode will accomplish your objectives:

```
RENAME CLIST(START) (STARTX)
RENAME CLIST(STARTO) (START)
```

Here it is assumed that member STARTX did not exist in this dataset prior to issuing these commands.

The LISTCAT Command

As its name implies, this command is used to list entries from a MVS catalog. In the MVS system, there is one master catalog and a number of user catalogs. For most purposes, an applications programmer need not concern himself with the catalog where his datasets reside. The catalog where datasets with a given prefix are defined depends on which user catalog that prefix was assigned to by the MVS Systems Programmer when he defined that prefix (also called alias) in the Master catalog. Of course, if a prefix is not defined in the Master catalog, and you try to allocate a dataset with that prefix, the system will attempt to define that dataset in the Master Catalog, and, since the master catalog is usually password protected, you will not be able to allocate that dataset.

Another thing to remember about catalogs is that there are various kinds of entries defined in the catalog, some of which are:

- User Catalogs which are defined in the master catalog
- VSAM cluster names
- VSAM data component names associated with corresponding VSAM clusters
- VSAM index component names associated with corresponding VSAM clusters
- Generation data group (GDG) Base names
- Non-VSAM datasets that may or may not belong to a GDG
- VSAM data spaces
- Alias entries that specify user catalogs to which aliases are connected
- MVS page spaces

The syntax of the LISTCAT command with the most commonly used operands only is as follows:

$$\begin{Bmatrix} \text{LISTCAT} \\ \text{LISTC} \end{Bmatrix} \quad \left[\begin{array}{l} \begin{Bmatrix} \text{ENTRIES(entryname[/password] [. . . . .])} \\ \text{ENT(entryname [/password] [. . . . . .])} \end{Bmatrix} \\ \begin{Bmatrix} \text{LEVEL(level)} \\ \text{L(level)} \end{Bmatrix} \end{array}\right]$$

$$\left|\begin{array}{l} \text{OUTFILE(ddname)} \\ \text{OFILE(ddname)} \end{array}\right|$$

$$\left[\begin{array}{l} \text{ALL} \\ \underline{\text{NAME}} \end{array}\right]$$

Let us now look at some examples of the LISTCAT command and realize the immense usefulness of this command.

Example 1.   Suppose your TSO prefix is Z2BKN and you wish to list the names of all datasets that have the first qualifier of your TSO prefix. One of the following commands can be used:

```
LISTCAT
LISTC
```

If you change your prefix to say Z3MFD, then the LISTC command will display all datasets with prefix Z3MFD. And if you set your prefix to null through the PROFILE NOPREFIX command, then LISTC will give you all entries in the master catalog, which is most likely of little use to you.

Example 2.   To list names of all datasets that have the first qualifier of TRPPY and second qualifier of PDS, use the following command:

```
LISTC L(TRPPY.PDS)
```

Example 3. To list all information from the catalog for datasets that have the first qualifier of Z3DTC, use the following command:

```
LISTC L(Z3DTC) ALL
```

Example 4. To list information from the catalog for datasets with the first qualifier of PRPPY and have the output written not on your terminal but into a dataset Z2BKN.LISTC.OUTPUT, do the following:

1. Allocate dataset Z2BKN.LISTC.OUTPUT using option 3.2 of ISPF or through the ALLOC command discussed above, with the following characteristics:

    *   Record Format: VBA (Variable Blocked with ASCII control characters)
    *   Logical Record Length =125, that is 121 + 4
    *   Block Size = 6254, that is 10 * (121+4) + 4

    This means that each record is of 125 bytes, with the first 4 bytes being record descriptor word (RDW). The fifth byte of each record is the ANSI carriage control character, and the remaining 120 bytes are for printed data. Note: The blocking factor here is 10, but you can choose any other value for it. However, the record format should be VB and the logical record length should be 125.

2. ALLOC this dataset under DDname ANYDD by issuing these commands:

```
FREE F(ANYDD)
ALLOC F(ANYDD) DA(LISTC.OUTPUT) SHR
```

3. Now issue this command to list information from the catalog and write the output into dataset Z2BKN.LISTC.OUTPUT

```
LISTC LEVEL(PRPPY) ALL OFILE(ANYDD)
                      or
LISTC L(PRPPY) ALL OUTFILE(ANYDD)
```

(Remember if OFILE or OUTFILE operand is omitted, the output from LISTCAT command is displayed on your terminal.)
4. Now you can browse the dataset Z2BKN.LISTC.OUTPUT and you will find that it contains LISTCAT output with names of all datasets with prefix PRPPY. It is not necessary to issue FREE F(ANYDD) in order to browse this dataset. However, executing the FREE command will not hurt.

This variable record length dataset can be read by a utility program which will write each record to an output dataset with the following characteristics:

```
Record Format = Fixed Blocked (FB)
Record Length = 121
```

This dataset with fixed length records can be easily manipulated by a COBOL, a SAS or an EASYTRIEVE program for producing reports.

Example 5. To determine if TRPAY is an alias defined in the master catalog, and, if it is, with which user catalog it is associated, issue the following command:

```
LISTC ENT('TRPAY') ALL
```

If it is a valid alias, output similar to the following will appear on your terminal:

```
ALIAS ──────── TRPAY
   IN-CAT - ICAT.SYSCATA
   HISTORY
      RELEASE ──────────2
   ASSOCIATIONS
      USERCAT - ICAT.SV001A
```

What this display indicates is that alias TRPAY is defined in master catalog named ICAT.SYSCATA and it is related to user catalog ICAT.SV001A. This means that all datasets with prefix TRPAY will be defined in this user catalog.

And if it is not a valid alias, output similar to the following will appear:

```
ENTRY TRPAY NOT FOUND
** TRPAY NOT LISTED
- - - -
- - - -
```

Example 6.   To list names of all entries with two-qualifier names in the catalog that have TRPAY as the first qualifier and anything else as the second qualifier, issue this command:

```
LISTC ENT('TRPAY.*')
```

To list all information about all entries with three qualifier names in the catalog that have PRPAY as first qualifier and COBOL as the third qualifier, issue this command:

```
LISTC ENT('PRPAY.*.COBOL') ALL
```

The following considerations should be kept in mind when using the LISTCAT command

1. Either ENTRIES (ENT for short) or LEVEL (LVL or L for short) operand should be specified. If neither LEVEL not

ENTRIES is specified, only the entries with the first qualifier being identical to your TSO prefix will be listed, assuming that your dataset name prefix (as shown by PROFILE command) is not null.

2. The name under ENTRIES operand can be fully-qualified; that is, enclosed within quotation marks, or qualified, for example ENT(PDS.COBOL) in which case the entry name searched will be prefix.PDS.COBOL. It can also be a generic name as shown in Example 6 above. A qualified name can be made into a generic name by substituting an asterisk for one qualifier.

3. You may direct the system to write the output to a destination other than your terminal. This is done by specifying the OUTFILE or OFILE operand. For example:

```
ALLOC F(LISTING) DA(LISTING) DSORG(PS) RECFM(V B) LRECL(125) +
      BLKSIZE(6254) SPACE(2,2) TRACKS
LISTC L(PRPAY.PDS) OFILE(LISTING)
```

Consult an appropriate IBM manual for the complete syntax of this command and detailed discussion of the various operands.

Appendix B
REFERENCE SUMMARY OF CONTROL VARIABLES AND BUILT-IN FUNCTIONS

Figure B.1 gives a summary of the most commonly used control variables available for writing CLISTs. For other control variables, refer to an appropriate IBM manual in the TSO/E library.

Figure B.2 gives a summary of the most commonly used built-in functions available for writing CLISTs. For other built-in functions, refer to an appropriate IBM manual in the TSO/E library.

Symbolic Variable	Use	Can be Changed by the Writer
&LASTCC	To obtain the return code from the last operation whether TSO command, subcommand, or command procedure statement. (See Note 1)	Yes
&MAXCC	To obtain the highest return code issued up to this point in the command procedure or passed back from a nested command procedure. The return code is in decimal format. (See Note 1.)	Yes
&SYSDATE	To obtain the present date in the format mm/dd/yy, where mm is month, dd is day, and yy is year.	No
&SYSDLM	To identify which character string, of those specified on the TERMIN statement, the terminal user entered to return control to the command procedure.	No
&SYSDVAL	(1) To obtain any parameters the terminal user entered, besides the delimiter, when he returned control to the command procedure after a TERMIN statement. (2) To obtain the terminal user's response line when a READ statement requests terminal input.	Yes
&SYSENV	To indicate whether the command procedure is executing in the foreground or background environment respectively. (This variable cannot be modified by a command procedure.)	No
&SYSICMD	To obtain the name by which the user implicitly invoked this command procedure. This value is null if the command procedure was invoked explicitly.	No
&SYSNEST	To determine if the currently executing command procedure was invoked from another procedure. &SYSNEST is replaced with "YES" if this is a nested procedure and "NO" if it is not.	No

Figure B.1.   Commonly used control variables.

Symbolic Variable	Use	Can be Changed by the Writer
&SYSPCMD	To obtain the name (or abbreviation) of the most recently executed TSO command (with the exception of the TIME command) in this procedure. The initial value is "EXEC" (or "EX") in the command environment and "EDIT" (or "E") in the subcommand environment.	No
&SYSPREF	To obtain the dataset-name prefix from the user profile table (UPT) for the command procedure user.	No
&SYSPROC	To obtain the procedure name specified when the command procedure user logged on.	No
&SYSSCAN	To obtain the maximum number of times that symbolic substitution is allowed to rescan a line to evaluate symbolic variables. The default is 16 times. The maximum value is two to the 31st power minus one (+2, 147, 483, 647); the minimum is 0.	Yes
&SYSSCMD	To obtain the name (or abbreviation) of the subcommand currently executing. The initial value is null if EXEC was issued in the command environment and "EXEC" (or "EX") if EXEC was issued as a subcommand of EDIT. The value is null whenever the procedure is in the command environment.	No
&SYSTIME	To obtain the present time in the format hh:mm:ss, where HH is hours, mm is minutes, and ss is seconds.	No
&SYSUID	To obtain the userid of the user currently executing the command procedure.	No

Note 1: The command procedure statement return codes are in Figure 18. The TSO command and subcommand return codes are:
    0   Normal completion
    12   A terminating error occurred during execution; however, the command processor might have been able to prompt for information necessary to recover from the error.

Figure B.1.   Commonly used control variables (concluded).

Symbolic Variable	Use
&DATATYPE (expression)	To find out whether an evaluated expression is entirely numeric. &DATATYPE is replaced by 'NUM' if the expression is all numeric or by 'CHAR' if there is at least one non-numeric character.
&EVAL(expression)	To find the result of an arithmetic expression. &EVAL is replaced by the result of evaluating the expression.
&LENGTH(expression)	To find the number of characters in the result of an evaluated expression. &LENGTH is replaced by the number of characters in the result. (Leading zeroes are ignored.)
&NRSTR	To define a Non-Rescannable character string for symbolic substitution. The primary use of &NRSTR is to handle variables, whose contents have been set from an external file. This function is useful if you are reading a file that has records containing ampersands, such as Job Control Language (JCL) records. If the &NRSTR built-in is used when setting symbolic variables, only one level of symbolic substitution will take place within the parenthetical expression. Within the parentheses, substitution will occur only on the first scan of the statement. No attempt will be made to evaluate the expression after the single symbolic substitution scan.
&STR(string)	To use the indicated string as a real value. Nested built-in functions and symbolic substitution are performed but no other evaluation is done. &STR is replaced by the string.
&SUBSTR (expression[:expression], string)	To use the indicated portion of a string as a real value. Nested built-in functions and symbolic substitution are performed but no other evaluation is done. &SUBSTR is replaced by the specified portion of the string (substring). The start and end of the substring are indicated by the two expressions. To select a one-character substring, you need to enter only the first expression.

Figure B.2. Most commonly used built-in functions.

Appendix C
REFERENCE SUMMARY OF CLIST STATEMENT ERROR CODES IN DECIMAL

Figure C.1 gives a summary of the CLIST statement error codes. These are also called return codes. The TSO command and subcommand return codes are:

   0   Normal completion
  12   A terminating error occurred during execution; however, the CLIST might have been able to prompt the user for information necessary to recover from the error.

16	Not enough virtual storage
300	User tried to update an unauthorized variable
304	Invalid keyword on EXIT statement
308	Code specified, but no code given on EXIT statement
312	Internal GLOBAL processing error
316	TERMIN delimiter greater than 256 characters
324	GETLINE error
328	More than 64 delimiters on TERMIN
332	Invalid file name syntax
336	File already open
340	Invalid OPEN type syntax
344	Undefined OPEN type
348	File specified did not open (for example, the filename was not allo⁻ cated)
352	GETFILE — filename not currently open
356	GETFILE — the file has been closed by the system (for example, file opened under EDIT and EDIT has ended
360	PUTFILE — file name not currently open
364	PUTFILE — CLOSFILE — file closed by system (see code 356)
368	PUTFILE — CLOSFILE — file not opened by OPENFILE
372	PUTFILE — issued before GETFILE on a file opened for update
400	GETFILE end of file (treated as an error, which can be handled by ERROR action)
8xx	Evaluation routine error codes
800	Data found where operator was expected
804	Operator found where data was expected
808	A comparison operator was used in a SET statement
812	(Reserved)
816	Operator found at the end of a statement
820	Operators out of order
824	More than one exclusive operator found
828	More than one exclusive comparison operator
832	The result of an arithmetical calculation is outside the range extending from -2,147,483,684 to +2,147,483,647.

Figure C.1.   Command Procedure Statement Error Codes (Decimal).

836	(Reserved)
840	Not enough operands
844	No valid operators
848	Attempt to load character from numeric value
852	Addition error — character data
856	Subtraction error — character data
860	Multiplication error — character data
864	Divide error — character data or division by 0
868	Prefix found on character data
872	Numeric value too large
900	Single ampersand found
904	Symbolic variable not found
908	Error occurred in an error range that received control because of another error
912	Substring range invalid
916	Non-numeric value in substring range
920	Substring range value too small (zero or negative)
924	Invalid substring syntax
932	Substring outside of the range of the string, for example, 1:3,AB; (AB is only two characters)
936	A built-in function that requires a value was entered without a value
940	Invalid symbolic variable
944	A label was used as a symbolic variable
948	Invalid label syntax on a GOTO statement
952	GOTO label was not defined
956	GOTO statement has no label
960	&SYSSCAN was set to an invalid value
964	&LASTCC was set to an invalid value and EXIT tried to use it as a default value
968	DATA PROMPT-ENDDATA statements supplied, but no prompt occurred
972	TERMI command cannot be used in background jobs
999	Internal command procedure error
*Sxxx	A system ABEND code
*Uxxx	A user ABEND code

*Printed in hexadecimal

Figure C.1. Command Procedure Statement Error Codes (Decimal) (concluded).

Index